The Mechanics of Optimism

Mining the American West

Boomtown Blues: Colorado Oil Shale
Andrew Gulliford

Hard as the Rock Itself: Place and Identity in the American Mining Town
David Robertson

*Industrializing the Rockies: Growth, Competition,
and Turmoil in the Coalfields of Colorado and Wyoming*
David A. Wolff

*The Mechanics of Optimism: Mining Companies, Technology,
and the Hot Spring Gold Rush, Montana Territory, 1864–1868*
Jeffrey J. Safford

Silver Saga: The Story of Caribou, Colorado, Revised Edition
Duane A. Smith

Thomas F. Walsh: Progressive Businessman and Colorado Mining Tycoon
John Stewart

Yellowcake Towns: Uranium Mining Communities in the American West
Michael A. Amundson

SERIES EDITORS

Duane A. Smith
Robert A. Trennert
Liping Zhu

The Mechanics of Optimism

MINING COMPANIES, TECHNOLOGY,
AND THE HOT SPRING GOLD RUSH,
MONTANA TERRITORY, 1864–1868

Jeffrey J. Safford

UNIVERSITY PRESS OF COLORADO

© 2004 by the University Press of Colorado

Published by the University Press of Colorado
5589 Arapahoe Avenue, Suite 206C
Boulder, Colorado 80303

 The University Press of Colorado is a proud member of
the Association of American University Presses.

The University Press of Colorado is a cooperative publishing enterprise supported, in part,
by Adams State College, Colorado State University, Fort Lewis College, Mesa State College, Metropolitan State College of Denver, Regis University, University of Colorado, University of Northern
Colorado, and Western State College of Colorado.

♾ The paper used in this publication meets the minimum requirements of the American National
Standard for Information Sciences—Permanence of Paper for Printed Library Materials.
ANSI Z39.48-1992

Library of Congress Cataloging-in-Publication Data

Safford, Jeffrey J., 1934–
  The mechanics of optimism : mining companies, technology, and the Hot Spring gold rush, Mon-
tana Territory, 1864–1868 / Jeffrey J. Safford.
    p. cm. — (Mining the American West)
  Includes bibliographical references and index.
  ISBN 0-87081-782-5 (hardcover : alk. paper) —   ISBN 978-1-60732-101-9 (pbk : alk. paper)
  1. Madison County (Mont.)—Gold discoveries. 2. Gold mines and mining—Montana—Madison
County—History—19th century. I. Title. II. Series.
  F737.M2S24 2004
  338.2'741'0978666309034—dc22
                                                                                2004013638

Maps by Dale Martin

Portions of this book are based on the author's two-part article "Baited by a 'Color' of Gold to a Mountain
of Granite," *Montana: The Magazine of Western History* (summer, autumn 1997). Used with permission
from the Montana Historical Society.

Contents

Illustrations

Photographs

Maps

Preface

MY INITIAL INTEREST IN THE HOT SPRING DISTRICT WAS NOT CONCEIVED AS A calculated effort to address the history of western mining or Montana's early territorial period. Rather, it stemmed from a lifelong passion for historic preservation dating back to the late 1930s when as a toddler I accompanied my parents and other members of the Staten Island Historical Society as they labored to restore life to the historic structures of Richmondtown, a community dating back to the Dutch occupation of New York. In Montana my interests were fed by appointments to the Montana Historic Preservation Review Board, the Montana Heritage Preservation and Development Commission, and the Montana State University (MSU) Historic Preservation Committee.

The latter was formed to study the significance of historic properties under MSU's jurisdiction, including the sites of three frontier military posts and a gold mining camp.

It was the MSU Agricultural Research Station at Red Bluff, Montana, that provided the spark for this current analysis. Red Bluff, situated midway between Bozeman and Virginia City, had been a viable late-nineteenth-century gold mining camp. Many foundations and two still-standing stone structures spoke of busy times. But Red Bluff's history had never been documented; what remained of its past was largely reminiscence tending toward speculation and wild inaccuracy. In 1980 I organized two graduate seminars whose enthusiastic members examined the background of the university's 1956 acquisition of the town site, produced an outline of Red Bluff's history, and fixed an accurate dating and function for its stone structures. An archaeological dig and historical architectural, geologic, and field surveying classes furthered our analysis of Red Bluff.

It was soon apparent that Red Bluff and the surrounding area was but part of a whole, that prior to its naming it had developed in the 1860s as one of several subdistricts within the larger Hot Spring Mining District, and that these subdistricts were inextricably connected such that independent analysis of each or any of them was impracticable. In consequence I redirected my study to a history of the entire Hot Spring District, specifically to a much smaller time frame—the 1860s, or that time frame when the Hot Spring District went through a tumultuous five-year period, from being heralded as among the finest for gold values in the entire territory to becoming the subject of derision for the failure of its developers to profit from its ores.

At its outset, this study relied on contemporary newspaper accounts and public records. Montana's first newspaper, the *Montana Post* (Virginia City), commenced publication in August 1864, almost simultaneous with the development of the Hot Spring District. Although its existing files are badly fragmented, the *Montana Democrat* (Virginia City), which commenced publication a year later, offered a second accounting. Public records proved extremely useful, particularly grantor and grantee files in the Madison County Clerk and Recorder's office and depositions taken of principals and witnesses in civil cases contained in the Clerk of the Court's office. Then came the discovery of a large collection of personal correspondence and business reports tracing the aspirations and failures of the district's most prominent hard-rock mining enterprise—the Midas Mining Company of Rochester, New York. Housed in Rush Rhees Library at the University of Rochester, these papers were made available with assistance beyond call by Karl Kabelac, head of special collections. Subsequently, Hot Spring rancher J. Peter Jackson introduced me to the correspondence of his grandfather, Peter V. Jackson, secretary to the Midas Company's works in the Upper Hot Spring district. Other Madison County descendants and relatives of Peter V. Jackson also assisted me, including the late Gayle Jackson, the late Peter V. Jackson III, Steven Jackson, and Ward Jackson. A full-fledged study was made possible through a grant-in-aid from the American Association for State and Local History and several research leaves generously provided by Montana State University.

One of the advantages of having taken a score of years to complete this study has been the opportunity to bring my entire family into its compilation. Over time my wife, June Billings Safford, and our four children, Hugh, Meredith, Alexander, and Brooke, took part in numerous ways—researching, tramping over the hills with me, and contributing their thinking and expertise. Above all, my lovely spouse, who creatively dubbed this long project the family's "ore-deal," in her wonderful way gave me the time and encouragement to keep at the project, despite the numerous delays, deterrents, and distractions that seemed to crop up consistently.

Others helped in special ways. I am particularly indebted to the encouragement and advice given me over time by the late Michael Malone, president of Montana State University, and by Paula Petrik and the late Richard Roeder—all three former colleagues in the MSU Department of History. Clark Spence, Robert Spude, Duane Smith, Robert Trennert, and Sally Zanjani gave generously of their time and wisdom to constructively critique the manuscript. Linda Peavy and Fred Quivik read portions of the study and made significant recommendations. Charles Rankin, former editor of *Montana: The Magazine of Western History*, published a small segment of the manuscript in 1997. State Historical Society librarians Robert Clark, Brian Shovers, and David Walter and head of Montana State University special collections Kim Scott always bent over backward to help.

At the Madison County courthouse in Virginia City I had the pleasure of working with public servants who went far out of their way to extend the scope of my research. Of these many officials I am most obliged to Jerry Wing, former clerk of the court, and Dorothy Brown, former head of the Clerk and Recorder's office. Yet another Madisonian to whom I am obliged is John Ellingsen, who allowed me use of the Charles Bovey Papers while they were housed at Nevada City, Montana.

I thank especially Ursula Smith, editor par excellence and distinguished author of western history, for her remarkable ability to identify my weaknesses, point out my strengths, and keep me on course. And to Sandy Crooms, acquisitions editor at the University Press of Colorado, I owe a great deal of gratitude; I especially appreciate her consistently positive and cordial support. To all the above I give my most ardent thanks, with the understanding, of course, that I alone am responsible for the final product.

Finally, this work is dedicated to J. Peter Jackson (1908–1996). Without his friendship and unselfish assistance—including accompanying me on numerous on-site analyses of the physical and industrial geography of the Hot Spring area and introducing me to his family papers—this study would have fallen far short of what it eventually became. If I have one regret, it is that I did not complete this history while he was still alive.

Prologue

WHEN THE RICHEST PLACER GOLD STRIKE EVER MADE IN MONTANA, SOME SAY IN the United States, took place on May 26, 1863, in Alder Gulch— fifteen miles of mountain gulch and streambed situated on the west side of the Madison and Jefferson River divide in southwestern Montana—it was only a matter of time before the surrounding terrain would receive the same kind of frenzied attention. The extraordinary values extracted from Alder Gulch, an estimated $30 to $40 million in 1863–1864, produced a stampede of thousands of gold hunters who, in the words of one observer, were so plentiful—like "bees around a hive"—as to appear hopelessly in "each other's way."[1] Despite the gulch's expanse, this swarm of miners soon saturated its bars and banks, inducing would-be millionaires to seek wealth elsewhere.

Accordingly, new districts proliferated rapidly—up Alder Creek to include Highland City, Pine Grove, Junction, and Summit City; down the creek below the original strike to Central City, Nevada City, Adobetown, and Junction City; and in the gulches along the western slopes of the Tobacco Root Mountains: Brown's, Granite, California, Bivens, Ramshorn, Wisconsin, Barton, and Mill Creek, the latter a full twenty-two miles distant from William Fairweather and Company's fortuitous discovery.

Then, in the spring of 1864, the area's gold seekers spilled eastward over the divide into the Madison River Valley and onto the eastern slopes of the Tobacco Root Mountains. In short order the Hot Spring District, located between the Tobacco Roots and the Madison River, was organized. Expectations for all of these districts on both sides of the mountains were uniformly high, and Madison County, created to encompass the whole, took the lead in Montana demographics and economy—with Virginia City, its own "metropolis," supporting an estimated population of 10,000 in 1864 and serving as territorial capital.

The proliferation of camps satellite to initial strikes and the organization of communities to supply their needs is a development hardly new to historians and gold camp buffs, and the pattern is amply documented in the history of the major western mining states and territories. But the attention given historically to this notable phase in the development of the frontier has tended to center not so much on mining as on topics relating to social history. Recent years, for example, have seen the publication of excellent accounts of the social phenomena associated with the West. Some of these studies—such as Elizabeth Jameson's account of Cripple Creek, Colorado; Sally Zanjani's study of women prospectors; Linda Peavy and Ursula Smith's stories of gold rush widows; and Malcolm Rohrbough's analyses of Aspen, Colorado, and the California Gold Rush camps—are the result of painstaking mining into the particulars of social structure. Elliott West's recent expansion of Rodman Paul's classic, *Mining Frontiers of the Far West,* is also an examination of gold camp society.[2] In contrast, comparatively few studies are concerned with the gold discoveries themselves, the nature of the mining technology, and the importance of the financial and administrative organizations associated with mining endeavors. For Montana this paucity of details on such matters is striking.

Yet this gap in our knowledge is not surprising. When one of the Hot Spring Mining District's most committed 1860s entrepreneurs reminisced thirty years later, he recalled not his laborious and disappointing efforts to wrench wealth from the earth but the upbeat social flavor of those times. "There was

lots of life to the minute in those days," he mused. "Miners, Mills, Men, Road
agents, Vigilantes, Overland Coach, Wagon trains, Bullwhackers and all."[3] As
for Virginia City, the fact that the mining camp rarely suffered a dull moment
became the thing to memorialize. The consequent emphasis on such subjects
as claim jumping, shootouts, dance halls, hurdy-gurdies, and saloons—on
living life to the hilt—contributed to a riotous, brawling environment that has
continued to capture the imagination of both the historian and the reading
public.[4] Indeed, the more colorful—and too often violent—social interactions
associated with Montana's early territory years have been given prominence
at the expense of other equally important events and developments.

It is not only in Montana's history that mining has been given short shrift
by this focus on the sensational. No one has underscored this better than Duane
Smith in his standard account of Rocky Mountain mining camps. As Smith put
it, compared with other contemporary western phenomena—mountain men,
fur traders, cattlemen, Indians, gunfighters, outlaws—the mining frontier has
fared poorly in its effort to capture popular attention. In particular, Smith observed, with these elements missing, it "has been hard to sustain great interest
in the contest of capitalistic corporations over control of a mineral deposit."[5]
Although Smith's study was produced over thirty years ago, his lamentation,
especially for Montana, still rings true—to this date, technological and corporate investments in early territorial Montana quartz mining and milling have
received but scant attention.

This study attempts to introduce some balance to our understanding of
Montana's early territorial history by examining the rise and decline of one
of Virginia City's satellite mining camps—the Hot Spring Mining District
that emerged roughly thirty miles northeast of the territorial capital in 1864.
Although not ignoring social factors, *The Mechanics of Optimism*'s major thrust
is to bring into prominence the nature and extent of the work of the miners
and mill operators who gave life and meaning to this geographically small
district during the mid- to late 1860s, a time-encapsulated boom-bust period
inaugurated with high expectations but concluded with dismal results.

Above all, it is a study of the investment of eastern capital in western
mineral exploitation and of the technological means by which these capitalists
sought to enrich themselves and their backers but, for diverse and numerous
reasons, uniformly failed. And because those who attempted to exploit Hot
Spring's minerals left behind a treasure trove of documentation, a study of
this particular district offers an unusually rich perspective.

To take it a step further, a study of the exciting rise and ignominious decline of the Hot Spring Mining District epitomizes patterns of development

in the majority of the West's mining districts. Hot Spring was just one of countless boom-bust gold and silver mining camps characteristic of the 1860s Rocky Mountain region. When Colonel Alexander K. McClure—traveling west in 1867 to look after his investments in Alder Gulch quartz milling—made a brief visit to the gold mines of Central City, Colorado, he was brought up with astonishment at the "abandonment and decay" he found in a district that only five years previously had been touted as one of fabulous wealth. Arriving in Montana, he found a similar pattern in the making.[6] Subsequent studies by Joseph King and Harvey Gardiner on Colorado, Merle Wells on Idaho, and Paul Fatout on California mining camps further document the phenomenon and serve as a reminder that Hot Spring District had numerous counterparts going through approximately the same experience at approximately the same time.[7]

Thus, an analysis of Montana's Hot Spring District strengthens our understanding of the entire western gold mining experience. Adding Montana to the mix fills out the regional picture of a national development. Moreover, a study of the Hot Spring District offers something of value in and of itself. These short-lived and frequently overshadowed bonanza camps were the rule rather than the exception, and, as W. Turrentine Jackson observed in his analysis of territorial Nevada, they often "consumed far greater human effort and suffering, more money and equipment, than the occasional successful mining district that gained lasting fame."[8]

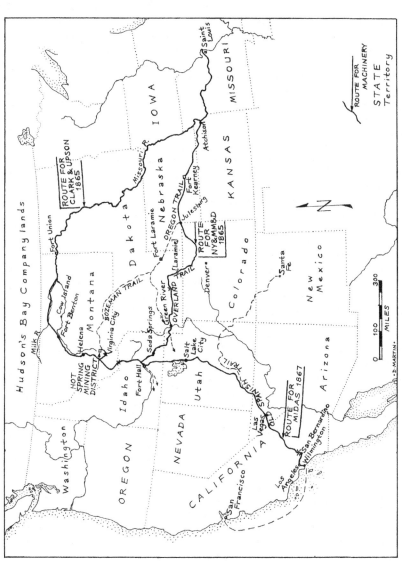

1 *Boundaries in 1865: Western states and territories, with routes taken by three companies in transporting their machinery to the Hot Spring District*

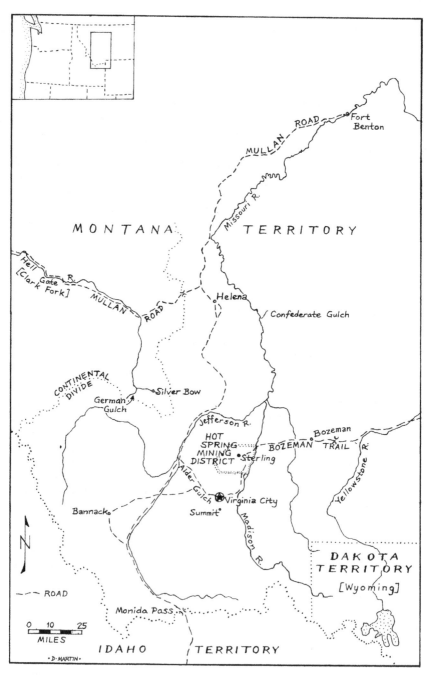

2 *Principal gold mining districts, Montana Territory, 1865, including Hot Spring Mining District*

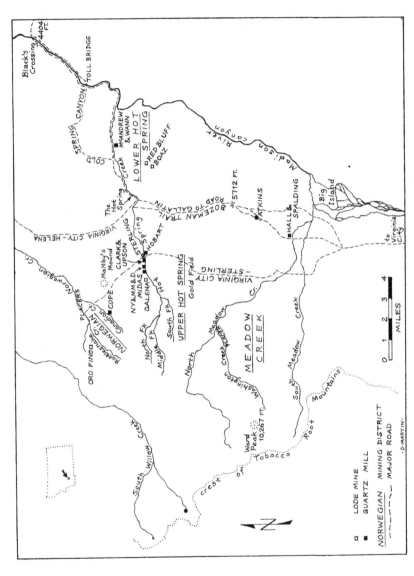

3 *Hot Spring Mining District, Madison County, Montana Territory, 1868, including sites of quartz mills*

CHAPTER 1

Patterns of Discovery

1863–1864

"Emigrants are pouring in and the whole country is one bustle
of excitement."

—James H. Morley

THE HOT SPRING MINING DISTRICT LIES IN THE NORTHEAST CORNER OF MADISON
County, Montana. The district's epicenter, today's tiny settlement of
Norris, lies thirty-five miles equidistant from Virginia City, to the
southwest, and Bozeman, to the east. Roughly speaking, the district is approximately fourteen miles in length, varying from fourteen to twenty miles
in width. On the east an undulating plateau ends abruptly at steep bluffs
overlooking the deeply cut canyon of the northward-flowing Madison River.
On the south the district looks down a thousand feet to the broad valley of
the upper Madison River. The south boundary of the Hot Spring District follows the bed of South Meadow Creek westerly—from its confluence with the

1

Madison River near McAllister to its headwaters high in the Tobacco Root Mountains. From here the district's western boundary follows the crest of the Tobacco Roots northward. The thickly forested slopes of these mountains are steep; the rounded, treeless summits pronounced. Ward Peak, at 10,267 feet, towers over the district; in the 1860s, before other Montana mountains were found to be of superior elevation, it was ranked as the territory's second highest. Along its west line the district follows this mountainous divide to the Norwegian and South Willow Creek drainages and then proceeds east to Black's Ford on the lower Madison River, the district's lowest at 4,404 feet. Altogether, the district embraces the entirety of four townships and portions of nine others, totaling 267 square miles.

The Hot Spring District's quartz lodes, or hard-rock mines, are located predominately in its rolling hills and plateaus, whereas its placer mines, or gulch workings, are found along two streambeds—Meadow Creek in the south and Norwegian Creek in the north. Between them Hot Spring Creek—named for a much-noted fount just east of Norris and the source of the district's name—cuts an easterly ravine through the plateau before it joins the Madison River at its effluence from the Madison River Canyon.

Geographically, little has changed in the 140 years since the discovery of gold in the Hot Spring District. Of course, modern roads have been constructed and different courses have been adopted. And small settlements exist where none existed before. In the 1860s the district was bordered on the western mountain slopes and gulches by thousands of acres of heavy stands of timber. Although much of this was cut to support mining and ranching, regrowth and management have returned the quantity of timber to virtually its mid-nineteenth-century state. In 1900 the Madison River, which in Montana's territorial period was a large, meandering, many-channeled meadow stream above its formidable canyon, was dammed to create energy for a hydroelectric facility. Six years later the reconstruction and enlargement of the dam inundated several substantial river islands noted frequently in early reports of the settlement and agricultural development of the area. And in 1944 the headwaters of South Meadow Creek were dammed. But other than these reconfigurations of the district's topography, much remains as it was in the 1860s. Nor has its beauty been marred; one still stands in awe, as a contemporary put it, of its "wild" range of mountains, crowned by Ward Peak, its "monarch and sentinel"; of its "leaping and rushing . . . streams of crystal waters," which cut ravines through the plateaus; of its rocky ridges, grassy hills, slopes, and "many fantastic domes and pointed towers stand[ing] often on bases far smaller than their upper parts."[1]

Today, at the dawn of the twenty-first century, the district is heavily engaged in the raising of livestock and the growing of grain, with periodic efforts to resuscitate its gold lodes marking it as an area of continued mineral potential. The current population of the Hot Spring District is little larger than it was during the heyday of its existence in the mid-1860s.

TO UNDERSTAND THE 1860s HISTORY OF THE HOT SPRING DISTRICT, ONE MUST APPRECIate it for more than its quartz milling phase. For the district had been in development for almost two years before the capitalists and their quartz mills came to the area. Indeed, Hot Spring was first inhabited not by prospectors or eastern entrepreneurs but by preemptors of agricultural lands. Although the first Hot Spring District mineral discovery claims on record were made in May 1864, a full year after William Fairweather and Company's fortuitous strike in Alder Gulch, settlement of the valley's agricultural land commenced less than three months following the Alder Gulch discovery, or two years before the arrival of the first quartz-crushing mill. How many of these original preemptors of land came with the sole intention of farming, how many came in expectation of profiting from mining and then switched to farming and ranching, and how many simply claimed land for speculative purposes is difficult to say. For certain, some of these pioneers saw the area as highly suitable for the raising of foodstuffs and fodder essential not only to themselves but also to the welfare of the thousands who inhabited Virginia City and the mining camps around it. As one early settler expressed it: "Mining even in good mining countries is uncertain business. Probably not more than one in fifty of the mining population ever get rich at it. While farming in a good mining country has almost universally proved profitable."[2]

The fact is that many of the men who emigrated to the Montana goldfields had been farmers, and once it became clear that opportunities in mining were not unlimited, a goodly number turned back to their former vocations. The territory's first newspaper, the *Montana Post* (Virginia City), made development of the farming and ranching community one of its earliest editorial priorities. "Montana can never be a home, strictly speaking," its editor, Thomas Dimsdale, wrote, "until it becomes in a great measure self-supporting. . . . In every land there must be a diversion of labor. All cannot be miners."[3]

Quarter-section land preemptions in the Hot Spring District were first made in late August 1863, when Montana was still part of Idaho Territory. A quarter section, a parcel of land 160 acres in size, or one-quarter of a square mile, was the figure set in the 1841 Preemption Act and again in the Homestead

Act signed into law by President Abraham Lincoln in 1862. The Homestead Act was the culmination of almost seventy-five years of agitation on the behalf of free-land advocates; it gave "any person who is the head of a family, or who has arrived at the age of twenty-one years, and is a citizen of the United States, or who shall have filed his declaration of intention to become such" the privilege of obtaining 160 acres of land free of charge—except for a small filing fee—in return for living on the land for five years, cultivating it, and making certain improvements.[4]

In Montana in 1863 the Homestead Act could be applied only in theory, for the official surveying of land was a requisite for full entitlement. But Montana's settlers had moved in faster than the surveyors had. When the official territorial survey was finally undertaken in 1867–1868, settlers had occupied significant portions of the territory for as much as five years. In reality, these settlers were not in full legal possession of their properties—they were in effect squatters. But to westerners squatters were, as Richard White put it, "noble pioneers."[5] And in Montana the principle applied was to secure possession for the territory's occupants and as much title as could be given prior to governmental surveying and patenting. In short, Montana practice, as in other western territories and states, legalized and protected squatters' rights in the early years of settlement.[6]

In adherence to the provisions of the Homestead Act, preemptions made in the Hot Spring District were for land suitable for agricultural purposes. The Meadow Creek area of the district received attention early, as it possessed good soil, ample water, and excellent stands of timber. That it was a beautiful and fertile valley could not be disputed. As important, its location gave it reasonable access to markets on both sides of the Tobacco Root Mountains. In realization of this, by December 1863 at least six preemptions had been made in the district, all of them on Meadow Creek. The following year—paralleling the discovery of gold, the influx of prospectors, and the formal organization of county government—witnessed intensified movement into the area by seekers of preemptable land. During the summer and early fall of 1864, twenty-one additional preemptions of agricultural land, totaling 3,360 acres, were filed for the Hot Spring District. Most of these were in the Meadow Creek area, but land to the north along Hot Spring and Norwegian creeks was now under cultivation. Other ranches most certainly were established in the Hot Spring District in 1864 but were filed on later—or not at all. At the same time, large parcels of land adjacent to the district, including property east of the Madison River and on both sides of the river south of the district, were also being preempted.[7]

An agricultural stamp was being pressed rapidly upon this formerly wild environment. One emigrant, accompanying a wagon train passing through the Meadow Creek area in early August 1864 after a long trek over Bozeman's Trail, was delighted to hear, for the first time since leaving civilization, the "sound of a [hay] reaper" and to see some fencing and a good garden.[8] A month later, when Richard Owen, accompanying a wagon train from Omaha to Virginia City, camped on Meadow Creek, he described the Hot Spring District as "a mountainous country [with] fine valleys between the mountains." Most of these valleys, he noted, were "occupied by white settlers, mules and oxen."[9] Another member of the same wagon train was equally impressed, citing the presence of ranchmen and the abundance of hay in the Meadow Creek area.[10] Where land was broken by plows, it predominately produced wheat, hay, and vegetables. Dairying and grazing of livestock were equally prominent—and economically feasible—as the mountain valleys remained remarkably clear during the winter, affording a lengthy grazing season despite the elevation and cold. In 1865 and 1866, when large cattle drives brought range livestock into Montana and the Madison River Valley, agriculture became firmly established in the Hot Spring District.

MEN WITH MINING INTERESTS ADDED PROMINENTLY TO THE AREA'S POPULATION IN 1864. These were the peripatetic prospectors who, defying the odds, sought to profit from the discovery of gold. Precisely how many prospectors operated in the Hot Spring District in 1864 is difficult to determine, but by year's end sixty-six different persons had claimed discoveries on ninety-two placer or quartz lodes. Untold others had been in on these discoveries or had labored without success. Numerous others bankrolled and supplied the prospectors from businesses located in and around Virginia City. Still others simply stockpiled lode property for speculative reasons.

Although agricultural labors had been centered mostly in the Meadow Creek area, the activities of mineral seekers stretched all along the eastern slopes of the Tobacco Root Mountains, from Meadow Creek in the south over the plateaus and divide directly north to Hot Spring Creek and its headwaters, culminating in Norwegian and Rattlesnake gulches and in the upper South Willow Creek area. Of the ninety-two lode discovery claims made for the district, twenty were in and around Meadow Creek, thirty were in Revenue Flats and Upper Hot Spring, and forty-one were located in the Norwegian Gulch–Willow Creek area. One bore a geographic description so vague that it is impossible to place. In short, by the end of 1864 the mineral properties of three of the Hot Spring District's principal subdistricts had been prospected:

Meadow Creek, Upper Hot Spring—including Revenue Flats [or Gold Field]—and Norwegian. Only the Lower Hot Spring District remained undeveloped; it would be "discovered" two years later.

What attracted prospectors to the Hot Spring District was its ample and easily accessed and worked surface values. Geologically, prospectors in the 1860s found in the Hot Spring District quartz vein outcroppings at the surface that held so much free gold it could be separated from the gangue (minerals with no economic worth) by mere pick and shovel. What had caused this was the oxidation, or chemical weathering, of the mineralized veins. After emplacement of the granitic Tobacco Root Batholith into the earth's crust and subsequent pulses of hydrothermal mineralization from the slowly cooling magma, millions of years of uplift, glaciation, and erosion gradually exhumed miles of quartz- and mineral-filled rock fractures, or veins. Veins that lay above the water table were exposed to oxygen and rainwater and were heavily weathered. Through time, many of the original mineral constituents were chemically altered and washed down to the water table, leaving quartz, which is almost indissoluble under normal conditions, and gold, which was freed from weathered pyrite (iron sulphides, also known as "fool's gold") and a number of usually economically unimportant accessory minerals. This geological process not only left the gold in a form easier to extract but also resulted in enriched (high-grade) ores because of the downward leaching of much of the gangue.[11]

"This region would be the delight of a geologist," remarked a knowledgeable contemporary observer. William Y. Lovell—probate judge, erstwhile assayer, and investor in Madison County mines—described the country rock as basically granitic in nature and metamorphic in appearance, "cut into irregular blocks by seams as straight and clean as if made by a knife." Most of the Upper Hot Spring District's quartz veins were found in the level fields of the plateaus: "Here they crop out through the yellow bunch grass, showing themselves at one or more points, then sinking below the surface." Nearer the Madison River the whole surface of the district, especially on or near the summits of hills or ridges, was "dotted with snow white quartz, while at the foot of the hills and over the plateaus, can be seen the quartz in place, running in every possible direction."[12]

Lovell found quartz specimens to be charged with "oxides of iron, and copper, as also with bright crystals of iron and copper pyrites, and blue glistening galena." Molybdenum, manganese, and plumbago (lead) headed the list of other ores he identified. The dissemination of these metals was considered a "most favorable feature, being as they are the constant companions of the precious metals." The oxidation of most of these metals had left gold in the surface quartz in a free state, rendering them susceptible to easy separation. Water was plentiful for use in processing the ores, and the accessibility of the mines was a distinct plus, as wagons could be driven to most of them at any season because they were located east of the mountainous snow zone.[13] Although Lovell was concerned uppermost with profits to be gained through corporate mining, such advantages were boons as well to prospectors and to modestly budgeted mining endeavors. In short, from every appearance, over the years nature had worked to render Hot Spring's surface gold remarkably pure, plentiful, accessible, and easily worked.

THE FIRST HOT SPRING LODE DISCOVERY CLAIMS ON RECORD WERE THE GENERAL LEE Lode and the Lawreance Lode, claimed by the Independent Quartz Mining Company on May 17, 1864—slightly more than three weeks following the establishment of the Madison County Clerk and Recorder's Office in Virginia City and just nine days before Montana was given territorial status independent of Idaho.[14] Precisely when these Meadow Creek claims were discovered is unknown, as initially the recorder's office did not require lode discovery claimants to disclose discovery dates. In those early months of development, Madison County's recorders, unquestionably overworked, were often quite lax in enforcing the rules. Although prospectors were obliged to file their claims within ten days if the discovery was located within thirty miles of the county seat—or fifteen days if located farther than thirty miles away—some claims were not legalized for weeks, months, and even entire seasons.

Nevertheless, prospectors were expected to adhere to clearly set procedures governing the preemption of mineral claims. These codes had been established on California precedents, which had been adopted as the mining frontier expanded to Nevada, Colorado, Idaho, and Montana. Prospectors were not only obliged to file their claims before the county recorder within a specified period; they had to bring a sample of ore with them, they had to pay a fee, and they had to swear that they had staked their claims in a precise and clearly marked manner. For quartz lodes this meant driving substantial stakes (usually five inches wide) at each end of the discovery claim; upon each stake was to be "written in legible characters the name of the lode as well as the names of the claimants thereof." For quartz properties, eleven claims in all were authorized for each lode; a discovery claim and five additional claims stretched out on either side of the discovery, each 100 by 200 feet in size. Discoverers were obligated, moreover, to have sunk on the discovery claim, to a depth sufficient to reveal at least "one well defined wall rock," the wall or side of a vein of ore. The claimant also had to attest that the sample of quartz deposited with the recorder had been "taken out of the discovery claim on said lode by the discoverer."[15]

Finally, the person filing the claim had to pay the recorder for the privilege of filing on the discovery and one additional claim on either side. The recorder then issued to each claimant a certificate of ownership—a possessory right to real estate. So the process of locating a lode and filing on it was no easy matter. Unless a fraudulent claim was being made, one had to have put in earnest work on the site, devoted up to two days of travel to Virginia City and return, and had access to the filing fee, which could total as much as $24.50 if the prospector—at his own expense—had chosen to write in friends and relatives or to pay off debts or obligations to businesses or public officials.

One way to mitigate the requirements was for miners to combine their efforts. Both the General Lee and Lawreance Lode discovery claims were made by a group of men from various states—including Vermont, Georgia, and Illinois—who called themselves the Independent Quartz Mining Company. Both discoveries were placer claims in the Meadow Creek drainage, thus showing prospectors' natural inclination to seek out placer diggings in preference to the harder-to-work hard-rock quartz mining properties. Contrary to common belief, however, placer gold was not found "literally lying at one's feet." After the surface had been skimmed, placer miners had to sink shafts down to bedrock—the rock or solid clay underlying the gulch. Gold, by its superior weight, found its way to this level. It was not unusual for bedrock shafts to reach depths of fifty to sixty feet, and when bedrock had been reached it became necessary to erect hoists or to excavate drain ditches sometimes miles in length to obtain the precious metal.

Once procured, placer gold came in various sizes and shapes. In every case it is relatively pure, mixed in with sand, dirt, gravel, and rock. This gold was separated from its host by simply washing it with water. The most elementary means of recovery was through panning. Under normal circumstances a prospector could wash fifty pans a day. Another crude method of recovery was through use of a rocker, built something like a child's cradle but with cleats (also known as riffles) fixed to the bottom to catch the gold, which, weighing nineteen times more than water, worked its way to the bottom. Placed streamside, a rocker was generally worked by two men; one rocked and applied water, the other provided the dirt.

Both panning and rockering were arduous and slow. Sluicing improved the system significantly. Sometimes hundreds of feet in length, wooden sluices carried considerable water at great force, enabling more miners to process much larger quantities of dirt and gravel. The length of the sluice increased the number of riffles, thereby increasing the prospects of capturing gold. If the gold was unusually fine, as it was in Madison County, mercury (quicksilver) was poured into the mixture of dirt and water. The mercury amalgamated with the gold it contacted, later to be separated by heating. The mercury could be used repeatedly, since most of it was recoverable upon cooling.[16] Until 1867, when hydraulic mining was introduced to the Hot Spring District, panning, rockering, and sluicing were the placering methods employed at Norwegian Creek and at Washington Bar on Meadow Creek—the sites where Hot Spring's placer gold was located.

As Elliott West has pointed out, however, placer gold represented merely "crumbs brushed from the table," whereas the major objective was the metal's original source.[17] Once the placer mines were fully staked out, miners who had missed out on the initial strikes or who dreamed of finding the "mother lode" headed for higher ground often well removed from the streams and riverbeds. Hard physical toil in itself did not necessarily generate rewards. Quartz lode prospecting was far more complex than placering. The prospector for quartz gold had to understand the geology of the country he was exploring and had to have sufficient knowledge and experience to recognize signs of its mineralization. That prospectors often worked in teams proved the maxim that group effort generated a greater chance of success.

A good prospector possessed very special capabilities. As Otis Young has observed, these might be so highly developed as to enable him to "detect . . . trifling changes in the kind of color of the scrub [brush], or even the speedier melting of light snowfall upon a band of mineralized rock." More commonly, the prospector centered on the kind of mineralization prominent in the district and then sought its indications.[18] In the Hot Spring District this was so-called float rock, gold mineralization that could be found on the surface and that was free of base metals. As one prospector reported, Hot Spring was rich in "free gold," and the outcroppings were heavier and better defined than in any other district known to him.[19] Coloration was also quite specific to Hot Spring ores. White quartz surface rock was conspicuous in its association with Hot Spring gold, and the district's float rock—and other rock contiguous to it—often bore a distinctive reddish orange tint caused by the action of descending waters, a clue that assisted prospectors in locating promising leads.[20]

Having ascertained the presence of gold, the prospector was then compelled to determine the extent and value of his find. Would it pay to develop it? Here he relied on skills long honed in history. "Indeed," Young noted, "his eyes, teeth, nose, saliva, and sense of 'heft' alone could force the rocks to give up much information. [A] bit of metallic-yellow mineral placed between the teeth gritted noisily if it was anything but native gold. Saliva dabbed upon a pebble or specimen enabled one to peer 'into' it . . . so as to detect the yellow specks of gold." The sense of heft was important, as rock containing gold was heavier than that without it. Color was the most important of all, with the "possession of an 'artistic' eye for shades . . . deemed essential to successful practice."[21]

The prospector then tested the float rock by crushing and panning it. If panning proved unsatisfactory, he was likely to crush a second sample of ore and boil it, applying salt, soda, and a small amount of mercury. If gold existed, it would adhere to the mercury. This pellet would then be roasted over a fire. The mercury would vaporize—leaving behind a bead or button of gold. From this the prospector could estimate, by proportionate means, just how much gold could be obtained from the ore at hand. Although this test was reliable, many prospectors were so adept at gauging colors that they bypassed it, certain that by mere eyeballing they could accurately assess the profitability or nonprofitability of their discovery.[22] Needless to say, a prospector who had acquired these skills—often meaning a miner with previous, particularly California, experience—would be in heavy demand when the capitalists arrived.

Once convinced he was on to something of value, the prospector might simply skim off the surface, taking the exposed ore and going no farther. How many did this in the Hot Spring area will remain unknown. For the most part, Hot Spring's prospectors appear to have gone beyond to examine the lode's values up to six or eight feet below the surface, digging with pick and shovel, perhaps even using dynamite. More often than not, superficial subsurface digging did not pan out, and the prospector was compelled to start the process over at another location. But if the prospector uncovered quartz indicating satisfactory value and if he didn't bound off to locate something even more profitable, he would take samples, pace off his claim boundaries, and set his corner posts. On these he'd attach a location notice and make notes, written or mental, on the relationship of his discovery to area landmarks. Frequently, he would note other discoveries nearby. This process completed, he had so many days to proceed to Virginia City to present his samples, pay his fee, and record his claim at the county recorder's office. Some prospectors might, prior to that and provided they could afford it, have their specimens assayed by a professional. Overwhelmingly, these assays would have been undertaken in Virginia City.

Relatively few prospectors were enamored of development beyond what it took to determine the value of a discovery. Prospecting, not mining, was in their blood, and few were inclined or had the financial means to undertake a mining operation. If they ran out of grub, they would likely sell their claims for what they could get and go back to prospecting. As often as not, they sat on their discoveries, preempting and holding them as real estate pending the arrival of capital and stamp mills to work them out. This tendency was characterisitic of lode owners in the Hot Spring District and would eventually prove a detriment to the district's success, as it was difficult for capitalists to know if deep digging on these mines would prove profitable, surface indications not always bearing witness to true value.

Prospectors were not the only sort to populate the gulches. The May 27, 1864, claimants of the Lexington Lode up the north fork of Meadow Creek had also preempted a mill site.[23] They were not the first to do so, as previously a party of five men had claimed ground on a branch of Norwegian Creek—including all of its "water, springs, and seepage"—for milling and mining purposes.[24] Shortly, two more mill site claims were made on the south fork of Meadow Creek.[25] All of these early mill preemptions are poorly described and very difficult to place. In any event, no record exists of any of these enterprises materializing. Another did: on August 24, 1864, William H. House recorded his purchase for $1,200 of one-third part of a sawmill site and "all the fixtures thereto belonging to the mill *now being constructed*."[26]

All told, Madison County records of preemption—agricultural, mineral, and mill—indicate that by the end of 1864 the Hot Spring District had been impacted significantly by human endeavors. Agriculturally, at least twenty-six homesteads had been preempted. Cabins had been erected on many of them. These farmers and ranchers were concentrated in the Meadow Creek area, where more than 3,000 acres had been filed on. These claims extended along the Madison River above its canyon and four miles up the Meadow Creek drainage. Meadow Creek also featured a sawmill, one of the territory's first. Other quarter sections of land had been preempted to the north of Meadow Creek, across the divide, on the upper stretch of Hot Spring Creek, and in Norwegian Gulch.

Although farmers and ranchers were conspicuous in fertile areas, in number they were greatly exceeded in 1864 by those who labored throughout the district as prospectors and developers of gold-bearing soils. Just how many comprised this group is difficult to say, but when the Rev. Learner B. Stateler, a southern Methodist-Episcopalian minister from Kentucky and an unabashed secessionist, chose the Norwegian District in mid-July 1864 in which to establish his pastorate and, with his family, escape the passions of the Civil War, he did so because the camp not only contained a group of families of similar political and religious persuasion—mostly from Missouri and Iowa—but because Norwegian Creek was the Hot Spring District's most heavily populated camp. By Stateler's estimate some "two-to-three hundred men" had established themselves in Norwegian Creek "taking out gold."[27] These men, working mostly in placer diggings along Norwegian Creek and its tributaries—notably Rattlesnake Gulch—produced four of every nine claims made in the Hot Spring District in 1864. Although population estimates for Upper Hot Spring and Meadow Creek are lacking, taking the Norwegian figures as a base it is likely that at the height of 1864 the Hot Spring District as a whole was worked over by 400 to 600 men—some with wives and families—who prospected, labored in the mines, or scoured out ditches to provide water to diggings.

Some of these were pilgrims, prospecting the district's mineral wealth as they passed through. June through September 1864 witnessed the arrival in Montana of large numbers of wagon trains. "Emigrants are pouring in and the whole country is one bustle of excitement," reported a prospector from Virginia City.[28] Although most emigrants traveled over the southern wagon or northern river routes, four wagon trains in 1864 chose Bozeman's Trail or Bridger's Cutoff, newly blazed trails that left the old road just west of Fort Laramie in Wyoming. These trails proceeded in a northerly direction on either side of the Bighorn Mountains to the Yellowstone River. Reaching Bozeman City in the Gallatin Valley, the wagon trains either traveled west to the Madison River, crossing the river at Black's Ford, or followed the East and West Gallatin Rivers to the three forks of the Missouri River and then came up the Madison Valley and through the Norwegian Gulch area. In either case trains destined for Virginia City by way of Bozeman's Trail had to come right through the Hot Spring District. Since Hot Spring was more than a full day's wagon train journey from the Alder Gulch diggings, the emigrants all seem to have camped in the Hot Spring District—taking a day or two or even more to rest there and in numerous cases to survey its assets.

One of these emigrants was William E. Atchison. Fresh from a remarkably trouble-free passage over Bridger's Cutoff and Bozeman's Trail, Atchison reached the Madison River on July 25, 1864, where his ears were filled with reports of rich discoveries at Norwegian. Atchison noted that fourteen of his fellow travelers left the train to check out prospects there.[29] Another member of the same company, Charles W. Baker, joined ten others in a trip to the placer diggings in Washington Gulch, about six miles west of their camp on the south side of North Meadow Creek. Here Baker's group staked out claims. The next day Baker and several others left camp for Virginia City. Two days later he came back to the Meadow Creek camp for one more day of prospecting.[30]

Within the month another wagon train bound for Virginia City—with A. A. Townsend as wagon master—camped four days in the Hot Spring area to enable members of the train to prospect. One of the prospectors, Benjamin W. Ryan, visited the Norwegian diggings. "Found quite a number a mining; about 100 claims taken," he jotted in his diary the next morning.[31]

Although some of Hot Spring's lode discoveries were made by members of emigrant trains, most of the prospecting energy came from men who extended their operations to Hot Spring from established mining camps. County preemption and court records provide an example of a team of miners, mostly from Wisconsin and largely from a family named Crawford, who branched off into Hot Spring from their Alder Gulch base in July 1864 and who would become important to the subsequent development of the district.

On May 7, 1864, two of the Crawfords, Andrew and Alexander, joined with P. G. Carter, Henry C. Crowell, Reuben Barringer, and Gilbert B. Weeks to form and incorporate the Virginia City Mining Company.[32] This nucleus was augmented shortly by the addition of Samuel Farrar, Fred F. Myers, J. C. Otto, William Florkee, and five more Crawfords—Henry F. ("Hank"), J. B., Alphonso, J. H., and Daniel W. Although the company had promising properties on Fairweather Bar in Alder Gulch, when its members heard of discoveries in the Hot Spring District, several journeyed over to evaluate the prospects. In July 1864, Andrew Crawford, the company's patriarch, began prospecting, along with Farrar and Myers, on the north side of Hot Spring Creek in its upper canyon above the juncture of that stream and Pony Creek, a smaller feeder from the north. Here they found rich prospects, and, returning to Virginia City, they filed a discovery claim on the Galena Lode, one of the most important discoveries ever made in the Hot Spring District.[33] Over time the Galena would develop into one of the district's steadiest performers, producing good values and enticing periodic interest in its prospects up to the present day.

Shortly after having filed on the Galena, the company, in various combinations of membership, made twelve more discovery claims on the upper reaches of Hot Spring Creek or within two miles to the north of it. Even though the group would subsequently claim the Alameda Lode in Fairweather District—soon one of the county's most celebrated quartz properties—the Crawford Company had found Hot Spring prospects enticing and would eventually shift much of its energy to that district, in the process becoming involved in the fortunes of the milling enterprises soon to be established there.

Prospectors, of course, were not the only ones to seek interests in mining districts removed from Alder Gulch. The variety of men who banked claims all over the county is remarkable. Government officials were conspicuous among those who sought to profit from discoveries. Neil Howie, U.S. marshal for Madison County, rarely missed such an opportunity, irrespective of his duties. Whether Howie was tending to the law or not, he seemed often to be in the field looking for lodes to stake out or invest in. In mid-June 1864, when Howie was compelled to ride over to Norwegian Gulch to attach some property and make an arrest, he might well have checked in on a claim he had filed earlier on the Grandmother Lode, west of Hot Spring Creek.[34] Howie's deputies, John Featherstun and John X. Beidler, also had claims in Hot Spring.[35] Hardly a sheriff, deputy, or marshal working out of Virginia City during the mid-1860s failed to acquire property in the districts surrounding the county seat, Hot Spring among them.

County and territorial officials observed these developments with eagle eyes and took liberal advantage of their offices to become heavy speculators in mining properties. Some officials, such as county clerks and recorders, received their entire salary in fees—mostly those paid by lode claimants and preemptors of land. By any measure these were fabulous salaries. At $24.50 a lode claim, for example, the clerks and recorders could make many hundreds of dollars a day. Considering that common laborers were fortunate to receive $5 a day for grueling work, clerks and recorders could make that much in minutes. Territorial supreme court justice Ezra Munson's observation that strategically placed recorders could earn salaries exceeding that of the president of the United States was not an exaggeration.[36] Appointment to territorial public office represented one of the most blatant practices of political patronage. When territorial attorney general Edward B. Nealley described the clerk and recorder's office as an "office of great influence and in the present quartz excitement of great value," he was speaking not only of the direct profit to be had for the recorder but also of the ability of the recorder both to obtain claims and to pinpoint good investments for his cronies.[37] Familiarity with a recorder and the continuity of that favorable relationship, once established, could pay handsome dividends.

Most clerks and recorders either pocketed the $24.50 fee or took a lode claim instead of, or for a reduction in, the fee. And as clerks and recorders were privy to mining developments through the claiming process, they understood all too well where the values were and made purchases accordingly.

Colonel Robert M. Hagaman, Madison County's first clerk and recorder, worked this system assiduously. By late October 1864, or six months after having been appointed to office by territorial governor Sidney Edgerton, Hagaman had accumulated more than two miles of claims on sixty-eight lodes in seventeen districts or gulches. Of this footage, 10 percent was located in the Hot Spring District. All of this he put on the New York City market, granting power of attorney to Walter C. Hopkins, a resident of that city and soon to be affiliated with one of Hot Spring's major milling enterprises.[38]

The courts were strongly represented in this group of absentee claimants. On December 5, 1864, when newly appointed territorial chief justice Hezekiah L. Hosmer administered the oath of allegiance to the United States to the twenty-three lawyers desiring to practice in his court, nineteen of the twenty-three—some of whom had been in the territory only a few weeks—held mineral claims in the Hot Spring District.[39] Hosmer soon joined the ranks, obtaining a claim on the Hale Lode, a Norwegian Gulch discovery, the very next month.[40] Hosmer's investments in Montana gold mining enterprises, including those in Hot Spring, eventually became extensive.

Virginia City–area businessmen also took heavy speculative positions in Hot Spring discoveries. Three of the earliest discovery claims in the Hot Spring District were made on Meadow Creek by the Eagle Mining Company.[41] The Eagle Mining Company consisted of ten men, seven of whom made notable contributions to Montana history: George Higgins, Captain Nicholas Wall, John Thomas Conner, Colonel John J. Hull, John A. Creighton, Thomas W. Cover, and Perry W. McAdow. This group contracted with one or more of the other members of the company to do the fieldwork while they provided the financial backing—grubstaking the agent or agents in the field and paying for costs of development, including the fee charged for filing a discovery and ten additional claims. The Eagle Mining Company would be but the precursor of several groups of entrepreneurs that would form for the purpose of profiting from Hot Spring gold mining. Having secured footholds in the district, some of these men—in particular Creighton, a well-known Nebraska freighter, stockman, and telegraph line contractor—would become active developers of the Hot Spring District in 1865.

For all the human energy at work in Hot Spring, most of it was concentrated within a very few months. By late August and September 1864, many emigrants had lost their enthusiasm for the mountains and started for home. When Richard Owen came through the Hot Spring area on his way from Omaha to Virginia City in late August, he observed that Norwegian's miners were leaving daily.[42] The Reverend Stateler also noted that many of the miners in Norwegian left the region for the winter.[43] When the Territorial Poll Census was taken in November, only twenty-five persons were listed for the Norwegian/South Willow Creek area, a reduction of as much as 90 percent over estimates made in July.[44] The preacher himself moved his family fifteen miles northeast to the Jefferson River Valley where the winter climate was more temperate and snowfall less severe.

Most of the people cited on the Norwegian/South Willow Creek poll list returned to the area the following spring, including the Statelers. And so would others who had worked in the Upper Hot Spring and Meadow Creek areas. The winter of 1864–1865, although limiting the ability of land and mineral holders to develop their preemptions, did not diminish interest in Hot Spring properties. Indeed, the Hot Spring District was on the verge of becoming one of the territory's most touted gold-bearing regions; over the next few years it would experience increased population growth and an explosion of energy, coupled with—and encouraged by—the infusion of eastern capital for the development and improvement of the district's many mines.

CHAPTER 2

Mills to Montana: 1865, I

THE RAGLAND, COPE, AND NAPTON

MINING COMPANY OF BOONVILLE,

MISSOURI, AND THE NEW YORK AND

MONTANA MINING AND DISCOVERY

COMPANY OF NEW YORK CITY, NEW YORK

"[I]n point of number, richness, and superior facilities for working, the auriferous veins of Hot Spring district [are] unequalled
by any in the Territory."

—Asahel K. Eaton

AS TWO CONTEMPORARY ANALYSTS OF THE TERRITORY'S EARLY MINING HIS-
TORY remembered it, "The Spring of 1865 . . . broke upon Montana
as the dazzling brightness of an almost unexampled prosperity."[1]
Not only were Alder Gulch's renowned placers still going strong, but numerous other gulches had been developed with gratifying results during
the fall and winter of 1864–1865. The most important of these was Last
Chance Gulch, located within present-day Helena. Confederate Gulch, up
the Missouri River from Helena, was also attracting much attention. Over
the Continental Divide important discoveries had been made at Silver Bow
and in German Gulch, both in Deer Lodge County. Rich and extensive

17

placers had been discovered in the neighborhood of Blackfoot City.

As productive as placer mining was, quartz mining was fast coming into a prominence, even a superiority, of its own. Those who sought the origins of the gold being worked out of gulches, streams, and rivers were discovering untold prospects of wealth in the hills and mountains above. Virtually all of the placer districts mentioned previously had their counterparts in quartz lode, or hard-rock, development. In Madison County numerous leads of great promise had been unveiled high in the gulches south of Virginia City, up in the Tobacco Root Mountains stretching north, and in the rolling hills of the Jefferson and Madison River valleys.

Hot Spring's place in this proliferation of discoveries was one of the notable developments of 1865. As its mineral wealth was realized and proclaimed, it became the working place for increasing numbers of prospectors and developers. By year's end 338 new discoveries would be recorded for Hot Spring, and their discoverers and claimants were convinced that the district was no less rich in promise than any in the territory. If Last Chance, Confederate, Silver Bow, and Blackfoot were the recipients of increased attention, attracting more and more emigrants, Hot Spring, with its remarkable development in quartz lodes, was equally the beneficiary of the extraordinary radiation of mining activity out into the territory in 1865.

There were good reasons to deem Hot Spring's potential as unrivaled in Montana. Hot Spring surface and near-surface ores were indisputably rich. Here oxidized ores, enriched and left in a more or less free state by exposure to weathering, paid handsome profits. Many assays from the weathered zone had already produced results unmatched anywhere in Montana Territory. Many thought these remarkable gold leads would multiply in value with depth. This was believed not only by residents of Montana but by increasing numbers who resided in the populous and wealthy states to the east. Capitalists who had hitherto considered Colorado and California suitable places for investment now had Montana in mind; some, as we shall see, would focus on the Hot Spring area in particular.

Accompanying these developments was the general realization that for placer or lode gold mining to produce desired values, the basic methods of mineral extraction would have to be improved. Panning and sluicing on placer claims would have to yield to hydraulicking, and successful hard-rock mining would necessitate the construction of quartz mills. Significant amounts of capital would have to be introduced to underwrite these improvements. Both processes represented a secondary phase in the development of gold mining—that of applying improved technology and organized capital to the procurement of the precious metals. The first phase in the history of gold mining, the exploitation of soil and stream with pick and shovel by the fabled argonauts of the nineteenth century, is well-known. These early prospectors were found almost exclusively in areas where the gold was most plentiful and easily obtained. They partook in the so-called placer phase of the gold rush era—the working out of free gold from gulches, basins, streams, and rivers. Placer mining sometimes produced phenomenal profits, but it was wasteful and inefficient. Using crude methods of extraction, miners skimmed off only the best and most accessible gold. They failed to capitalize on the presence of other valuable minerals, and they often stampeded to any district that promised them a better return.[2]

To counter such inefficiency, miners sought to increase the scope and thoroughness of their labors. One means was hydraulic mining, the powering of water through high-pressure hoses and nozzles onto stream banks and hillsides to wash them down and produce a supply of auriferous gravel and dirt much more readily than could be obtained by panning and sluicing. With an efficient hydraulicking operation, one or two miners could achieve in an hour what scores scarcely achieved in a day.[3] By contrast, hard-rock mining was much more complex, expensive, and demanding. It required extensive subterranean excavation, timbering, hauling, and the construction of steam- and water-powered stamp and crushing mills. Most early prospectors lacked the resources necessary to develop their holdings profitably. For the vast majority, the only hope lay in persuading capitalists to improve their claims for them. Indeed, the displacement of individual miners with corporatively capitalized operations represented the most significant development in mining during the 1860s.[4]

Although the Hot Spring District possessed two areas in which placering was prominent—Norwegian Gulch in the north and Washington Bar on Meadow Creek—the advance to hydraulicking would not be applied in Hot Spring until the summer of 1867. In contrast, hard-rock miners in the district, like hard-rock miners everywhere on the western mining frontier, quickly realized how inadequate their prospects would be without the introduction of machinery. This can be documented for the Hot Spring District as early as September 1864, when the Virginia City partners of the Eagle Mining Company discussed the desirability of acquiring a quartz mill and putting it up on the waters of Meadow Creek.[5] Shortly after, Rider, Hunter and Company, which held numerous claims on both Meadow and Hot Spring creeks, commissioned one of its members to "proceed to the States and use all endeavor to secure and bring out a quartz mill . . . said mill to be put up as soon as practicable during the year AD 1865, the dangers of navigation on the Missouri River, the casualties of [the Civil] war, and Indian depredations on the plains excepted."[6]

Neither of these mills was constructed, but others would be. Before 1865 was out, three companies, operating on capital secured overwhelmingly from investors in the States, had installed or begun construction of quartz mills in the Upper Hot Spring and Norwegian districts. The first of the companies to erect a working mill was the firm of Ragland, Cope, and Napton; the capital supporting construction came mostly from Boonville, Saline County, Missouri. The New York and Montana Mining and Discovery Company, another firm that began operations in the district in 1865, was heavily capitalized by men from Gotham. The third entity to build a mill in the Hot Spring District, the Clark and Upson Mining Company, was bankrolled by entrepreneurs from in and around Hartford, Connecticut. Not coincidentally, these same Hartford capitalists simultaneously organized a second company, the Nelson Mining Company, to underwrite Alder Gulch's first hydraulic placer mining venture.

The Ragland, Cope, and Napton Mining Company was organized by George Frederick Cope, a native of Boonville. At an early age Cope had tried his hand at gold mining in Colorado. Having heard of rich strikes in Montana, he left Black Hawk, Colorado, for Bannack in the spring of 1863, arriving on the Fourth of July. He was just twenty-one years of age and diminutive in stature.[7] Sometime that year he relocated from Bannack to Alder Gulch.[8] Cope understood the advantage of quartz milling and returned to Missouri in the winter of 1864–1865 to persuade others to invest their resources in such an enterprise. Cope found two men willing to take the risk: William Napton and William Ragland.

William Barclay Napton Jr. was the oldest of ten children born to a Missouri supreme court judge in Saline County. At age eighteen Napton had caught western fever; in 1857 he joined a company hauling freight to Santa Fe, New Mexico.[9] The following year young Napton penetrated even farther into the interior, working on a steamboat between Missouri and Fort Benton, Montana.[10] Subsequently wandering home to Missouri, he turned to the study of law, but before completing his studies he was caught up in the Civil War, joining Confederate forces. In the fall of 1861 he was captured by federal troops and, as he put it, "given the alternative of going to prison or taking the oath of allegiance." Napton chose the latter option and commenced practicing law in Boonville. It was while he was thus employed that George Cope persuaded him to join in a quartz mill venture.[11]

William N. Ragland was forty-five when Cope approached him in early 1865. Prior to the Civil War, Ragland had achieved considerable success and affluence as a farmer in Boonville. But Boonville was located strategically on the Missouri River 125 miles west of St. Louis; caught between Union and Confederate forces and ravaged by guerrilla warfare, it suffered badly during the sectional conflict. Despite suffering personal loss and property damage, Ragland got caught up in Cope's enthusiasm and was persuaded to take the lion's share in the fledgling enterprise.[12] Pooling their capital—with Ragland contributing $17/38$, Napton $11/38$, and Cope $10/38$—the partners purchased a fifteen-stamp quartz mill for $26,000 in St. Louis and arranged for the mill's passage to Madison County on the first boat up the Missouri River to Fort Benton in April 1865.[13]

Cope set out across the plains to beat the mill to Montana, as he and his partners needed to select a site for its construction. Arriving in Virginia City in late May 1865, Cope visited the office of the *Montana Post* and informed its editor that he had a fifteen-stamp mill—with power to drive fifty stamps, if needed—on its way up the Missouri. Using the paper as his forum, Cope let it be known that he had much experience as a mill owner in Colorado and that he had on hand all the auxiliaries necessary to carry out a successful operation, including copper and quicksilver. The company bore no prejudice toward any gold-bearing district, he said, but would allow the mill's location to be determined by any party or parties "possessing rich lodes" and desirous of contracting with his firm for the crushing of their ores. Cope added that he was also willing to sell a quarter interest in the mill to any interested party. This was actually an open call for an additional partner to underwrite 25 percent of the company's costs—and an admission that the resources of Ragland, Cope, and Napton were limited and that the enterprise was undercapitalized.[14]

Unfortunately, Cope did not succeed in finding a party or parties willing to take a quarter share in his company. Strapped for the cash necessary to erect the mill, he was compelled to accept a much less desirable alternative: a loan of $5,000 plus a working agreement from the Oro Fino Mining Company, a Virginia City–based investment venture holding title to quartz lodes almost entirely contained within the Norwegian mining region of the Hot Spring District. The company's prize possession, the Oro Fino Lode, had been discovered about half a mile north of the Rattlesnake branch of Norwegian Gulch in late August 1864.[15]

The Oro Fino Mining Company was composed of some of the territory's most notable public and business figures, including the territorial chief justice, Hezekiah L. Hosmer; the territorial attorney general, Edward E. Nealley; the Internal Revenue Service's territorial collector, Nathaniel Pitt Langford; William

Chumasero, the county's district attorney; Robert C. Knox, sheriff of Madison County; General Andrew P. Leach, county treasurer; and Richard Leach, Virginia City treasurer. Colonel William Maner Stafford, a Virginia City attorney, presided over the company. Other notables bought into the company, including Stafford's partners in law and several capitalists: Joseph Mallard, a local banker; Samuel T. Hauser, a young aggressive investor and later governor of the territory; and Henry Hauser, Samuel's brother. By any measure this was a group with considerable clout.[16]

The agreement between Ragland, Cope, and Napton and the Oro Fino Mining Company was drawn up in late June 1865.[17] By this understanding the Oro Fino Mining Company loaned Ragland, Cope, and Napton $5,000 to assist the company in erecting its fifteen-stamp quartz mill, "convenient to the Oro Fino Quartz Lode," on the condition that the mill be "erected on or before the 10th day of September." Ragland, Cope, and Napton furthermore was obliged to sink shafts to the depth of fifty feet on eight selected lodes— with special emphasis on the Oro Fino Lode—and to have prospected and developed any that could yield $50 per ton or more by the first of March 1866. Deeds to the Oro Fino's holdings on the eight lodes were then transferred to the Missouri company.[18] Although the recorded agreement doesn't stipulate it, the loan carried what Napton later complained was "heavy interest."[19] In every way this deal was highly favorable to the Oro Fino Mining Company. For $5,000—loaned at substantial interest—the company had secured a mill, had underwritten costs of operation and production, would obtain the development of its properties, and would receive profits taken from the eight lodes in question. Henry Hauser, who had bought into the Oro Fino company with his brother, anticipated good earnings from his investment. The Oro Fino Mining Company's prospects in Norwegian, he noted in his diary, were said to be "the best thing in the Territory."[20]

Although George Cope now had additional capital with which to install his mill and commence operations, he knew this agreement in itself would not guarantee profit to his company. Consequently, Cope courted additional arrangements to provide the mill with steady business and a paying income. These arrangements were complex and demanding. One such agreement took place between Cope and two Norwegian Gulch prospectors who agreed to deed over claims to Cope for a specific siting of the mill on Canadian Creek in the Norwegian District. Cope also agreed to crush at least one cord of ore, or about seven tons in quartz rock, each week from these miners' holdings from the time the mill went into operation until July 1, 1865, "at as low a rate as any other Mill in the Territory."[21] Another agreement obligated the Missouri company, in exchange for deeded property, to "devote three eighths of one year's running time" to the crushing of quartz furnished by a group of local prospectors.[22] Yet another agreement with four area miners obliged Ragland, Cope, and Napton to "crush quartz one day in each alternate week for one year," whereas a fourth contract required the company to crush quartz "three days in each and every month" for a year.[23]

True to Cope's word, the Ragland, Cope, and Napton quartz mill arrived at Fort Benton from its journey up the Missouri in early August, having made the river passage without serious mishap or delay. Indeed, the steamboat was one of the very last to successfully complete the entire trip to Fort Benton in 1865. The company's freight must have left Benton at once, for the mill was on-site in Canadian Gulch—an offshoot of Norwegian Gulch—preparatory to erection on August 21.[24] William Napton and William Ragland accompanied the mill on its passage from St. Louis to assist Cope in erecting the mill and arranging for production contracts. Ragland, Cope, and Napton had put in considerable effort to provide work for the mill and to secure revenues with which to pay off the company's debts and make good on its investment—although the partners were sure to experience difficulty in shifting from one ore-crushing assignment to another and in sinking shafts and developing mines. Unwilling to trust their prospects to walk-on trade, they had made and would continue to make extensive, formal, and precise contractual arrangements, recording them with the county—a practice and process that proved unusual compared with the subsequent work of other mill operators in the Hot Spring District. Whether these arrangements would prove worthy of their intent remained to be seen.

WHILE RAGLAND, COPE, AND NAPTON ERECTED ITS QUARTZ MILL IN CANADIAN GULCH IN the Norwegian District, a wagon train bearing a second quartz mill for Hot Spring District—that of the New York and Montana Mining and Discovery Company (NY&MM&D)—was laboring its way across the plains. By every measure the NY&MM&D Company was a much larger and much more heavily capitalized enterprise than Ragland, Cope, and Napton. That entrepreneurs from New York City should take an interest in such a venture is not difficult to understand. New York City was the undisputed commercial capital of the United States. More wealth resided there than in any other metropolis in the country. New York was the nation's greatest distribution center for both domestic and foreign goods; by itself it imported more grain, meat products, and textiles than its three leading competitors combined. New York ranked first in the nation in the value of its manufactures and in its capacity for providing shipping, merchandizing, and credit. Although this capability had been built over many years, the Civil War had provided it with a significant boost, not only by expanding the city's industrial capacity but also by bringing about the infusion of money to support activity on an unprecedented scale. Numerous New York bankers and banking houses either got their start or expanded during the war years. Ready cash produced speculation in stocks, money, and enterprise at record levels. It was not that enterprising New Yorkers had become individually richer than people in other cities; because of New York's population—over 1 million, including Brooklyn—there were simply more persons in the metropolitan area who had achieved prosperity before and during the war.[25]

The inclination to invest some of this surplus wealth in internal enterprise was definitely boosted by war-related factors. Formerly, New York had enjoyed extremely lucrative ties with southern enterprise, most notably the cotton trade—the nation's leading export commodity. But initial hopes of re-engaging in trade with the South after the war were dashed by the chaos of federal reconstruction and by many southerners' hatred toward their northern conquerors. Western ventures, by contrast, faced relatively fewer impediments and benefited from the growing rail linkage between New York and the interior, spurring the organization of numerous development companies and the human and financial resources to support them. One has only to scan the annual directories for the City of New York for venture-company advertisements during the immediate postbellum years to appreciate the breadth and depth of those commitments. New York would continue to reign as the nation's greatest seaport, but increasingly its commerce was concentrated at railroad depots rather than at the docks. For the most part these stations serviced points west.[26]

IN THIS ENVIRONMENT WAS BORN THE NEW YORK AND MONTANA MINING AND DISCOVERY Company. Founded in early 1865, "under and by the laws of the State of New York and doing business in the City of New York," the company had come about through the energies of Edwin R. Purple, a native New Yorker and veteran of California and Montana gold-seeking ventures.[27] Purple had stampeded to Bannack in 1863, where he acquired valuable stakes in the fabled Dakota Lode and in potentially valuable silver ore deposits near Bannack. Purple then followed the next stampede to Virginia City, where he developed a reputation for intelligence in mining matters.

Returning to New York City in late 1863, Edwin Purple met with New York entrepreneurs to outline a strategy he was contemplating for the upcoming season. He felt strongly that the group, which appears to have been unnamed initially, should purchase a twelve-stamp mill brought into Bannack in 1863 by E. D. Pitt. He received support for the idea, and in the spring of 1864, Purple set out for Montana to examine the Bannack prospects in the company of Walter C. Hopkins, previously cited as a noted promoter of Montana mines, and Professor Asahel K. Eaton, a chemist, geologist, and mineralogist. Satisfied by Eaton that profits were in the offing and that the mill and mines would suffice for the purpose, Hopkins purchased Pitt's mill in addition to an enlarged interest in the Dakota Lode. By November 1864 the group had the mill up and operating in Centerville, later renamed Marysville, about a mile down the gulch from Bannack. According to the *Montana Post,* around $60,000 in gold had been expended to purchase and erect the mill, secure gold-bearing ore, and put everything into operation.[28]

But the company was not content with Bannack alone. As the mill was being erected, Hopkins and Eaton expanded their pursuit of investment opportunities. Locally, they were attracted to silver deposits in Beaverhead County's Rattlesnake District. That Edwin Purple had interests in these lodes assuredly influenced the company's decision. But Eaton concurred: the silver ore could be satisfactorily smelted, he said, and the clay needed for the construction of a furnace to test the ores was present in the vicinity. Eaton and Hopkins immediately commenced to increase their holdings in Rattlesnake preparatory to construction of a furnace in 1865, which helped foster the development of a town near the mines called Montana City, later renamed Argenta.[29] Elsewhere, Eaton and Hopkins examined prospects in districts satellite to Virginia City. In October Eaton was actively purchasing and selling shares in lodes in Wisconsin Gulch on the west side of the Tobacco Root Mountains and in Meadow Creek on the east side.[30] Purple, Hopkins, and Eaton returned to New York City in November 1864, but not before Purple had informed Thomas Dimsdale at the *Montana Post* that his confidence in his findings had "succeeded in interesting some of the monied men of Gotham sufficiently to induce them to authorize and venture an investment in [the company's] quartz lodes."[31] The "monied men" referred to would become the backers of the New York and Montana Mining and Discovery Company.

There is no record of the NY&MM&D Company's letters of incorporation in the Secretary of State's Office in Albany, New York, nor of the company's initial public announcement. But matters of this sort followed a standard procedure. For instance, a joint stock company organized in New York at exactly the same time as the NY&MM&D Company and with almost identical interests in Montana issued a prospectus that hyped the remarkable character of the territory's ores, which were "known [to be] richer, apparently more abundant, and less expensive in working than any hitherto found in any State or territory of this country." This "opportunity for the profitable employment of capital, either by individual or Company expertise," the prospectus continued, "has never been excelled, and equaled only in exceptional instances, since quartz mining has become a source of wealth to the country."[32]

The cash—$75,000—necessary to underwrite a discovery expedition was to be raised by sale of the organizers' properties to the corporation's stockholders. The company concluded its announcement by backing up its remarkable assertions with supportive letters from prominent men who knew Montana, including Hezekiah L. Hosmer and two of the men who were principal in organizing the New York and Montana Mining and Discovery Company—Asahel K. Eaton and Edwin R. Purple. Hosmer, whose insatiable thirst for profit at least equaled, if not exceeded, his passion for justice under the law, provided the company with an ecstatic late December 1864 endorsement:

> My confidence in the means of making large amounts of money in a short time and in a legitimate way in this territory increases daily . . . as I believe there never will be another time on this continent when opportunities so inviting will be presented for investment as are now open here. You can know nothing of it now, but next year, when the true nature of our mineral resources [is] known in New York, you will not *then* deem me enthusiastic.[33]

Hosmer's endorsement of the extravagant get-rich-quick assertions made by the company, which virtually guaranteed profitable earnings in a short time, described the tactics of the stereotypical promoter of his day and age. For many, caution in undertaking investments was thrown to the winds when measured against the prospect of making the quick returns Hosmer and others were assuring their New York clients. The hype attached to the advertising of Montana and the territory's mineral wealth was so effective that thousands of men and women were willing to pay extravagant prices for property of which they had not the slightest knowledge, save for the boasts of the promoters they were led, or wanted, to believe.

The aforementioned serves as a good example of the way numerous speculative enterprises were inaugurated in New York City during this period. War profits and inflation had created balmy days in Gotham. William W. Fowler, a veteran of Wall Street, gave a colorful, highly opinionated, but not inaccurate account of the orgy of speculation at work in lower Manhattan in the mid-1860s:

> [Speculative enterprises] proceeded to organize companies in all manner of those useful, costly, and beautiful things, which bountiful mother earth

pours out of her lap in the rough. Samples of these things could be seen in Wall Street; brokers and bankers appeared to have been suddenly smitten with a passion for mineralogy. Their offices were transformed into cabinets of minerals, containing very fine specimens of sulphuret of lead, carbonate of copper, and oxide of iron, besides blocks of quartz bespangled with virgin gold, and lumps of coal which burned like a candle. Their talk was in mining slang, and "pockets," "fissure veins," "faults," "spurs," "lodes," "pyrites," "chimneys" ran all through their vocabulary. The press teemed with advertisements of these various enterprises, and some of the daily journals devoted columns to the record of what had been done, was doing, or was about to be done, in this new field of speculation. . . . In fine, far off in the wilderness, as well as close to the fringes of civilization, there were hidden treasures without number, materials for wealth without stint, ungarnered, unminted, unmoulded, almost unwatched.[34]

In much the same fashion, and undoubtedly on the basis of like rhetoric, the New York and Montana Mining and Discovery Company was organized and stock issued on February 1, 1865. Eaton's recommendations were critical in shaping the company's action policy, for he had concluded that the company should go beyond its Bannack gold and silver interests. He was particularly pleased with what he had seen in Madison County and urged the company to install a second quartz mill there as soon as possible. Eaton especially favored the Hot Spring District, and even before the company was officially organized, its backers acquired a number of Hot Spring claims from men who—like Eaton, Hopkins, and Purple—had returned east for the winter.[35] To carry this effort to Montana, the company created a discovery corps, for which Eaton, listed as a geologist and mineralogist, was appointed superintendent. At the same time, Eaton, Hopkins, Purple, and Willard Oliver, the company's treasurer, helped found "The Montana Territory Society," an organization formed in New York City to promote investment opportunities in Montana.[36]

Professor Asahel K. Eaton, on whom much of this company's story will turn, is one of many persons who impacted Montana's early territorial period. Although trained as an agricultural chemist, Eaton, a balding man in his mid-forties when he began work for the NY&MM&D Company, had broad scientific interests and capabilities. One account credits him with having perfected a process for smelting iron.[37] Another portrayed him as having been engaged for a number of years "in prospecting for different Eastern capitalists and companies among the gold and silver mines of New Mexico, Arizona, Australia, California, and Montana." Facile in many subjects, Eaton was said to speak with authority on the topics of "climate, soil, timber, water, coal, fruit, grain, [and] facilities of traveling."[38]

Eaton's breadth in scientific matters was indeed remarkable. Although not a mining engineer per se, in effect he was one and more—a composite chemist, geologist, surveyor, agriculturalist, metallurgist, and mineralogist. He not only knew how to locate, identify, remove, and develop ores taken from the ground, he also took on responsibility for reducing the metal from the ore. He devised machines to improve such operations, and he actively engaged in promoting and marketing his work. Employed in New York City at the United States Assay Office, Eaton also ran an assaying school in Brooklyn, New York. Not content to apply all these skills locally, he had carried his profession abroad. With his versatility an acknowledged fact, he had caught the attention of capitalists in New York and was engaged by the NY&MM&D Company to serve as its expert in the field.[39]

Now formally organized, the company proceeded to contract with H. R. Worthington and Co. of Brooklyn for a forty-stamp, water-powered quartz mill, cost unknown but certainly in excess of that built for $26,000 for the Ragland, Cope, and Napton Mining Company. After consideration, a standard rather than a newer or improved mill was chosen, since experience had demonstrated that such a model should work easily and effectively in the field; and particularly because it was so simple in construction, with duplicate parts on hand, the company felt it could avoid "serious loss of time from breakage or derangement of machinery." This was a "decisive consideration," the company argued, for operating in Montana, "a locality remote from foundries and machine-shops."[40]

In addition to the quartz mill, which would be driven by a water-powered turbine installed under the mill itself, the company purchased a considerable amount of supplementary equipment. This included sixteen arrastras—primitive, beast-of-burden–driven, ore-crushing devices intended for use while the mill was under construction, when it was inoperative as a result of malfunction or lack of water power, or to add to the mill's capacity for any reason; twenty amalgamators, devices that conveyed the gold in the pulverized ore into a union with mercury; and seven sets of duplicate dies and shoes, the latter the heavy metallic pieces that were fastened to the end of the stamps. Worthington completed the order in seventy days, whereupon the entire lot, including 3,000 pounds of mercury in forty large flasks, was shipped by rail to the Missouri River town of Atchison, Kansas. In the meantime, while the mill was being constructed and shipped, Eaton and a group of employees, designated the "discovery team," left New York in advance to catch a boat up the Missouri to canvass Montana for an ideal mill location.[41]

ALTHOUGH EATON AND HIS DISCOVERY PARTY WERE ABLE TO GET TO MONTANA THROUGH a combined Missouri River and overland route, the two-and-a-half months it took to assemble the mill and its parts, the late arrival of the company's machinery at Atchison, its size and weight, and the rapidly decreasing depth of the river forced the NY&MM&D Company to forgo conveyance by water for the much slower, laborious, and more expensive passage over land. To undertake this, Edwin Purple and Enfield Loring Pratt, superintendent of the company's field operations, accompanied the company's freight to Atchison, where they sought to purchase an outfit—wagons and teams of oxen to pull them, men to guide the teams, and provisions to feed and supply both. This was a formidable undertaking, as many hundreds of pioneers and numerous outfits had converged at Atchison and were competing for the same services and goods. It being a seller's market, wagons and teams were in short supply, and the company had to pay exorbitant prices to get what it required.

After much difficulty, Purple put together a sizable outfit—324 oxen and thirty-eight wagons tended by a crew of forty-five men, including Enfield Pratt who took over as wagon master.[42] The costs were formidable; before the train had moved a foot west, another $39,041 had been added to the cost of the mill. The costs included $6,191 for rail and personnel expenses associated with freighting the mill to Atchison; $23,235 to purchase the 324 oxen and yokes, bows, and chains; $6,630 for thirty-eight ox wagons; $502 for six horses with saddles, bridles, and cinches; and $2,483 for various odds and ends to round out the outfit, including cooking gear, tents, wagon covers, whiplashes, 130 additional yokes with irons, a branding iron, and extra axle trees and tongues.[43] Salaries excluded, the NY&MM&D Company had expended a considerable amount of money as the train readied itself to set out west through Kansas and Nebraska for the Montana goldfields. Finally, after vexatious delays, the train moved out of Atchison on July 10, 1865, in the humidity of a wet and oppressively hot summer. Purple chose not to accompany the train. Falling ill, he seems also to have fallen into the background of company actions.

The trek to the goldfields is one almost all of the major companies destined for Hot Spring had to plan, underwrite, and undertake at considerable expense. For the journey to Montana—which in itself rivaled in its geographic remoteness and isolation virtually any other part of the United States—involved numerous hazards beyond length of passage alone, many of them unpredictable and uncontrollable. These could make or break the fortunes of mining companies even before they had commenced crushing quartz. Just how many hundreds of companies shipped the components of their quartz milling enterprises over the plains, over the mountains, up the Missouri River, or inland from the West Coast before the completion of the transcontinental railroad system in 1869 might never be known. But in the case of Hot Spring, the supply routes and journeys of three of the principal companies that erected mills in the district in the mid-1860s can be traced with fair accuracy. As it turns out, each of these companies suffered adversely from the journey to the Hot Spring District.

The route chosen by the New York and Montana Mining and Discovery Company was at its outset the traditional one employed by western sojourners for twenty-plus years: the Oregon Trail. This took the train slightly northwest from Atchison through the Little Blue River country of Nebraska to Fort Kearney on the South Platte River. At first, it would not have been easy going. The northeast section of Kansas is deeply cut by numerous slow-moving streams that would have caused much inconvenience in that summer's rainy conditions. Farther west, however, travel through the plains of southern Nebraska along the South Platte would have been more pleasurable, following the bluffs and undulating plains along the river, turbulent and murky at the time. And travel westward from Fort Kearney to Julesburg, in the very northeastern corner of Colorado, would have been relatively free of burden, provided the train did not meet up with hostile natives.

In this regard, members of the train must have felt great apprehension, for earlier in the season Indian depredations had caused much injury, death, and general grief along the entire South Platte River route. One wagon train foreman vividly recollected that his passage that same year from the Little Blue River in Kansas all the way to the foothills of the Colorado Rockies had presented scenes of incredible carnage. Over a distance of seventy to eighty miles on the Little Blue River, "Every house was burned and most every person killed. Their bodies were left scalped and lying in the yard, some yards would have one to ten graves." Conditions had been no better farther west. Julesburg had been sacked at least twice; only one house remained. Every stage station west of that outpost had been burned to the ground.[44] It is hard to believe that the Pratt train did not encounter some of the same devastation.

No doubt influenced by these experiences and by recommendations from the military, the NY&MM&D Company's wagon train decided at Julesburg to continue along the south bank of the South Platte on a bowed route southwesterly to Fremont's Orchard and then northwest to Fort Collins along the eastern face of the Rocky Mountains, rather than follow the shorter overland route through Cheyenne to South Pass.[45] Topographically, west of Julesburg the ground cover changes dramatically. Extremely arid and covered with sagebrush, this northeastern corner of Colorado is an area inhabited by a paucity of humans even to this day. In fact, with the exception of a very few oases along the route, the absence of grass and trees between this location and Monida Pass on the Idaho-Montana border, roughly 800 miles distant, is a conspicuous feature of the landscape. It would take considerable effort, in this grass-poor environment, to maintain the oxen teams in serviceable condition.

At Fremont's Orchard wagon trains traditionally crossed from the south to the north bank of the South Platte River. Anxiety about this crossing would have been building for days. The river was extremely wide here—as much as a mile—with a treacherous bottom of shifting sands, potholes, channels, quicksand, and bars. The NY&MM&D Company's train appears to have accomplished the crossing without notice. At Fort Collins the emigrants forded the beautiful Cache La Poudre River, likely the first true mountain course of water many members of the train had ever encountered. From Laporte to Laramie the trail grew exceedingly rough, full of canyons, hills, and rugged, if spectacular, multicolored terrain—the first truly mountainous going.

At Laramie, wagon master Pratt was obliged to take the overland route to Idaho. A year earlier he would have had alternatives—the newly blazed Bozeman and Bridger routes north through Wyoming to the Yellowstone River in Montana. These cutoffs were shorter by at least 400 miles, and they avoided the necessity of crossing the Continental Divide. But the Bozeman and Bridger routes traversed land inhabited by Native Americans, and in 1865, Indian opposition to travel on them had proven so dangerous that not a single wagon train attempted to challenge their dangerous gauntlets. Further, the military authorities at Laramie would not have authorized such a foolish venture.[46]

Consequently, Pratt was obliged to continue west rather than turning north, knowing that the train faced not only two crossings of the Continental Divide—first in Wyoming and then back over the divide between Idaho and Montana—but at least four to six more weeks of laborious travel. It would mean that the NY&MM&D Company's wagon train, already running late, would face the possibility of being impeded or even halted by mountain snow. Heading up and over the windswept and devegetated slopes of the 7,000-foot divide directly west of Laramie—along the route followed roughly by today's Interstate 80—the company faced the much-feared 80-mile descent down Bitter Creek toward Green River, Wyoming.[47]

Named for its acrid alkali taste, Bitter Creek became fixed in the minds of emigrants for their bitter memories after attempting to traverse down its steep and torturous course. The unpalatability of its water was not the only impediment. Grass was scarce or nonexistent, and the sand and dust along the route were, as a wagon master recalled of his trip through the region in 1865, strongly impregnate with alkali. Our men often bleeding at the nose caused by the inhalation of the same. The water . . . has quite disappeared in the sand and left the bed of the bitter stream dry and dusty. . . . Our stock began to fall by the wayside. . . . Some of our horses began to yield to the pressure and would devour with ravenous appetite sage brush, grease wood, picket ropes and even wagon sheets. . . . All hands were sick, tired and almost worn out in body and spirits.

It took this wagon train nine days and nights to get through the "Bitter Creek desert."[48]

The NY&MM&D Company journal does not note its passage down Bitter Creek, but when the train arrived on or about October 15 at Hams Fork, about 30 miles west of Green River at the junction of Hams Fork and the Black Fork of the Green River, so many oxen had died—almost one-third of the original number—and the remainder were so exhausted that Pratt decided to leave behind thirty-four of the tired beasts of burden, eight wagons, and considerable equipment—twenty-five tons in weight—including sixteen of the forty stamps for the quartz mill. All this was left at the current site of Granger, Wyoming, named for the person who agreed, for a fee, to winter the livestock and care for the equipment until the company could retrieve both in the spring.[49]

It was the third week of October. While the wagon train rested at Hams Fork, the discovery team, under Eaton's supervision, had long since arrived in Montana by way of the Missouri River. The journey had not been uneventful, as low water had prevented their steamer from getting beyond the Milk River—still 300 miles short of Fort Benton—and the remainder of the passage to the river town had to be completed over land.[50]

From Fort Benton the discovery corps had started toward Virginia City but had stopped at Helena to look over the new and celebrated diggings at Last Chance Gulch and Big Prickly Pear. Prospects here were good, but in late September, on orders from Eaton, the corps moved its work to Hot Spring. In explaining to the company's stockholders his decision to move on, Eaton reported that he had become "satisfied that in point of number, richness, and superior facilities for working, the auriferous veins of Hot Spring district were unequaled by any in the Territory." He had found an excellent site for the mill, with abundant water power and with fuel and timber close at hand. Nature had, in the geologic configuration of Hot Spring Creek, provided the company with an excellent site upon which to construct a dam, high enough to furnish a head of water with a thirty-five-foot fall—far more than would be required by the mill's turbine. Having cast his company's fortunes with this site, Eaton purchased a downstream ranch of 480 acres on which was located in the district's most distinct landmark, the noted hot spring itself. With a temperature of 124 degrees F, it would be an indispensable source of heat for the process of amalgamation should the company decide to build a second mill there. The ranch was also valuable to the company as a range for its cattle and horses and was nicely suited for growing grains and vegetables. Having completed his research, Eaton moved the discovery team into the Hot Spring District on October 1 and immediately sent the men into the field to locate and secure quartz lodes for the company. By November 18, 27,000 feet of Hot Spring property had been claimed or purchased, all within 2.5 miles of the mill site.[51]

But this had not been the team's sole work in the field. During the fall Eaton traveled to Montana City, near Bannack, where he built a furnace to test the values of the silver holdings held in that region by the company and others. He was convinced that the construction of a mill there would benefit the company, for the costs of development had been borne by other parties, and the tests had revealed the company's ores to be of good value.[52] To sum up, the New York and Montana Mining and Discovery Company now had three operations at work in Montana: a gold mill at Centreville near Bannack, a silver furnace at Montana City, and a gold mill about to be constructed in the Hot Spring District.

It is doubtful that Enfield Pratt was aware of any of these developments as his wagon train broke camp at Hams Fork late that October. Pratt's mission was to bring his train to Virginia City, still 450 miles distant; much difficult ground lay ahead. Traveling north by northwest, the train encountered extremely difficult and arid terrain, for between Hams Fork and Soda Springs, Idaho, lie the Bear River Mountains—almost 200 miles of the most inhospitable ground imaginable, much of it above 6,000 feet in elevation. The stream and river courses through which the train had to labor were hellish, as the canyon walls come right down to the water. Sometimes the only way to negotiate these canyons was for the wagons to enter a stream and follow it to a favorable exit point. A sojourner who had passed on this route earlier in the season recalled this stretch as "the roughest country ever traveled in freight wagons."[53]

By contrast, Soda Springs, on the Bear River, proved a welcome sight, as the area was well watered and supplied the train with good grass. From here the train left the old Oregon Trail—which followed the Port Neuf River in a westerly direction to Fort Hall, Idaho—and proceeded northwest 30 miles to Blackfoot on the Snake River. Crossing the river at Eagle Rock Ferry, Pratt's train passed current-day Idaho Falls and carried on over toll roads to Market

Lake. After passing through the long and exposed Monida Pass into Montana, Pratt stopped at East Bannack on November 16 to purchase supplies. It would take the train another week to cover the 70 miles between Bannack and Virginia City, but on November 24 Pratt and his company arrived in the territorial capital, where the train learned of its final destination.[54] The train—which had shrunk from thirty-eight to approximately twenty-four wagons and from forty-five to twenty-six men—finally reached the Hot Spring Creek mill site, about 4 miles west of present-day Norris, on or about November 27, 1865, but the 140-day trip from Atchison had cost the company any hope that its mill would be erected that year. To add to the disappointment, when the freight was unloaded, the company's assistant superintendent, Colonel J. Talbot Pitman, rejected as "defective" more than $5,000 in machinery and supplies.[55] When the remainder of the train was brought up from Hams Fork the following spring, the total cost of moving the company from Atchison to Hot Spring had exceeded $55,000.

By the company's account, however, the wagon train's safe arrival after such a late start had been remarkable. To the trustees' knowledge, no other train leaving for Montana at a comparably late date with mining machinery had made it through; the others had suffered heavy losses and had been compelled to go into winter quarters somewhere in the mountains short of the territory.[56] The trustees, however, did not report one interesting development that would have concerned the stockholders. When the NY&MM&D Company's wagon train arrived in the Hot Spring District on November 27, it found a contingent of men unloading wagons for the construction of a competing quartz mill only 140 yards downstream. This was the wagon train of the Clark and Upson Mining Company of Hartford, Connecticut.

CHAPTER 3

Mills to Montana: 1865, II

THE CLARK AND UPSON AND THE
NELSON MINING COMPANIES OF
HARTFORD, CONNECTICUT

> "Said steamer grounding more frequently the farther we
> proceeded up the River . . . caused me great solicitude for the
> interests of our company."
>
> **—William J. Clark**

WILLIAM JUDSON CLARK AND MAJOR GAD ELY UPSON WERE NATIVES OF
Southington and Marion, Connecticut, respectively, two towns located fifteen to twenty miles south of Hartford. Hartford was Connecticut's capital and a national insurance center. Thriving iron and armament
works braced a vigorous and growing economy. Lucrative government contracts secured during the war had added substantially to the city's prosperity.
With a population of about 35,000, Hartford ranked second only to New Haven
as the state's largest city.

The incentive for establishing the Clark and Upson Mining Company for
a Montana quartz milling venture came from Gad Upson, who had been to

Montana and caught the gold fever. Born in 1823, Upson left Marion at age twenty for Jackson, Mississippi, where, with a brother, he set up a tinning and stove business. When the Mexican War broke out in 1846, Upson turned to soldiering, serving in the First Mississippi Infantry. Five years later he was back in arms with other Mississippi- and Louisiana-based Mexican War veterans and adventurers as a member of the 1850 Narciso Lopez filibustering expedition against Cuba, one of several efforts organized in the South before the Civil War to expand the slave economy. Somewhere along the way, Upson's mercenary exploits earned him the sobriquet of major. Following the Lopez expedition's miscarriage, Upson returned to Connecticut, his militaristic ardor considerably cooled. In 1857 he moved to Kansas, where, in an intensely hostile environment pitting free soilers against slavery advocates, he supported the Union cause. In 1860, Upson received a clerkship in the Department of the Interior. Three years later he was appointed Indian agent at Fort Benton, Montana, departing for that post in October 1863 by way of the overland route.[1] Upson arrived at Fort Benton—the head of Missouri River steamboat navigation—on December 21, 1863, only seven months after the discovery of gold in Alder Gulch.[2]

From Fort Benton Upson traveled periodically to Virginia City, selected Montana territorial capital in May 1864, to report to his immediate superior, territorial governor Sidney Edgerton. These trips between Fort Benton and Virginia City took Upson through Montana's most celebrated gold-bearing regions, and like many other government appointees he attempted to supplement his salary by speculating in gold properties. One of the routes from Fort Benton ran up the Missouri and Madison rivers, and by the summer of 1864 Upson had made claims and acquired holdings on quartz lodes in the Hot Spring Mining District.[3]

William J. Clark's path to Montana followed a similarly varied course. Following common and private school educations, Clark served for one year as principal of a high school in West Avon, Connecticut. He then shifted successfully into boating on the Farmington Canal and into grocery, lumbering, and coal businesses. In 1849, at age twenty-four, Clark abandoned everything to follow the Gold Rush to California. Joining fifty-six other area men in buying and sailing a schooner around the Cape Horn, he arrived in San Francisco in June 1849 after an eventful five-month journey. Like so many other argonauts who sojourned to California, Clark gained little from the venture. He fell ill, and, unable to do manual work, he returned home the following spring through the Isthmus of Panama.[4]

Clark then entered the manufacture of nuts and bolts, a fledgling industry for which the Southington Valley was gaining national prominence. In

1854 William J. Clark and Company was incorporated. As "Manufacturers of Clark's Patent Carriage Bolts, Machine Bolts, Coach Screws, Nuts, Washers, Etc.," the firm flourished. Clark's fortunes were improved substantially with the outbreak of the Civil War when his company was awarded a lucrative contract with the Springfield Arsenal to manufacture gun screws for the Union Army. By 1865 Clark was numbered among Southington's most affluent citizens.[5]

But Clark still suffered from gold fever. His failure to realize wealth in California, which he felt illness had deprived him of, only whetted his appetite for another venture. That appetite would soon be satisfied. In late 1864, Gad Upson was sent east to Washington, D.C., to lobby Congress for a territorial survey and subsidies for Montana. During congressional breaks, Upson twice visited Southington, where he got together with his old friend William Clark. Upson was high on Montana gold, and it took little to convince Clark that the two men should form a partnership to exploit the territory's mineral wealth by establishing a quartz milling and mining operation in Madison County.

The Clark and Upson Mining Company secured articles of incorporation on March 25, 1865, to conduct "the business of mining, refining, smelting, extracting and washing Gold, and other ore." Stock was issued initially in the amount of $130,000. Clark and Upson held 46 percent, and Hartford-area entrepreneurs—banking and insurance executives predominately—held the rest. But the real driving force among the stockholders—aside from Clark and Upson—was Samuel S. Woodruff, president of Woodruff and Beach Iron Works, Connecticut's largest manufacturer of iron and composition-cast high- and low-pressure steam engines, boilers, and pumps.[6]

A Southington native, Woodruff had been one of Clark's shipmates on the 1849 gold-seeking journey to California. Like Clark, he returned to Connecticut, rising rapidly within the ranks of the state's industrial and business elites. When the Civil War broke out, Woodruff and Beach enlarged already lucrative ties with the United States Navy as a supplier of steam engines, including machinery for the navy's celebrated sloop of war the *Kearsarge,* which obtained naval immortality by sinking the Confederate steamship *Alabama* off Cherbourg, France, in 1864. Woodruff and Beach also profited from producing armory machinery for the Colt Patent Fire-Arms Manufacturing Company's factory at Hartford.[7]

When Clark and Upson approached Woodruff in March 1865, they tapped the right man at the right time. Woodruff had earned enormous profits during the Civil War, but with war demands slackened he was ready to diversify.

Gold mining and insurance attracted him the most. The latter—the presidency of the Putnam Fire Insurance Company of Hartford—engaged his capital and managerial skills; the former—Montana mining—engaged his capital and mechanical resources. Woodruff likely also welcomed the opportunity to reenter the gold business on what appeared more favorable terms than he had experienced in 1849 and 1850.

With Woodruff and Beach machinery, Clark proceeded to Brooklyn, New York, where he purchased the additional equipage necessary to round out a sizable quartz milling operation. The company's outfit, which weighed almost fifty-seven tons, was then shipped by rail to St. Louis in early May 1865, preparatory to its journey up the Missouri River to Montana.[8]

Almost simultaneously, Woodruff and a core of Clark and Upson backers bankrolled a second Montana gold mining enterprise—the aforementioned Nelson Mining Company. Occasioning its formation was the arrival from Montana of another Connecticut returnee, Colonel John A. Nelson, who had come east seeking to incorporate Alder Gulch's first hydraulic mining operation. Although the Nelson Mining Company did not operate in the Hot Spring District, the two companies were governed by many of the same entrepreneurs, shared the same executive leader—Samuel Woodruff—and would undertake similar courses of development in Montana.

Born in the mid-1830s to Irish immigrant parents, John Nelson had developed a reputation as a capable machinist and in this employ had become familiar with various Hartford men of industry, including Woodruff and Henry Beach. At the outbreak of the Civil War Nelson was commissioned a captain in the Third Connecticut Volunteers, an all-Irish infantry unit recruited in New Haven. In spring 1863, Nelson, in his late twenties, was promoted to colonel and put in command of the Third Louisiana Native Guards (Colored)—who distinguished themselves in the siege of Port Hudson, Louisiana, in May and June 1863—and later of the Tenth United States Colored Troops, part of the African Brigade stationed in Virginia and North Carolina during the winter of 1863–1864. Nelson's rise through the ranks came to an abrupt halt on December 28, 1863, however, when he was placed under arrest and discharged from the army three months later for "having authorized and permitted the impressment of negro recruits into his regiment."[9]

First reports of Nelson's presence in Montana date from September 1864. That fall he made himself notable in Virginia City by acquiring a liquor store, undertaking military responsibilities pertinent to territorial Indian policy, running unsuccessfully as a Union candidate for the territorial assembly, and engaging in mining in the already legendary Alder Gulch.[10] Nelson also endeared himself to the sporting set by building an indoor arena, Leviathan Hall, for boxing, wrestling, and other sporting purposes. Some of the most notable prizefights ever staged in the Rocky Mountains were fought at Nelson's arena.[11]

In early February 1865 Nelson sold Leviathan Hall for $7,000 in gold coin, assumed Madison County quartz mining properties on consignment for sale in the East, and set out for Connecticut to convince his former employers to support a hydraulic mining venture.[12] Arriving in Hartford in mid-April, Nelson met with a small group of entrepreneurs, almost all of whom had committed to the Clark and Upson Mining Company only weeks earlier. The group's leader was Samuel Woodruff, and all of those present seemed well acquainted with Colonel Nelson. Samples of quartz Nelson had brought with him were sent to the United States Assay Office in New York City, and some of the returns were spectacular. Specimens from two quartz lodes situated in upper Alder Gulch above the placer diggings produced values from $2,000 to $3,000 per ton.[13] Eschewing the fact that an assay specimen does no more than reveal the contents of the specimen itself, the Hartford capitalists accepted Nelson's argument that these specimens were representative of his lodes in their entirety and bought into his scheme with enthusiasm. In doing so they were duplicating once more the way speculative excitement was capable of wresting all sense of caution from even the most accomplished businessmen when investment opportunities in western precious metals mining came on the market during the late nineteenth century.[14] Woodruff and his associates endorsed Nelson's plan with zeal, offering the colonel the capital and machinery necessary to equip Alder Gulch's first hydraulic mining enterprise, a joint-stock, steam-driven operation called the Nelson Mining Company. Their one-year agreement was dated April 29, 1865.[15]

Following the assemblage of the machinery pertinent to commence a steam-powered operation—engines, boilers, pumps, piping, and the like— Nelson left Hartford for St. Joseph, Missouri, where he planned to rendezvous with the freight shipment from New York and Hartford for the long trek by wagon train across the plains, it being too late in the season to take the river route.

In retrospect, Nelson's choice of mechanical technology over gravity is curious. The latter was preferred by far. In California, where hydraulicking was the most fully developed, water power built by gravity drop, not engine pumps, was the acknowledged means to success. Although expensive, once headworks, flumes, and penstocks had been constructed, gravity did not require engines, boilers, fuel, trained mechanics, and machine and blacksmith's shops to function efficiently. Moreover, gravity works could be constructed largely of natural materials at hand, whereas steam-powered hydraulic machinery had to be freighted to Montana at great expense. In addition, steam-pump operations, tied as they were to fixed engine and boiler plants, were difficult to move about.[16]

Despite Nelson's unusual and complex plan, Woodruff and company officers embraced it with optimism. One inducement was the company's ability to provide some of the machinery at cost. Another was the expectation that Nelson would prove a suitable director of operations. Woodruff was strong on Nelson, promising that the company had "unlimited confidence" in him. Extolling his leadership, Asa S. Porter, the company's new president, wrote to Nelson: "I have no doubt of your success, honesty, integrity, energy, determination & ability." Nelson, he thought, "was sure to succeed anywhere." All were, as Henry Beach summed up, "hoping for *big things* from the Nelson."[17]

The next phase of operations for the Clark and Upson and the Nelson mining companies involved the journey from Missouri to the Montana goldfields. The first shipment to depart for the mountains was Clark's. When it arrived in St. Louis in early May 1865, the company's machinery was transferred to the *Fanny Ogden,* one of a fleet of Missouri River steamboats owned by John G. Copelin. The *Fanny Ogden* departed from St. Louis on May 15 for Fort Benton, Montana, 2,300 winding and difficult miles upstream. Clark and two company employees accompanied the freight.[18]

The Missouri River was an unreliable conduit for trade. Not only did numerous snags from uprooted trees obstruct the river, but the Missouri's currents and crooked beds shifted continuously, forming treacherous sandbars. Its waters, among the muddiest in the world, obscured such hazards. Hidden snags could stove in a vessel, and uncharted sandbars could slow progress to a standstill. Only the most reckless river pilot dared to run the river at night, and except for a brief period in spring and early summer, the Missouri was untrustworthy for all but the shallowest draft vessels. As warmer weather progressed and water levels dropped, travel could become extremely laborious. Many excursions had to be terminated short of their objective. Such difficulties were compounded in 1865 because the previous winter's snowfall had been below normal. Spring runoff peaked prematurely on the Missouri, and water levels dropped precipitously at an early stage. The *Fanny Ogden's* mid-May departure from St. Louis proved far too late; in less than a month on the river the vessel had been grounded by low water several times, and it ran aground even more frequently as it approached Fort Union, just above the confluence of the Missouri and Yellowstone rivers on the present-day Montana–North

Dakota border. Understandably, these groundings and delays caused Clark to have "great solicitude for the interests of our company,"[19] and, indeed, the consequent failure of the river steamer's voyage helped undermine Clark and Upson's Montana venture.

A day before the *Fanny Ogden* reached Fort Union, about June 16, it was met by the *General Grant*, a smaller steamer sent downriver to help lighten its sister ship's load. Although it seemed clear that the larger vessel and its cargo would fail to reach Fort Benton unless it was lightened, the *Fanny Ogden*'s captain refused assistance. Clark and other passengers strongly protested the captain's decision. Some passengers even talked of mutiny, but their protests were in vain. In consequence, an adversarial relationship developed between Clark and the ship's officers.[20]

Four days later, on June 20, above Fort Union, the *Fanny Ogden* grounded so badly that its voyage had to be abandoned. Stuck 15 miles above the mouth of the Milk River, roughly 350 nautical miles short of Fort Benton—itself more than 200 miles north of Virginia City—the steamer was forced to tie up. Its cargo was placed ashore in a fortification built for the occasion and christened "Fort Copelin." Two smaller-draft steamers—the *Deer Lodge*, which took approximately 5 percent of Clark's cargo, and the *Roanoke*, which took on the *Fanny Ogden*'s passengers—attempted to go on. Several days later, however, both steamers failed to get up Dauphin's Rapids, just above Cow Island. Cargo and passengers were hauled overland to Fort Benton by mule and bull train, arriving sometime in mid-July. Assured that the remaining forty-eight tons of company freight left behind at Fort Copelin would be brought overland to Fort Benton as soon as possible, Clark proceeded to the Hot Spring District to select a suitable location for his mill.[21]

In mid-August Clark learned to his astonishment that the company's freight had not been forwarded. Despairing of getting any cooperation from Copelin, Clark decided he could wait no longer. If the mill could not be delivered before the late-fall freeze, its construction and operation would be set back until spring. That the Ragland, Cope, and Napton mill had arrived earlier at Fort Benton and would get a head start on working Hot Spring ores assuredly increased his apprehension. Deciding to hurry the freight from Fort Copelin at his own expense, Clark hired a bull train out of Fort Benton and sent one of his employees, Jesse Williams, to accompany it to Fort Copelin. There had been reports of hostile Indians in the vicinity, but the train reached Fort Copelin in September without mishap. Copelin's agent refused to release Clark's consignment, however, until Williams signed a bill of lading. Williams did so under protest, returning to Fort Benton with the company's freight shortly after mid-October. Here he was held up for four more days by another of Copelin's agents, who demanded full payment for delivery despite Copelin's failure to carry the freight through. Williams refused. Meanwhile, Clark had secured a mill site on upper Hot Spring Creek just east of where it exits its canyon. At the same time, he made modest purchases of gold discoveries to supplement the claims Gad Upson had recorded the previous year.[22] Upson, consumed by his responsibilities as Indian agent at Fort Benton and caught up in a futile effort to be elected territorial delegate to the United States Congress, appears to have taken a minimal part in the mining company's work during 1865.

BACK IN ST. JOSEPH, MISSOURI, JOHN NELSON HAD TAKEN LODGING AND AWAITED THE arrival of the company's machinery. The machinery, shipped from New York by rail to St. Louis and thence transshipped upriver to St. Joseph, did not arrive until early June. At St. Joseph it was unloaded once again and fitted to a mule-drawn wagon train. Three other men assigned by the company joined the train, one of whom, Edward J. Murphy, was a company agent sent to keep an eye on matters. The train got under way on June 21, five weeks after the *Fanny Ogden* had departed from St. Louis and just one day after the *Fanny Ogden*'s voyage had been discontinued upriver.[23]

The Nelson wagon train encountered numerous and sometimes serious Indian problems along the overland route. At Fort Kearney, Nebraska, the train was joined by others for safety by military mandate, and Colonel Nelson was elected captain of the conglomeration. He performed the role to satisfaction, losing no men or livestock. However, along the way Nelson became ill and left the wagon train for Montana by stagecoach. The next day seventeen of the train's oxen were run off by Indians, slowing progress. The colonel arrived in Virginia City on September 21, more than six weeks in advance of the wagon train, now wending its way through the mountainous plateaus of western Wyoming and southern Idaho. Pending its arrival, Nelson hustled his old liquor trade, leased claims in Alder Gulch, and, with the assistance of hired hands, prepared ground for installing the company's hydraulic works. Expectations ran high in Virginia City. Thomas Dimsdale's *Montana Post* promoted Nelson's enterprise vigorously; Nelson's company, the paper claimed, would increase community prosperity by working ground that "cannot remuneratively be operated upon by hand."[24]

Nelson's wagon train arrived in early November after a journey of slightly less than four-and-a-half months. Although inclement weather, including subfreezing temperatures, set in, Nelson successfully installed a portion of his machinery on leased claims in the lower gulch. Hydraulicking was not new to Montana, having been utilized at Bannack since 1863. Miners who had come to the territory from California were familiar with the process and its benefits. Moreover, Alder Gulch possessed all the advantages needed for its application—a good drop, steep gravel banks, and sufficient water. For those who had not seen hydraulicking before, Nelson's operations were impressive. The engines, reportedly ten horsepower each, were designed to throw water 80 feet high—300 feet high when combined as a quartet. The wrought iron piping, with 2.5-inch India rubber hose extensions, stretched 1,500 feet in length and was said to have a capacity for working a front 100 yards wide. Machine and blacksmith shops stood close by.[25] On November 28 Nelson and his crew started one engine and blew its steam whistle. Dimsdale proclaimed it "the first mining engine whistle that ever awoke the echoes of Alder Gulch." Despite subfreezing temperatures that prevented the engine from reaching maximum pressure, the results were dramatic. "The hoze nozzle," the *Montana Post* reported,

> was directed towards the compact, frozen bank. The resistance of the earth and gravel was but momentary; soon it yielded, and then, having opened the way, the stream bored into the orifice with magical rapidity—leaving holes thus eat [sic] away three, four, five, and even six feet in depth. With a full pressure of steam on, the stoutest bank would soon be torn away, and sent floating down with the returning torrent. Now, that the hydraulic process is introduced, we may expect it to become common.[26]

Nelson's plant was located up the western slope of Alder Gulch in close proximity to Virginia City, and the town's residents visited it regularly. Dimsdale reported on it frequently, sharing his readers' fascination with seeing "the steam hydraulic ripping up the bowels of mother earth."[27] But in late 1865, fearful of split hoses and ruptured machinery under harsh winter conditions, Nelson locked up his works for the season and left to prospect other diggings to the north, notably in Confederate Gulch on the Missouri River and on the Little Blackfoot River in Deer Lodge County to the northwest.[28]

Winter weather also stymied Clark and Upson's prospects. Only days after their agent had finally departed from Fort Benton with the company's freight, a heavy snowstorm halted the wagon train on or about November 6 at the base of a steep hill on Little Prickly Pear Creek. They were north of today's Helena, still more than 100 miles from Hot Spring Creek. The severe weather forced the train to encamp for two full weeks. Further, this was not an isolated storm. Winter arrived early in Montana in 1865. Snow and freezing temperatures became the norm by late October, and by mid-November the ground was frozen hard. The train finally arrived at the Hot Spring mill site about November 25—two days before the New York and Montana Mining and Discovery Company's train appeared.

For both companies it was too late; winter had set in. A Hot Spring miner reported that on the first of December it had "snowed and blowed like blazes all day and night." The following day, temperatures plummeted below zero, so cold that mercury was said to have frozen solid in Summit Mining District above Virginia City, and the *Montana Post* reported—not entirely tongue in cheek—that "alcohol liquor might have been sold in chunks."[29] The average temperature in December 1865 remained many degrees below what was necessary for a mill operation requiring copious supplies of water, and no break in the severe weather was to come for several months.

To add to Clark's discomfort, Copelin's agents appeared at Hot Spring in December with a bill for 95,315 pounds of freight. Not only would Clark not pay it, he told the agents to inform Copelin to expect a counterclaim for nonfulfillment of the original contract. Because the steamboat company had been negligent, Clark calculated damages to his enterprise of $26,307, including damage to and loss of goods while at Fort Copelin, the cost of freighting overland to Fort Benton, and other losses resulting from the "greatly delayed erection of the mill" and the "unnecessary expense of keeping a great number of hands, machinists, engineers and other workmen" over the winter.[30]

Then came another blow. Upson became critically ill. Suffering from an advanced case of tuberculosis, he was confined to bed in mid-January 1866. In anticipation of the worst, he transferred his Hot Spring mining claims to Clark and, hoping to return to Connecticut for medical treatment, left Virginia City in early February. Although he had planned to take a steamer from San Francisco, his illness prevented him from traveling beyond Sacramento, where he died in the company of his brother, Laurin, California's surveyor general, on March 30, 1866. The complicated administration of Gad Upson's estate—in Montana, Connecticut, and Washington, D.C.—now added to William Clark's burdens.[31]

The affairs of Ragland, Cope, and Napton and of the New York and Montana Mining and Discovery Company were in no better shape at the end of 1865. Although the Missouri company had the advantage of a working mill, business had not come close to satisfying needs. Ragland, Cope, and Napton had begun operations in September, but the company was heavily in debt—"behind hand," as Napton put it. Binding contracts had obliged the company to work on many lodes that had proved disappointments. One such was the Pony Lode, considered to be among the district's finest. At first the lode had paid well, but at fifty to sixty feet it had "capped," or narrowed down to a small seam. At the start of the new year the company was fighting its way down in an effort to get through the cap, but without success. The costs of the attempt were proving prohibitive. One report alleged that the company's mill was "imperfect" and that the company was not working with sufficient diligence to save as much gold as possible. At the same time, Ragland's health had deteriorated, and the trio's morale flagged.[32]

The position of the New York and Montana Mining and Discovery Company was hardly better. The same inclement weather that had forced Clark to postpone construction of his mill had brought about a similar decision by the New York outfit. Perhaps Asahel Eaton had anticipated this, for he had left the territory for the States on November 18, choosing not to stay to welcome the company's wagon train. Nevertheless, he retained the services of the discovery party on-site and readied work for several members of the wagon train—not only for the purpose of preparing the mill site but toward increasing the company's holdings in quartz properties, for Eaton was greatly optimistic about Hot Spring's future. He had found the ores there remarkably rich, "uniform in their yield," and easily broken down by the crushing process, he told the stockholders. Moreover, the district's gold-bearing veins were extraordinarily extensive; some lodes could be traced for miles on the surface. Values in gold ranging from $900 to $2,700 per ton had been assayed from lodes in the company's possession. The company's property in the Hot Spring District, Eaton argued, exhibited "a degree of richness that places the success of the mill beyond a question."[33]

Despite the professor's certitude, the fact was that almost nine months had passed without profit for these enterprises from the East, and another three to four months would be added by Montana's harsh winter climate. Consequently, there was understandably inescapable anxiety and even frustration among the principals—and their backers.

CHAPTER 4

Further Development of the District, 1866

THE HERSCHEL MINING COMPANY OF VIRGINIA CITY, MONTANA,
THE GOLDEN ORE MINING AND PROSPECTING COMPANY OF
MONTANA (BROOKLYN, NEW YORK), AND HALL AND SPAULDING
OF MEADOW CREEK, MONTANA

"It is scarcely possible to take up a piece of rock without finding
the free gold sticking out on every side."

—George Atkin

LTHOUGH CONSTRUCTION OF THE HARTFORD AND NEW YORK QUARTZ MILLS IN
the Hot Spring District was slowed down by the winter of 1865–1866,
the development of a town to support them was not. Where the name
Sterling came from is uncertain, but the camp was clearly in the making by
November 1865 when the Clark and Upson and the New York and Montana Mining and Discovery (NY&MM&D) companies arrived in the area.[1]

Located on the first-level ground below where Hot Spring Creek breaks
out of its rugged canyon into the rolling plains below, Sterling was a logical
place for a settlement. The site was strategically located astride the Virginia
City–to–Norwegian Gulch road precisely where it crossed Hot Spring Creek.

Moreover, as Asahel Eaton had pointed out to the NY&MM&D Company's stockholders, the topography of the canyon just above that point lent itself uniquely to the construction of a dam with which to impound water for use in quartz milling. Quartz milling required men—men to run the mills and men to locate, dig out, and transport the ore for processing at the mills. These men would, in turn, need commercial services.

Sterling soon achieved a size sufficient to rank it among the territory's larger mining camps. The one existing photograph, probably taken in March or April 1866, catches the town in a very early stage of development. Perhaps a dozen structures can be identified in the vicinity of the town site. Later that year a member of a wagon train provided a rough estimate of thirty structures, a considerably larger number than he had seen in passing through the village of Bozeman.[2] A year later a resident noted that a "large number of buildings of every shape and size, for store houses and residences, are being erected in every direction."[3] Business license receipts, a number of which have survived for Sterling, offer additional evidence of the mining camp's commercial size. Those for 1867, for example, document two boardinghouses, two hotels, four mercantiles, five saloons, two butcher shops, and three livery or feed stables. Licenses were also issued to a hatter, to a billiard hall owner, and to one of the town's merchants for a retail liquor business.[4]

Another source cites the existence of five blacksmith shops.[5] Inasmuch as the value of a mining district could be determined in part by the number of blacksmiths at work in it, the presence of as many as five in Sterling marks the community as one of some energy. In addition to the facilities at Sterling, the mining companies lying at its western edge had their own licensed boardinghouses, stables, and forges. Hot Spring District, with Sterling as its administrative base, had become sufficiently large as a population center by August 1866 to be designated one of Madison County's ten townships, with William Clark, George Cope, and Theodore Maltby elected township commissioners. Shortly thereafter Sterling acquired a justice of the peace and a constable. A deputy sheriff was added the following year. That the camp had come of age was certified when the U.S. government authorized the location of a post office in Sterling in October 1867.

As for inhabitants, a territorial surveyor who knew the Hot Spring area well recorded in his field notes that in 1866 and 1867 the town boasted a population of 500.[6] This is hard to corroborate; one is reminded that a round figure of 10,000 seems to have been fixed historically as Virginia City's heyday population, a figure that could be off by many hundreds, if not thousands. Most likely, 500 was a figure descriptive of the "greater metropolitan area," meaning the population existing anywhere in the vicinity of Sterling—including the miners who dug out ore for use at the Sterling mills, the camp's mercantilists, the farmers and ranchers who supplied the community with its food and fodder, and the families attached to each group. In any event, 500 seems to be the accepted figure, and when J. Ross Browne compiled his report on Montana's mineral resources in 1867, he credited Sterling with that number for its "estimated population." This ranked the modest mining camp among the territory's seventeen principal cities, with Helena's 8,000 leading and Virginia City next, with 4,000.[7]

Ethnically, Sterling's population was overwhelmingly white, Anglo-Saxon, and native born. Because the camp's rise and decline occurred before the first territorial census in 1870, when fewer than 5 percent of those earlier identified with Hot Spring still resided in Montana, ethnic identification has to be made mostly by conjecture through a hardly perfect analysis of names. Yet even on this crude basis, of 1,369 persons associated with Hot Spring during the years 1863–1870 and for whom data beyond mere lode ownership are available, fewer than 10 percent had surnames that were not of British, Welsh, Scotch, or Irish origin. German names (eighty-seven) led this small list, with French (twenty-three) and Scandinavian (six) following. Other ethnic names (Italian, Spanish, Polish, and Mexican in Hot Spring's case) totaled under 1 percent. Moreover, some of those with non-Anglo names were born in the States. To complicate matters, a sizable number of these early pioneers did not reside in Sterling but conducted their business with the camp from Virginia City. Nevertheless, this population breakdown was uncommon, as other western mining camps were inhabited by far more foreigners, with the California example the most graphic.[8] To be sure, early on, teams of German and French prospectors had worked the gulches on the west side of the Tobacco Root Mountains. But no such feature marked Hot Spring's demographics.

Hot Spring also failed to experience a Native American presence. Although members of the Bannock tribe continued to camp on the plains west of Alder Gulch throughout the 1860s and were often seen in Virginia City, documentation of an Indian presence in Sterling and the Hot Spring District is virtually nonexistent. However, as the Madison River was a corridor for tribes venturing to the buffalo plains to the east, Indians were assuredly among Hot Spring's transient visitors. Archaeological field surveys have uncovered numerous tepee rings along the Madison River in the Hot Spring District, for example; and during the so-called Indian campaign in the spring and summer of 1867, large numbers of "friendlies" moved into Montana's frontier mining camps to protect themselves from trigger-happy volunteers forming the Montana militia.

Members of the Bannock and Brule tribes were reported in unusual numbers in and around Virginia City, and thirteen lodges of Snake, or Shoshone, Indians set up camp along the Madison River in the Hot Spring District.[9] At roughly the same time, one Indian, identified as from the West Coast, worked in the district until he was killed in a fight with a white miner in a Sterling saloon.[10] But this was an exception, as by and large Native Americans in Madison County were seen as peaceable, especially compared with white roughs. As for blacks, no record exists of their presence. Chinese, always associated with placer mining and conspicuous in Alder Gulch after 1865, did not take up residency in Sterling, a hard-rock camp.

Of the overwhelming Anglo-Saxon element, men and women of southern origin appear to have been in the majority. One breakdown in 1867 noted a mining company workforce in Sterling composed of two-thirds southerners and one-third New Englanders, meaning those who had New England origins or family roots.[11] Most of the southerners whose roots can be identified were from Virginia, Kentucky, or Missouri. Inasmuch as virtually all of the camp's mining companies and commercial enterprises were run by northerners and the laboring force was composed largely of southerners, social and political tensions in Sterling were characteristically sectional, reflecting lingering Civil War passions and significant differences in lifestyle. Ethnic and religious factors played a very minor role in shaping Sterling's social character. A working-class identity, soon common in western hard-rock camps, was nonexistent in Sterling. Not surprisingly, with southerners in the majority, Sterling's political sentiments favored the Democratic Party, an expression characteristic of Montana as a whole during this period.

Aside from politics, it is important to understand that the Madison Valley and the eastern slopes of the Tobacco Roots were settled largely by old-stock emigrants from the East, or "pilgrims," as the experienced California miners pegged them. In all probability, lack of experience was a characteristic of Hot Spring miners, especially in the early years. The mill operators in Hot Spring preferred men who had prospected or had been engaged in milling in California and were pleased when they could report that they had some in their employ. But Californians were a distinct minority in Hot Spring, as they were in Montana as a whole. In contrast, the Idaho and Nevada mining districts were populated by significant numbers of Californians.[12]

Culturally, Sterling compared poorly with a community such as Virginia City, which had an opera house, a band, theaters, a library, resident poets, two Masonic Lodges (north and south), and a men's literary association. About the best Sterling could boast of was a subscription grade school. But if the "twin pioneers of civilization" were "the Church, and the School-House," as Nathaniel Langford, U.S. Internal Revenue agent, put it in 1866, then Sterling was less than fully civilized because it lacked a house of worship.[13] When territorial chief justice Hezekiah Hosmer noted that "no one has seen a mining camp in its glory who has not spent a sabbath in it" and that "men who at home have all their lives been accustomed to attend church soon learn to conform to the loose morality of the country," the irreverence he was speaking of strongly characterized Sterling and most, if not all, western mining camps as well.[14] There is no record of any effort to organize congregations in Sterling. Temperance did not take hold either. When members of the International Order of Good Templars succeeded in organizing temperance chapters in Virginia City and Nevada City and undertook a recruiting effort among Meadow Creek's ranching community in March 1868, they made no attempt to solicit support in Sterling, where drinking and drunkenness were a significant component of the camp's social fabric.

Like so many other frontier mining communities, Sterling lacked even the most basic medical and social services. There is no record of a physician taking up residence in the camp, although the county did keep a doctor on retainer during the mid-1860s to care for cases for which there were no resources other than public dollars. Sterling also lacked the basic welfare programs created in Virginia City to assist the needy, the ill, paupers, orphans, and the physically and mentally disturbed. Burials for indigents, care for the sick and poor, and the incarceration of criminals were all centered in Virginia City. There was no jail or organized system of protection against fire in Sterling. There was no central water supply system. Sanitation was virtually nonexistent—undoubtedly some of the camp's effluvia seeped into Hot Spring Creek. No traces of a cemetery remain; where the town's dead were laid to rest is unknown. All these factors reflected Sterling's indifference to services of this nature; most of the camp's residents—resident only as long as the camp proved profitable—cared little about such improvements, an attitude generally characteristic of the western ephemeral mining camp experience.

A MAJOR IMPETUS FOR STERLING'S EVOLUTION WAS THE WORK AND PROMOTION OF THE Herschel Mining Company, organized in Virginia City in August 1865 and describing itself as "engaged in the business of Mining and in the Discovery of Gold and Silver Mines, and in Working the same."[15] The company was not interested in putting up quartz mills but sought instead to profit by marketing its holdings to, or investing in, other companies engaged in that business. Although the Herschel Mining Company acquired properties in several locations, its emphasis from the start was on the development of the Upper Hot Spring District. Four men comprised the partnership, three of whom— John Creighton, William McK. Dennee, and John S. Rockfellow—were Virginia City businessmen. The fourth, Captain Theodore T. Maltby, was a veteran miner.

John Creighton, with his brother Edward, had founded an important freight business between Omaha and Salt Lake City in 1862. Two years later Creighton Brothers extended its business to Virginia City, but in name principally because Edward was not an active participant in the company's Montana extension. John broadened the company's stakes in Montana considerably, opening a grocery and liquor store in Virginia City, building stone commercial structures—the Creighton Block, for instance—and entering into an extensive stock-growing business. Mining captured his attention as well; as previously noted, he had made early 1864 investments in the Meadow Creek area as a member of the Eagle Mining Company. Simultaneously, Creighton began to appear on Upper Hot Spring mining claims with Maltby and Dennee.[16] Creighton and his brother had also received national attention as superintendents of the western division of the Western Union Telegraph Company, a communications service Montana craved. Creighton's wide business interests kept him on the move and often absent from Virginia City. In October 1866 he left Montana to supervise the construction of Western Union's transcontinental telegraph line.[17]

William McK. Dennee hailed from New Orleans, Louisiana. In 1866 he was approximately twenty-seven. He had arrived in Virginia City in May 1864 and soon entered into mining arrangements with Creighton and Maltby.[18] Somewhat later that year he became acquainted with John Rockfellow, another mercantilist. The two men formed Rockfellow and Dennee, wholesale and retail grocers and storage and commission agents. Rockfellow and Dennee carried just about everything and more required in a hungry and supply-dependent mining community like Virginia City.[19] Although from every account profitable, this partnership was short-lived. When the Herschel Mining Company was organized in August 1865, Dennee terminated his business relationship with Rockfellow and sold him a substantial portion of his interest in the mining company.[20] Although Dennee was still a minority partner, he did not play a significant role thereafter in the company's business affairs. Like Creighton, Dennee left for the States in the fall of 1865.

With Creighton and Dennee gone from the territory for the better part of fall and all of the winter of 1865–1866, the reins of the Herschel Mining Company were left in the hands of Rockfellow and Maltby. Both proved energetic and capable in their efforts. John Rockfellow was a native of Bound Brook, New Jersey. The same age as Dennee, Rockfellow had been in the merchandising business for at least nine years, seven of which had been spent in St. Louis, Missouri. In 1863, Rockfellow entered the freight business across the plains between St. Louis and Virginia City.[21] Settling in Virginia City permanently in the late summer of 1864, Rockfellow founded his mercantile partnership with Dennee, investing at the same time in mining and milling. To most Virginia City citizens Rockfellow proved a delightful addition to the community. He was not only respected as a businessman of remarkable entrepreneurial energy, he also established an agreeable reputation for his benevolence, his support of cultural events, and his ability to throw a good party. Considered eminently trustworthy, Rockfellow, a Union Democrat, was elected city treasurer in February 1865, a position he held for nearly three years. Simultaneous with the organization of the Herschel Mining Company, he was appointed territorial treasurer. It is safe to say that in Virginia City he was both appreciated and admired.

Theodore D. Maltby, or Captain Maltby as he was known in Madison County, was the field superintendent for the group. Like Dennee, Maltby hailed from the Deep South. During his youth he had been something of a mercenary, fighting in the Florida War against the Seminoles—where he received a leg wound—then in the Texas War of Independence, and finally in the Mexican War. Grievously wounded in the head during a clash with Santa Anna's forces, he had been captured and imprisoned for two years, during which period he was tortured by his jailers in a vain attempt to convert him to Catholicism. Maltby's battle wounds and imprisonment left him subject for life to periodic debilitating bouts of epilepsy and arthritis. Following his release from captivity, Maltby married a Texan who had nursed him during one of his seizures. They moved to Louisiana, but Maltby was soon off again, this time in search of gold—first to California and then to Montana, where he appeared in the Norwegian and Upper Hot Spring area in the summer of 1864.[22] At least two features of the Hot Spring District attribute their names to his influence. Maltby's Mound is a distinct conical hill rising singularly out of the plains between Hot Spring Creek and Norwegian Gulch, and Picayune Creek, located just west of Maltby's Mound, is a clear reference to a Louisiana namesake.[23]

Maltby early became acquainted with Creighton and Dennee—on his first discovery, recorded on July 30, 1864, he wrote them in as claimants.[24] In all probability it was Maltby who saw earliest among the Herschel group the richness of Hot Spring's gold values. Many of the claims made for the company in the district were the product of his hand. His preemption of 160 acres just below the Upper Hot Spring Creek Canyon gave the company its first land base.[25]

The Herschel Mining Company attached itself to the New York and Montana Mining and Discovery Company at a very early date; its organization simultaneous with Eaton's arrival in Montana is unlikely to have been happenstance. It is quite possible, in fact, that Eaton's August decision to purchase ranch land at the hot spring and to locate the mill on the upper portion of Hot Spring Creek was his response to the Herschel Mining Company's recommendation and initiative. With the close relationship that existed between the two companies it is hard to believe their actions were not constantly taken in concert. Properties acquired by the Herschel Mining Company, both mineral and land, were made available or turned over to the New York company at nominal prices, and the Virginia City group undertook projects that patently supported Eaton's efforts. The site on which the New York company would build its mill was ground originally preempted by Maltby and deeded to the Herschel Mining Company upon its organization. In 1866 the company conveyed the lot to the New York enterprise for a dollar.[26]

Within months of its organization, the Herschel Mining Company put together property holdings of a full square mile in the vicinity of Sterling.[27] The company also laid claim in September to its own mill site just above the site on which the NY&MM&D Company would commence construction.[28] This preemption became linked to the emergence of yet another Hot Spring quartz milling enterprise. The Midas Mining Company of Rochester, New York, had begun to center its interests in the district that fall, and in late October the Herschel group sold Midas its mill site and numerous Upper Hot Spring mining claims.[29] The Midas Mining Company would not deliver a mill to this site for another twenty-one months, but the announcement of its interest added measurably to the development of the adjacent community—Sterling—to service needs.

The Herschel Mining Company was astute in understanding the support systems these mills required. Toting up existing water supplies, it was evident that the flow of Hot Spring Creek would be insufficient to provide the necessary force—even with impounded waters—suitable to the needs of three mills, one of which, and the one the Herschel Mining Company had specific interest in, was water-powered and which anticipated running as many as forty stamps. On or about November 10, 1865—or two weeks before the arrivals of the Clark and Upson and the New York and Montana Mining and Discovery Company wagon trains—Rockfellow employed Captain Walter W. de Lacy, the territory's most eminent surveyor, to stake out a course for a 3.5-mile ditch that would divert 400 cubic inches of water from upper Meadow Creek over the divide in a northeasterly direction into the headwaters of Hot Spring Creek. Construction on the ditch would take place as soon as weather permitted.[30] In short, the investments and projects of the Herschel Mining Company assuredly contributed to the growing expectation that the upper portion of Hot Spring Creek would become the center of an important quartz milling endeavor requiring the services of significant numbers of workers.

As soon as spring weather permitted in 1866, the two Hartford firms—the Nelson Mining Company and Clark and Upson—and the New York enterprise began piecing together the components of their respective operations. John Nelson's hydraulic works in Alder Gulch was the first to function. With much excitement, the engines were started on April 19, only eleven days short of the conclusion of the Connecticut company's one-year contract with the colonel. Although a large number of onlookers witnessed the event and seemed pleased with the "highly effective action" of the hose, Nelson and his workers were not happy. Despite numerous alterations made to the machinery, the engines lacked sufficient power to project a stream of water with requisite force. Gold was procured, but given the energies engaged, it was of a volume and value far less than needed to cover investments, much less produce a profit.[31]

John Nelson may have already lost his enthusiasm for the company's commitment to Alder Gulch. From the previous December's brief trial, he must have sensed the inadequacy of his machinery. Moreover, bad blood had existed between Nelson and company agent Edward Murphy from the start. The two men clashed over authority and over the authenticity of the quartz lode titles Nelson had turned over to the company. In addition, Nelson had interpreted Murphy's presence as a form of unwarranted company surveillance and as a questioning of his competence.

Growing competition might also have been a factor. As the *Montana Post* had predicted, at least two other hydraulic companies had moved into the gulch over the winter. One situated itself directly above Nelson's works, the other directly below. Both were gravity-powered operations, and they seemed equally as capable as Nelson's mechanically complex enterprise. Perhaps because of this turn of events, perhaps as the result of his having seen promising prospects elsewhere, Nelson intimated even before resuming operations in mid-April that he had become interested in placer mining districts to the north, with or without the company's machinery.[32] The disappointing results of late

April seemed to convince Nelson that a different course would be more profitable, and in the first week of May, immediately following the expiration of his one-year contract with the company, he left for the Little Blackfoot District near Deer Lodge, Montana.

News of Nelson's departure reached Hartford quickly by stage and telegram, and on May 11, angry stockholders, led by Samuel Woodruff, filed notice that the company had abandoned the continuation of a joint-stock corporation with Nelson. Empowering Murphy "to take possession of, use, and improve on our behalf and our account any and all property . . . now or heretofore held by any person or persons for or on behalf of the Nelson Mining Company," the company also decided to withhold permanently Nelson's one-third share in issued stock.[33]

Under Murphy's management the company tried to carry on. The *Montana Post* continued to trumpet its efforts, commenting on the immensely pleasing sound transmitted to Virginia City by the ferocious "puffing, snorting and squirting" of the company's works. The newspaper's pronouncement was poorly timed, however, for on the day those words appeared in print, Murphy closed the works. He could see no profit from continued operations. An attempt several weeks later to restart mill operations was short-lived. A Montanan who had leased gulch property to the company sued Nelson for $1,300, claiming the colonel had absconded with that much in gold from his claims. In an attempt to get back something on its investment, the company turned to William J. Clark, directing him to sell the Nelson Mining Company's Alder Gulch machinery. Clark posted notices in territorial newspapers in August, but there were no takers.[34]

Nelson, meanwhile, had sold the company's herd of mules, but he refused to reimburse the Hartford trustees, alleging that he had been forced to sell the animals to underwrite his legal expenses. The Hartford group's decision to withhold Nelson's share of the corporation's stock, which Nelson might have sold for working capital, undoubtedly strengthened Nelson's justification for retaining the proceeds from the sale of the mules. By midsummer 1866, Nelson's relationship with his backers had soured completely. In Alder Gulch, Murphy had torn down his pumphouse, stored all of the company machinery, and been left, according to an observer, with an outfit of such little value that its sale wouldn't pay his passage home.[35] So ended Madison County's first hydraulic mining venture—a complete failure.[36]

WILLIAM CLARK'S ENTERPRISE IN THE HOT SPRING MINING DISTRICT SOON PROVED EQUALLY disappointing. Like Nelson, Clark had pieced together the components of his operation at the first break of winter. By May 1866 he had completed his mill, a seventy-by-thirty-foot structure built of native stone at a cost of $8,000, and was making experimental runs of ore. Although steam-operated, the Clark mill was unusual among Hot Spring mills for not using batteries of stamps. Instead, it employed a Gardner "Improved," or "Thunderbolt," mechanical crusher, supplemented by a Howland pulverizer. The Gardner machine, common to Colorado operations, crushed base ore by the vertical action of jaws.[37] The ore was then fine-graded by the Howland pulverizer's rollers. Clark claimed that the two were capable of reducing one ton of quartz per hour. Both were driven by a wood-fired steam engine, fuel for which was plentiful in the nearby Tobacco Root Mountains. Water for the boiler and milling system was brought up into the mill on a slight upgrade by steam-powered pump from Hot Spring Creek.

The separating tables, for segregating gold from coarser rock, and the amalgamators, which employed quicksilver to combine with and retain the almost imperceptible particles of gold, were the patented inventions of Asahel K. Eaton and James T. Hodge. Hodge, a chemist-geologist from Plymouth, Massachusetts, and former superintendent of the Cooper Institute in New York City, was field superintendent for the Roosevelt Mining Company of New York, which operated a quartz mill in Oro Fino Gulch near Helena. Although working separately in the field, Hodge and Eaton were partners in a laboratory-workshop in Brooklyn, New York, and Clark had likely purchased the separating and amalgamating equipment from them while assembling his mining outfit in Brooklyn the previous year. In any event, these were new inventions, and the mining community followed their installation with interest.[38]

In early June 1866 the *Montana Post* reported that "after a series of very satisfactory experiments, made with a view of testing the power of the machinery and balancing the speed of the different portions so as to equalize supply and demand all through," Clark's mill was "ready to run 'for keeps.'"[39] After several starts, however, Clark's mill proved unproductive. All three components of the milling system failed to produce profitable values. The Gardner crusher and the Howland pulverizer seemed incapable of reducing the district's hard granite either adequately or rapidly enough into the powdery substance required for separation and amalgamation. And the separators and amalgamators, once supplied with reduced ore, were not saving gold commensurate with assays. Reports that Clark's equipment was subpar began to circulate in Sterling.

In mid-July Clark confided to Theodore Maltby, who was running the Herschel Mining Company's operation out of Sterling, that he would try his crusher and pulverizer once more, and if they failed to operate well enough to suit him, he would change his method of operation. When the crusher and pulverizer again performed inadequately, Clark decided to replace them with stamps.[40]

Clark also disposed of his separators and amalgamators, selling them back to Hodge who, with superior stamp-crushing equipment in Helena, believed he could make them profitable. To replace them, Clark headed for California in early January 1867, admitting he had little to show for having spent $118,000 on machinery, a mill, and subsidiary structures—not to mention the costs of purchasing mining claims, of labor, of production, and of transporting at extraordinary expense all of the machinery to Montana Territory. He was leaving, he said, to survey milling operations in Nevada and to purchase new separators and amalgamators in San Francisco. From there he would take sea passage for Connecticut. He had been absent from Southington for eighteen months, and his business interests at William J. Clark and Company required his attention. During his leave, subordinates would oversee the Hot Spring milling enterprise. In late January 1867, Charles Hendrie, a noted millwright from Iowa who had constructed and equipped other mills in Montana, arrived at Sterling to remove the crusher and pulverizer from the Clark and Upson mill and to install twelve used stamps of his own. The *Post*, in its fashion, predicted handsome returns for its owners.[41]

NO SUCH PREDICTION COULD BE MADE FOR THE INTERESTS OF THE RAGLAND, COPE, AND Napton Company's enterprise on Canadian Creek in the Norwegian District. Over the winter of 1865–1866 the three partners had continued work on the Pony Lode, fighting down to over 170 feet, but they had not broken through the cap. The unsuccessful effort had cost them $9,000. As the mill had not operated during the inclement winter months, it too had produced no profit, and many of the agreements the company had made in its search for quartz had not materialized, as the majority of the miners—despite the contractual demands they had placed on the company—had not produced the ore.

To add to the burden, Cope had run out of money, and neither Napton nor Ragland was willing, as Napton expressed it, "to hazard any thing farther . . . having families at home, and much reduced in circumstances by events of the war." As Ragland's health had been "miserable" during his stay in Montana, he and Napton had resolved to give up entirely and return to Missouri. Cope did not support their decision, desirous as he was of starting up the mill again. But his partners had lost confidence in his ability to manage the company's affairs and would not advance him the funds to continue the operation. Cope, as it was, had already secured $1,328 from them by mortgaging his share of the mill. Ragland and Napton now concluded to sell it; they would be satisfied to recover the original cost of the mill—$26,000—they said, provided the purchasers would fulfill what few contracts remained in force from the previous year.[42] In effect, Napton and Ragland, having washed their hands of the venture, were hoping desperately to salvage something through the sale of their lodes and machinery. When the mill did not sell immediately, the two partners, holding the majority of shares, had it dismantled, or so the *Montana Post* understood—"the batteries remaining in place, but spiked by the absent partners."[43]

In some unclear manner Cope, operating under his own initiative, was able to restart the mill and run it satisfactorily through the remainder of 1866 and beyond. By year's end, in fact, Cope was running day and night, with twice as much ore offered as he could accept.[44] Where Cope secured his operating capital is uncertain, but his success during the summer of 1866 in making the Pony Lode profitable might have been the explanation. Unwilling to continue work on the lode's cap at 180 feet, Cope had made a side cut of 15 to 20 feet and had "struck the main vein 'heavy.'" Reports indicated that it was one of the richest in the country. Indeed, Cope's mill, the only one running through the winter of 1866–1867, was making a go of it, and the *Post* forecast prosperous times for the enterprise and for the nearby town of Sterling, now growing rapidly into a "Thriving burg."[45]

IN THE MEANTIME, THE NEW YORK AND MONTANA MINING AND DISCOVERY COMPANY had been tending to its own needs. Under the direction of its superintendent, Enfield Loring Pratt, the company had worked at its mill site during the winter of 1865–1866 and had increased its footage in quartz claims through purchase; whereas the discovery team, under the supervision of J. Talbot Pitman, assistant superintendent, continued—weather permitting—to search for new leads.[46]

At about this time, the corporation's headquarters issued an optimistic circular to its stockholders in which the trustees and Asahel Eaton described the previous year's work and forecast the unquestionable success of the enterprise. The trustees also announced that they had decided to sell off stock held in reserve and to enlarge the company's capital stock by issuing more shares. It was acknowledged that there had been a strong diversity of opinion among the trustees as to how the reserve stock—10,000 shares originally held back as a "Contingent Treasury Stock Fund"—should be disposed of. One group had argued that the shares should be sold on the open market at their enhanced value, "with the probability of dividends within the year to come" now that the company had firmly established itself in Montana, whereas others had favored their distribution as a dividend to the present stockholders. These two extremes of opinion were eventually satisfied with a compromise: the 10,000 shares would be made available to the company's stockholders for $3.50 per share, or the original price, with interest from February 1, 1865. A portion of the revenues raised from this sale within the company would be utilized to "insure the completion of the 40 Stamp Mill, now being erected in Montana, and for the building of necessary miners' houses at the mines."[47]

To satisfy the other group, the trustees had decided to increase the company's worth by issuing an additional $250,000 in stock, which would be sold on the open market at a significantly higher price than that at which the original stock had been offered. The moneys secured from this sale would be used "either for the erection of Smelting Furnaces for working the silver ores of Montana, or in keeping a Discovery Party in the field for another year—or for both." In sum, the trustees were bent upon substantially increasing their commitment to Montana.[48]

Asahel Eaton, having spent the winter at his residence and business in the New York area, started back to Montana in late April 1866. His course of travel took him through Ohio where he spoke to a Cleveland business group. In his presentation Eaton waxed eloquent about Montana, which he had found "equal, in richness of mines, to any place he had ever visited," including New Mexico, Arizona, California, and Australia. As for other aspects of Montana, the weather was "not severe," even in the off-season; there was an abundance of timber and immense beds of coal; and vegetables, if not fruit, could be grown readily and to prodigious size. Montana was not only a desirable place to live, Eaton assured his listeners, "it was a great field for the safe investment of capital and labor."[49]

In May the connection between the NY&MM&D Company and the Herschel Mining Company was strengthened when William Dennee, back in Montana, sold his remaining share to Pratt and the New York firm for $25,000. Singled out in the transfer was Dennee's one-sixth share in the full section of property his company held in and around the town of Sterling, which Dennee identified as "the principal place of business" and headquarters for the Herschel Mining Company.[50]

By mid-June 1866, Eaton had taken over supervision of the company's mill construction project and was estimating completion within weeks. Unlike the Clark and Upson mill, which was made of stone, the quartz mill of the New York and Montana Mining and Discovery Company was constructed as a wooden-frame building measuring forty-two by seventy-five feet.[51] Although forty stamps had been intended, the decision had long been made to reduce the mill's capacity to twenty, even after the arrival in July of the sixteen stamps left behind at Hams Fork. A large water-powered, under-the-mill turbine, described by one onlooker as a "novel structure," provided the energy to drive the stamps.

Although "novel" to this westerner, in the East, turbines, except in the smallest mills, were speedily replacing waterwheels. Turbines were placed horizontally under a mill and worked a vertical shaft. Durable, efficient, and with superior running speed, turbines could be better regulated as to power. These features enabled turbines to be operated at a lower cost than the old-style breast and overshot wheels.[52] All that was required to ensure a turbine's success was a head of water of sufficient force. For the New York company the motive power would come from water impounded behind a dam constructed about 1,000 feet west up the creek at the narrow entrance to the steep-walled canyon. There, as Eaton had informed the stockholders earlier, high and solid rock abutments anchored the dam. From the dam itself water was flumed the first 200 feet or so over swampy land. Reaching solid ground, the water was conveyed by ditch the remaining distance to the mill. Arrastras and amalgamators assisted the machinery, which was principally supplied with ore from the company's Thermopylae—Greek for "warm water"—Lode, reported to be "very rich in gold," and from the Orion Lode. Both of these lodes had been located by the company's discovery corps the previous fall.[53]

From the outset, a shortfall of water at the Hot Spring site impeded operations. Hot Spring Creek does not carry a great deal of water in its upper reaches. For the most part it runs about 4 to 5 feet or less in width, with an average depth of rarely more than a foot. Fed primarily by mountain runoff, in the heat of summer it greatly diminishes in size. Eaton had certainly assured his stockholders of the plentiful availability of water on the understanding that Hot Spring would be adequately supplemented by a diversion from Meadow Creek. John Rockfellow had deduced this necessity just as early, pledging immediate construction of a ditch to convey water into Hot Spring Creek. The 3.5-mile ditch had been staked out in November 1865, before the mill had arrived, and in early February 1866 Rockfellow had proudly displayed a map of its line and of the Herschel Mining Company's ledges in the Hot Spring District.[54]

But work on this ditch did not commence until late summer of 1866, in part because of strong opposition from Meadow Creek farmers dependent on irrigation water. Once undertaken, moreover, the work went slowly and the ditch was not completed until December 1866. By then it was too late in the season to be of assistance to the mill. Nevertheless, by earlier agreement with the ditch's owner, John Rockfellow, the NY&MM&D Company picked up the expenses of construction—labor, tools, and supplies, including dynamite, plus food and shelter for a crew of sometimes as many as twenty-nine men.[55]

The cutting of ditches to guide water to mining operations has always been an industry prerequisite, and the diversion ditch built by the New York and Montana Mining and Discovery Company in the late summer and fall of 1866 helped certify Hot Spring's "coming of age." When the *Montana Post* observed in October 1866 that "Hot Spring district is thriving, and seems to be the busiest section of the Territory" and that "more mills are actually and profitably working at this place than at any other," it was referring not only to the Ragland, Cope, and Napton; the Clark and Upson; and the New York and Montana Mining and Discovery enterprises.[56] For during the summer three new companies had selected the district as the site for operations of their own: the Golden Ore Mining and Prospecting Company of Montana, based in Brooklyn, New York; Hall and Spaulding, local entrepreneurs; and the Midas Mining Company of Rochester, New York.

The Golden Ore Mining and Prospecting Company of Montana made its initial appearance in the Hot Spring District in early August 1866, shortly before the NY&MM&D Company commenced work on its Meadow Creek diversion ditch. George Atkin, a British citizen and engineer, was the company's representative in the field, having been sent out over the plains to make a personal survey and estimate of thirty-two lodes in which the Brooklyn firm had taken speculative options. Atkin was to select one lode on which to commence work and to erect mill buildings preparatory to the installation of machinery.[57] Atkin had no intention of prospecting himself but depended on the discoveries and recommendations of others.

Atkin's immediate impression of Montana's gold prospects was expressed in euphoric terms. In three letters to his company in September and November 1866, Atkin raved about Madison County's riches. He reported visits to milling operations all over the county, including Brown's Gulch and Summit, where every lode was "first class." But Meadow Creek and Hot Spring held "decidedly the best rock" and the easiest to work. Atkin had thoroughly canvassed the Hot Spring District. Visiting Norwegian Gulch, he had come away from George Cope's operation convinced the Pony Lode was a winner but that the Canadian Gulch mill was quite wasteful, leaving 50 percent of the gold in its tailings. In fact, miners there had offered Atkin 400 feet on the Senator Lode if he would put up a competitive mill in the region. Atkin had looked at all the lodes the company had expressed interest in, and he was ecstatic about them: "I have seen the rock from the different lodes, all so rich that it is difficult to decide without seeing the lodes [themselves] which is the best, as all contain free gold in great quantities." The fact was, he continued, "[i]t is scarcely possible to take up a piece of rock without finding the free gold sticking out on every side." Atkin reported assays as high as $1,800 of gold per ton in quartz taken from one of the district's more highly touted lodes.[58]

Atkin finally settled on a mill site on the northern slopes of Meadow Creek. His decision was based on three factors. First, the site lay adjacent to the "public road" between Meadow Creek and Hot Spring Creek, allowing easy access to the mill. Second, the site was located near a small spring, sufficient, Atkin believed, to provide water for a steam-powered operation. Third, Atkin was convinced that lodes offered him by two Meadow Creek miners were just the ticket and that the owners were prepared to transfer their titles only if Atkin agreed to locate in their vicinity. Atkin justified his commitment: "I am pretty sure I can give to the company seventy five to one hundred thousand dollars clear in twelve months, above all expenses." For the right amount of money, Atkin promised to "guarantee success that it will pay right away from the first day the mill runs."[59]

In truth, Atkin's forecast of the profits to be made from Hot Spring mining defied sensibility. Could he really have believed what he wrote? Certainly, he must have known the situation was not that rosy. Others, in fact, thought his reports were frightfully exaggerated. When his letters were picked up by the *Montana Post*, one of those who knew better wrote home that Atkin had written "so foolishly" and had made such "loose statements" that the reader of his letters should dismiss him as an authority.[60] Yet such were the ways in which men in the field, paid to make promising reports, complied. It is little wonder that numbers of speculators in the East were attracted to the district. Given the fabulous prospects forecast by "experts," high expectations easily eclipsed normal precautions.

Having settled on a site for operation, Atkin purchased a mill from Charles Hendrie, the Iowa foundryman who would install new stamps in the Clark and Upson mill early the next year. Atkin's mill was a twelve-stamp steam-driven machine delivered to the Meadow Creek site on December 24, 1866. In preparation for its arrival Atkin built several cabins, and his workmen named the place "Atkinville." Atkin planned to adopt the Wyckoff Process for the reduction of his ores, approximately 100 tons of which would be extracted for crushing by the time the mill was operational.[61]

The Golden Ore Mining and Prospecting Company was not the only firm interested in locating a quartz milling operation in the Meadow Creek area in the summer of 1866. After almost two years of residency as prospectors and farmers, Don O. Spaulding and Andrew Hall announced their intention to go into the business as well. The Ohio-born Spaulding and Hall, a native of New York, would be important fixtures in the commercial activity of the Hot Spring District throughout the 1860s and 1870s. Sometime in midsummer of 1866, about the same time George Atkin appeared in Meadow Creek for the Golden Ore Mining Company, Hall and Spaulding were reported to have purchased a stamp mill and amalgamators from the [Hezekiah] Hosmer Mining Company of New York. This mill was to be erected on lodes the partners had discovered.[62] But the arrangement to acquire a quartz mill from the Hosmer Mining Company did not materialize when the company's superintendent changed his mind about Meadow Creek and placed the machinery in Ramshorn Gulch instead. Strongly disagreeing with the decision, Hosmer brought suit against his partners, but that was of little assistance to Hall and Spaulding.[63] Nevertheless, the announcement of Hall and Spaulding's intentions in the summer of 1866 added to the district's growing reputation as the territory's busiest milling district.

CHAPTER 5

Expansion of the District and New Investors, 1866

The Midas Mining Company
of Rochester, New York

"A pretty thorough examination of the several gold producing regions satisfied me that the lodes of Hot Spring District were, in point of richness and superior facilities for working, unequalled by those of any other part of the Territory."

—Henry Augustus Ward

DESPITE THE SETBACK IN GEORGE COPE'S OPERATION, WILLIAM CLARK'S DIFFIculty getting adequate results from his mill at Sterling, the postponement of Andrew Hall and Don Spaulding's aspirations, and the late start of the New York and Montana Mining and Discovery (NY&MM&D) Company's water-diversion project, interest and investment in Hot Spring gold continued at an extremely high level. One reason for this was the "discovery" in the summer of 1866 of the Lower Hot Spring Mining District.

Why the Lower Hot Spring District had not found favor prior to 1866 is hard to determine. In 1865, Asahel Eaton had looked it over but, surprising for a man with his powers of observation, had not been impressed. So had others with similar, if regrettable, results.[1] And few had considered it valuable for agricultural purposes, with the only settlement occurring west along Burnt Creek and around the hot spring, in that area where Norris exists today.

Topographically, the lower district constituted the leg of a rough T. Across the top of the T, from south to north, were the Meadow Creek District, Upper Hot Spring (including Revenue Flats—or Gold Field, as it was often called), and Norwegian Gulch. Lying east of these subdistricts was the Lower Hot Spring District, with Hot Spring Creek forming the T's spine. This district extended from the hot spring itself to where the creek empties into the Madison River. The area has limited acreage available for growing crops, but its rolling ranges can nicely sustain livestock. Probably because gold had not been discovered there in the years 1863–1865 and because its use for agricultural purposes was limited to grazing, land in the lower district had seen few preemptions prior to 1865; those claims that were taken centered mostly in the area west and south of the hot spring—an area much larger and better suited for conventional agricultural use. It was for this reason and for the 124-degree waters of the hot spring that Eaton had purchased 480 acres, encompassing an original homestead, in late August 1865.

It took another six months for men to realize that the Lower Hot Spring Creek area held promising mineral leads as well as grazing land. Prospectors seem to have concluded as much in early 1866. By May and June dozens of prospectors were making claims throughout the area east and southeast of the hot spring. The bonanza discovery, made by Jonathan P. Rodman, James Watson, and Watson Forst on June 19—that of the Boaz Lode—shook the whole district.[2] By every measure the Boaz discovery was deemed the most valuable Hot Spring District lode to date. Access to and the success of Boaz ores would be a major means by which all the milling companies located on Hot Spring Creek would calculate the success or failure of their enterprises. In fact, Boaz ores would figure prominently in the ups and downs of the Hot Spring District for the next seventy years.

Within days of the Boaz discovery, Lower Hot Spring became the object of a ministampede. On June 20, Gilbert B. Weeks, a principal member of the Crawford brothers' company, claimed the Atlantic and Great Western Lode, one-half mile east of the Boaz; discovery of the Victor Lode by the same men who had filed on the Boaz followed quickly.[3] Within the week, eight additional lodes were discovered in the vicinity. Between July 1 and the beginning of September, half of all lode discoveries for the entire Hot Spring District (twenty-three of forty-five) were made in the lower district, most within a mile or so of the Boaz, which became the most common geographic reference point for legal location descriptions. This miniboom was capped on September 3 with the discovery of the Red Bluff Lode.[4] Soon to be compared with the Boaz, the Red Bluff Lode eventually gave its name to the community that developed in the early 1870s around these lodes.

THE DISCOVERY AND DEVELOPMENT OF THE LOWER HOT SPRING DISTRICT COINCIDED with the decision of the Midas Mining Company of Rochester, New York, to locate its operations on Hot Spring Creek. The story of the Midas Company, by far the most significant company to commence work in the area, can be told because of the remarkable record-keeping habits of its field superintendent, Henry Augustus Ward. Ward, thirty-one years old in 1865, was another of those extraordinary jacks-of-all-trades personified by Asahel K. Eaton. Basically, Ward was a naturalist in the business of gathering vertebrates, fossils, and other specimens for natural history museum collections, or "cabinets" as they were called then. Ward earned his living by marketing his specimens through his own museum supply business in Rochester—Ward's Natural Science Establishment—a firm that continues to service geology and earth science departments in schools, colleges, and universities to this day. In fact, Ward has been given due credit as having inaugurated the natural history museum movement in America. His zoological and paleontological interests were international in scope; he had traveled extensively throughout Europe, the Near East, and Africa as a collector; and he would soon develop an international reputation for his accomplishments in meteorology—becoming, literally, an around-the-world collector of meteors and meteor fragments. Most important to our story, Ward had studied geology at the École des Mines in Paris, France; he had close connections with the Columbia School of Mines in New York City and was familiar with many U.S. mineralogists and geologists.[5] He knew and respected Asahel Eaton. But there was one major difference between Ward and Eaton. Eaton lived his life in historical anonymity; Ward lived a life documented to its fullest. For Ward was a collector, and as specimens piled up on his shelves, so too did his filing cabinets bulge with letters, telegrams, memoranda, and reports.

Henry Ward's first contact with Montana had come in the winter of 1864–1865 through Moses M. Sperry of Rochester, one of Bannack's early pioneers. Although not a mining person himself, Sperry had purchased a considerable number of mineral claims from other parties; some of these claims had changed hands three times before Sperry acquired them, and Sperry had never personally examined most of them. The claims were located in several counties, including Edgerton (now Lewis and Clark), Beaverhead, Deer Lodge, and Madison.

Back in Rochester, Sperry had offered some of his holdings for sale. Two of Ward's acquaintances had taken an interest. Putting down $4,000 on approval, the men asked Ward to go to Montana for them to ascertain the authenticity of the claims. Sperry was to pay Ward's expenses.[6] Ward accepted the offer; he could draw a fee as a consultant and have his expenses paid while at the same time securing specimens of western wildlife—specimens he was short of—for his museum collections. In May 1865, Ward embarked on a steamship from New York City to San Francisco by way of the Isthmus of Panama, arriving in Montana by stage over the overland route from California in mid-June.

Ward's investigation found his sponsor's properties in Bannack disappointing, as the claims available were undeveloped and distant from discovery, something Sperry either had not known or had not told Ward. None of Sperry's Beaverhead County claims, moreover, had been filed with the county recorder. From Bannack, Ward moved on to Sperry's holdings in Madison County, where he met further disappointment. Some of the lodes Sperry had acquired and then sought to sell to the Rochester investors were little known to the locals, and Ward had difficulty locating them. Once located, Ward found that the ores had not been tested by a reliable assayer; some that he panned out had no value at all. Ward regretted having to give such an unfavorable opinion of the lodes: "But they are like thousands of others which parties pick up at random here. . . . There are, all over the hills here, unprincipled men who fasten on to anything which they can call a lode, record it, and sell their 'claims' for any price which they can get. A buyer not watchful in these matters is sure to be taken in."[7] Ward was not the only one cognizant of these practices; Thomas Dimsdale, editor of the *Montana Post*, put it this way:

> The racing hither and thither from one prairie dog hole to another and thence to the Recorder's office—there to swear to a crevice as visionary as Macbeth's "dagger of the mind"—must receive a condemnation at the hands of every man who has at heart either the welfare of the community or his own final success. . . . [The territory was suffering] from the flagrant violation of truth by men of large swearing power and small digging propensities.[8]

Ward was understandably leery of purchasing anything but discovery claims. Where prospects were good, however, the owners would not sell or were asking far too much. What they were selling were the less valuable and unproven outer claims to finance their work on the discovery itself. Ward would purchase nothing of this sort for his Rochester clients. Having canvassed Beaverhead and Madison counties, Ward prepared to visit Sperry's properties in Helena's Last Chance Gulch and at Big Prickly Pear.

Although Ward's report home had not been enthusiastic, he could not deny that he had seen much to encourage him. The Sperry claims were worthless, but many others were "sure to make their owners rich." Such claims were available, but they required "time and care, with close, cautious observation." To his sponsors Ward broached the subject of a quartz milling endeavor—the reduction of quartz might pay as well as or better than speculation in lodes. For $15,000, admittedly $5,000 more than he had been authorized to spend, he believed a twenty- to twenty-five-stamp mill could be purchased that would suit their needs. For another $100 to $200 he could buy a mill site. He would await their counsel.[9]

The fact is that Ward had become hugely enthusiastic about Montana gold. He had caught the gold bug. Friends at home received amazing descriptions of the territory's wealth. "You have no idea of the quantity of gold which they get here," he wrote. He had ridden on one occasion in a stagecoach with a miner who foolishly displayed a satchel containing $30,000 in nuggets, one of them the size of a fist. He had seen enough gold to pave a walk approximating the longest in a notable Rochester city park "two inches thick."[10]

Doubting his present supporters' ability to finance what he had in mind and aching to find such capabilities elsewhere, Ward went right to the top, penning a long letter on July 12, 1865, to Hiram Sibley, the driving force behind the great Western Union Telegraph Company, headquartered in Rochester. "I take the liberty of writing to propose to you an investment in gold property in this Territory," Ward opened. The letter continued:

> I believe that there are here opportunities for large profits upon sums invested, much beyond anything to be found in the Eastern States. . . . It is barely three years since the first "prospectors" crossed the mountains to the south, and discovered gold in this Territory. Now there is here a population of about 20,000 people, who find their entire support in the mineral products of the soil. They are, in the main, gulch miners, who wash the gravel clean across the bottom of the narrow vallies [sic] and along their entire length, and gather up the dirt, and grains, and nuggets of gold. You would be astonished at the amount of the precious metal which these gulches yield. You can only estimate it by the ton. Many single "claims" of 100 feet along the line of a stream have yielded from $50,000 to $100,000. . . . The whole territory, in a broad belt running from here north to Fort Benton—some 300 miles—has its narrow vallies thus profusely filled with gold. . . . The hills and plateaus contain, over many large areas, the same rich quantities of gold which have been found in the ravines. The gold exists there in quartz veins ("leads," or "lodes") which cut thickly through the strata, and can sometimes be traced for long distances. These lodes are now attracting a good deal of attention, for they are to prove the lasting source of gold after the gulches have all been exhausted. Several hundred

practical miners are now "prospecting" these hills for lodes of gold-bearing quartz. Several thousand of these lodes have already been found in this and the adjoining counties, and of it perhaps one fourth will pay handsome returns for working. . . . I have spent considerable time in the . . . examination of these lodes, and have been quite astonished at their richness. There is nothing in the least like it in California, or in many European countries where I have studied mines. Few of them show gold to the naked eye, but yield it abundantly when crushed. The other day I took rock . . . from 46 successive lodes on a hill-side. Crushing this rock in a mortar and "panning" it, I found visible gold in 42 of the lodes. I found average results of from $100. to $200. per ton. They would yield much more than this in a careful chemical assay.

Ward went on to discuss ore he had assayed at $5,000 to the ton from the Oro Cache Lode in the Summit District above Virginia City. A year previous, the first claims from discovery had sold for $100 each. Now those same claims were selling for $10,000 and more. Ward estimated that in a year's time their value would double or triple. There was much competition for these properties among buyers; parties he knew of from New York City had been empowered to spend up to $100,000 for claims of such value.

Ward further observed that few of the lodes he had examined were worked to any depth and that the great need was for crushing mills and separators. These would bring relief to the lode owners who were unable to meet the costs of such machinery. To be effective, such mills would have to be of steam because winter conditions and the unreliability of water militated against water-powered operations. Wood for fuel was more readily available and could be obtained for labor only.

Ward professed disinterest in profits for himself. His life's concern was the collection of "shells, corals, fishes, reptiles, birds and quadrupeds" for his museum cabinets. But it bothered him immensely

to see the wealth which I see here . . . without wishing that my friends in Rochester shall have a part of it. I can but be moved when I see property which can be bought today for $10,000, and which I expect to see, if I live for five years, valued at $100,000. to $500,000. Never was there a better chance to make a rich investment. . . . If these gold mines will not pay, and pay richly, then no mines in the world will.[11]

Ward suggested to Sibley that he invest $20,000 to $100,000 in Montana gold lodes, with the intent of crushing and working them himself or holding on to the ores as speculation on their rise in value over time. He would stay in the territory for two to three months more, he told Sibley, and during that period he would inspect everything within 200 miles of Virginia City. He would use his geological experience to select only the best claims, open lodes and

have their rock assayed before acquiring them, and see to all the legal requirements associated with purchase and title. John Creighton, Western Union's
supervisor in the West, could probably serve as banker for the enterprise.
Ward suggested a figure of $10,000 to give himself a start.[12]

Hiram Sibley did not respond to Ward's letter. Unknown to Ward, Sibley
had retired from Western Union Telegraph and was vacationing abroad in
Heidelberg. But as Ward had sent the letter to his family's banking house for
forwarding, Ward's uncle, Judge Samuel L. Selden—a founder of and major
shareholder in Western Union—intercepted the letter and accepted the challenge. Selden's cryptic August 31 response to Ward marked the inauguration
of the Midas Mining Company of Rochester, New York: "You may purchase
as stated in your letter, to an amount not to exceed, including all expenses,
ten thousand dollars ($10,000). Take title in my name as trustee; have sent
one thousand dollars ($1,000) to Holiday & Hasley. Will furnish balance as
required. Answer."[13]

Samuel S. Selden, esteemed Rochester jurist and owner of and shareholder
in Rochester newspapers, had also gained distinction for his long-standing
involvement in technological development. An inventor of some note—machinery to produce cheap lead piping for the conveyance of water and gas was
one of his more notable achievements—Selden had been one of the nation's
first citizens to promote the development of telegraphy.[14] Other members of
his extended family, including the Mumfords and the Wards—the latter heavily into banking—had joined in the communications enterprise. After more
than a decade of intense competition to monopolize the lines between New
York and St. Louis, in 1856 these efforts had produced the Western Union
Telegraph Company, of which Selden was a trustee.

The Civil War increased the company's position and fortunes immensely.
Because Western Union's lines ran east and west through Union territory and
not north and south, as did the lines of its major competitor, the company
was able to escape war damage almost entirely and emerged from the conflict
with its commanding position greatly improved. Just as important, during the
war Western Union executives were employed by the Lincoln administration
to head the military's and government's telegraphic communications system.
Military telegraphic traffic in itself was extremely profitable.

The war had also accelerated construction of the transcontinental telegraph
line, the contract for which was let in its entirety to Western Union. It was
completed in 1862 by contractors, including John Creighton who, with his
brother Edward, constructed the eastern link from Nebraska to Salt Lake City;
the total cost had not exceeded $500,000 and had provided its backers with

many millions in profit. Government subsidies paid back virtually the entire cost within ten years. Additional profits were reaped by the trustees through the sale of watered stock to thousands of enthusiasts. At war's end, Western Union controlled lines from coast to coast, possessed a brilliant future, and had become "one of the largest and most comprehensive private enterprises in the world."[15]

That Western Union was headquartered in Rochester, the nation's twentieth most populated city in 1860, spoke to that community's prominent place as a center of commerce. Called America's first boomtown, Rochester had developed initially on the fortunes of its flour milling trade and then had grown dramatically—and been given a western orientation—with the opening of the Erie Canal. Relative fortunes had been made subsequently in milling, fruit and flower farming, farm journals, clothing, the manufacture of clothing and shoes, leather, wool, woodworking, tobacco, liquor, and perfume. At the close of the Civil War at least twenty-seven of Rochester's capitalists had annual incomes of between $20,000 and $100,000, extraordinary for that day and age. Of these, Hiram Sibley, former chairman of the board of Western Union, paid the most in taxes.[16] Samuel Selden was close behind. Retired from the bench in 1862, he had the time and the resources to make an investment in mining.[17]

During the time between writing his letter to Sibley and receiving Selden's response, Ward made a trip to Helena and reported on his findings in the mines around Last Chance Gulch and Big Prickly Pear. Moses Sperry's prospects were no better there; many lodes could not be located, and most of those that had been found had proven barren. Ward anguished over the wildcat behavior of prospectors, "staking every little spur of quartz which protruded above the ground, never testing the rock to see what it contained, but selling the 'claims' to whoever would buy." This kind of property was being rushed into the eastern markets in "immense quantities" and "was not worth the deeds that transfer it." Many other men like himself, representing eastern investors, had met with like results and formed similar opinions. Ward concluded that Sperry's Helena properties were virtually worthless. By comparison, he thought Beaverhead and Madison County properties much superior.[18] Within these counties Ward was focusing on one district in particular—the Hot Spring District on the east side of the Tobacco Root Mountains.

When Ward first became acquainted with Hot Spring is not clear, but he clearly knew of it once he met William J. Clark and Major Gad Upson in late July 1865. This meeting had obviously proved satisfactory to Ward, for on August 10 he, Clark, Upson, and John Gill, superintendent of the Silver Mountain

Mining Company, had entered into an agreement to associate themselves "for the purpose of Discovering, Mining, Purchasing and Selling Mining property located in Montana Territory."[19] Clark and Upson's commitments to the Hot Spring area were quite solid, and Ward had just taken a significant step in that direction. No doubt Thomas Dimsdale would have applauded Ward's decision. "[I]t is not a matter of difficulty where to find a fortune," observed the *Post*'s editor, "but which place to select as a base of operations." Properly located, a "thousand quartz mills" would find sufficient work in Montana to make millionaires of their promoters.[20]

Selden's backing, coming four weeks later, was used to supplement and cement Ward's growing commitment to the Hot Spring District. Ward had met with the members of the Herschel Mining Company, was impressed with their work and holdings in Hot Spring, and had concluded to purchase a one-fourth share in their properties, including lodes and two mill sites. For this Ward paid $10,000 in gold dust, or $11,111 in greenbacks—a portion down, with the balance of $6,000 to be paid by Selden in three installments by February the next year. Ward purchased additional Hot Spring property from private individuals. He also made a smaller investment in Wisconsin Gulch on the western side of the Tobacco Roots.[21]

From these lodes Ward wanted to get out as much ore as possible as far in advance as possible, for he anticipated a milling business of many years' duration. In fact, he believed that for the time being, ores could be stockpiled easily by the rudimentary method of pick and shovel and bucket and windlass. Little blasting would be required, as the ore was remarkably soft and hardness was not anticipated. Once on-site, a forty-stamp mill would crush fifty tons of this quartz per day almost without cessation. Ward estimated that at the bottom level, $40 per ton would be the minimum result. Perhaps that seemed low, given the figures he had previously quoted, but he had taken the figure from reliable mill men, averaging out the good and the bad. It was better to stay on the conservative side, he said. Cost of crushing would not exceed $10 per ton. Ward assured his uncle that without a doubt the company would clear $336,000 annually.[22]

Ward hoped Selden would honor his estimates, decide to enter into mining, and agree to get a mill to the territory at the earliest possible moment. But the choice of route was of concern. Aware of what Clark and Upson had gone through, he was not enthusiastic about the Missouri River. As for the overland route, the mills that had been transported across the plains had only just arrived and stood small chance of becoming operational before next June. San Francisco offered the best source; mills there were cheaper and even better than East Coast mills. If such a mill could be put on the road from Los Angeles to Salt Lake in February, he reasoned, it would be in Hot Spring by June, with a mill building ready on the site.

In communicating with Selden, Ward was insistent that only the best sort of mill should be purchased and that all the accessories (amalgamators, separators, plates, screens, and the like) be "suited to the kind of rock in question." The mill should have a power at least one-quarter in excess of need, and because the territory lacked foundries and machine shops, duplicates of many parts had to be on hand. As for costs, the mill and its accessories would not exceed $30,000, he told his uncle; its transportation and erection in a substantial building would be about $40,000. It could fall short of that, but in this business there were many unpredictable expenses. Putting all anticipated costs together, including purchases of quartz properties, Ward estimated that $100,000 of working capital would do it. He "was entirely satisfied of the great value" of Selden's Montana property, he advised his uncle, "and of the great dividends which it will pay under proper working."[23] This was Ward's last report from Montana in 1865, for shortly thereafter he was off—with a brief stop in Nevada Territory—to San Francisco, narrowly escaping a road holdup on the way. Ward, like the chap who possessed $30,000 in gold nuggets, carried wealth of his own—a solid gold brick with which he intended to impress Selden and others interested in a Montana enterprise.[24]

The Midas Mining Company of Rochester, New York, was organized shortly after the start of the new year. George Mumford, an officer of the Western Union Telegraph Company and related to the Ward family by marriage, was elected secretary of the company and chairman of the board of directors. On February 9 the company issued to its stockholders a report provided by Henry Ward covering his Montana explorations. The nine directors, duly impressed with Ward's gold brick, which now lay on exhibit in the banking house of Ward and Brothers, emphasized that they were convinced that the professor had "understated rather than overstated" the richness of the company's gold properties and that "the enormous profits estimated by Prof. Ward—over 100 per cent., namely, for the first year—can be relied upon, if the additional capital requisite for putting up a mill and working the quartz, can be immediately obtained." Sixty thousand dollars had already been offered for Ward's purchases, but the trustees were of the opinion that the stockholders should hold on for even better profits through development. To raise the capital necessary to undertake a mill operation, the company was issuing 20,000 shares at $10 each, which, added to the capital already invested by the trustees, would give the company a worth of $300,000.[25]

Ward's appended report was in essence a reiteration of much of what he had already conveyed from Montana to Samuel Selden:

> [The] extraordinary richness of yield, together with the great facilities which the country affords, (abounding as it does with wood and water, and productive land already under cultivation in hundreds of places) makes present or future mining operations in Montana more promising of favorable results, and liable to fewer drawbacks, than those in almost any other point in the Great West. . . . A pretty thorough examination of the several gold producing regions satisfied me that the lodes of Hot Spring District were, in point of richness and superior facilities for working, un-equalled by those of any other part of the Territory.[26]

Ward had chosen Hot Spring, he reported, because the district's foundation rock was fragmented and decomposed to a "great depth below the surface," therefore making it easier to work. The terrain in which it was found was gentle and undulating, allowing easy access by road. Hot Spring Creek provided "abundant water for all mill and other purposes," and the nearby mountains furnished for the taking an "inexhaustible supply of wood for fuel and build-ing." The adjoining agricultural and grazing lands of the district were capable of supporting a large mining population. A small settlement was already in the making, "with many houses, [a] store and [a] tavern." Three other gold milling companies had selected Hot Spring as their site of operations.[27]

Ward scaled down some of his earlier estimates. The mill would be of twenty stamps, he said, and after all expenses the first year's costs would approximate $200,000. This represented a halving of the mill's size and a doubling of the costs anticipated for the first year. The directors can only have assumed that Ward's initial call for a forty-stamp mill was excessive and that his original costs had been greatly underestimated. Still, Ward assured the stockholders that the mill would pay for itself and all the company's prop-erty in the first nine months of operation. Gold bullion would be produced within a fortnight of the mill's commencement and would continue without interruption. "I do not hesitate to promise," Ward concluded, "that every reasonable expectation of the stockholders of the Midas Mining Company will be fulfilled."[28]

During the winter and spring of 1866, Ward spent most of his time tend-ing to his museum business, even taking a trip to Europe. While the Midas Company was filling its stock subscriptions, there was little he could do in Hot Spring. But Theodore Maltby kept him informed about matters. In early April, Maltby reported on his work in opening and developing the lodes his company had sold to Ward, noting that extreme cold had curtailed all work on the surface. Clark's mill was near completion, but water had flooded one of the

Hartford company's best hopes, the Ivanhoe Lode, forcing its abandonment until spring. Both Clark and Maltby were doing better on the Richmond Lode up on Gold Hill. The Ragland, Cope, and Napton mill had just crushed some ore with values of $40 a ton but had done a poor job of making a thorough cleanup. The superintendent of the NY&MM&D Company, Enfield Pratt, had bet Maltby a basket of champagne that he would have the New York mill in operation on or before the Fourth of July; Maltby was not sure where Pratt expected to secure the champagne. Over in Meadow Creek, opposition to the Rockfellow diversion ditch had arisen among the farmers, and Pratt had needed time to placate them and secure their assent. With that accomplished, Maltby was optimistic that work on the ditch would commence as soon as the mountains were clear of snow. The map Captain de Lacy had drawn of the entire Hot Spring District had been forwarded to John Creighton to be lithographed. Ward would have a copy as soon as it was printed. Maltby concluded his note with the news that he and Rockfellow would take fifty shares each of the Midas Mining Company's stock.[29]

In the meantime, the Midas Mining Company had been unable to move fast enough to secure a mill and equipment in time for installation and operation in the 1866 season. The task of raising capital sufficient to underwrite the project had been undertaken too late. Ward had originally believed that for a mill to be operational and remunerative in 1866, it would have to be shipped from San Francisco in February. But the company's public stock offering had not even been announced until that month. Then there was difficulty getting the stock subscription filled. These matters affected the decision on the size, make, and cost of the mill to be purchased and on its accessories. Ward remained convinced that buying the best mill attainable was the proper course, but others were of a different mind.

In spite of these difficulties, the Midas Mining Company sent supplies and equipment to Hot Spring by the Missouri River route in June; the cargo departed from St. Joseph, Missouri, on the 26th of that month. Water levels were much improved in 1866, and travel on the river was possible much later in the season than it had been in 1865. Ward also left Rochester for Montana early that summer but by the overland route, as he planned to visit Denver. In the interim, events within the Midas Mining Company led Samuel Selden to harbor serious doubts about what he and Ward had gotten the company into, and, hoping to catch Ward before he made too many concrete decisions, the judge wrote the professor on September 18 in care of Denver.

Selden wondered if perhaps a different strategy ought to be considered. Why couldn't the company purchase the mill of Ragland, Cope, and Napton instead of a new one? In August Napton had offered the mill for only $20,000; there could be substantial savings in time and cost by adapting the Missouri machinery to Midas's needs. Selden knew full well Ward's argument that better economy would be achieved by purchasing a new, "first-rate" mill, but it was becoming more and more a concern to the judge that time was perhaps of greater consideration than long-term economies, for Selden feared a delay in operations would result in a withdrawal of support: "Already one or two of the members of the Company give indications of backing out," he advised his nephew. One of these dissidents had delayed interminably in paying for his stock, and the other appeared ready to forfeit all he had already purchased. Several others had advanced as little as 5 to 25 percent on their subscriptions, and such behavior was bound to affect the backing of others. As prospects for commencing a milling operation were now delayed until 1867, the potential for a falling off of support had increased. Holding to a new-mill policy would only exacerbate the problem. "If, by taking an inferior mill at the outset, at a low price, you can demonstrate that money can be made by mining it, although the percentage of profit may be comparatively small," Selden reasoned with Ward, "then will there I think be no difficulty in getting all the money you will need. Show them a little gold actually realized as profit from running a mill & you will reach minds that dare not trust the results of this reasoning[,] however well grounded it may be." Selden was not afraid to admit that he could be wrong, but as the company was having difficulty meeting its subscription goals and he did not want to terminate the enterprise, he would "prefer to make a little sacrifice in the outset, in point of economy, for the sake of putting an end to speculation by an actual test."[30]

Ward, who by remarkable coincidence arrived at Sterling in late September just as the company's freight train from Fort Benton came up the road, gave sober consideration to Selden's concerns and made some adjustments, but he would not budge from his desire to obtain a new mill. Having looked over the operations of his competitors in Hot Spring and taken into consideration the work of other territorial mills, of which around forty now existed, he was convinced that only new machinery could avoid the excessive losses currently reported. Clark, he noted, had given up entirely on his crusher and pulverizer and was preparing to purchase new equipment, sacrificing a $40,000 investment. Pratt had discovered that the engineer who had designed the water-driven turbine for the NY&MM&D Company's mill had overestimated the water power obtainable from Hot Spring Creek. Consequently, Pratt had been compelled to build up a full day's water supply behind his dam to work the company's stamps for just two hours! The Meadow Creek ditch, intended to bolster the creek's capacity, was being completed too late to be of service that season. Moreover, throughout the territory, reports of great losses of gold to sheer slovenliness and inefficient amalgamation and separating processes certified Ward's conviction that the company should use only the newest and best apparatus.[31]

Ward, however, was not insensitive to the growing difficulties the company was experiencing in Rochester. He was also, for the first time, willing to acknowledge that his earlier evaluation of the profits to be made had been somewhat exaggerated. Nevertheless, he still felt confident that good profits, if somewhat reduced, were there in Hot Spring for those who worked diligently and scientifically. The district still retained its good name and prestige. The old miners Ward relied upon—from Mexico, California, and Nevada—were still strong on the district's prospects. Ward had much faith in their reasoning. He wanted to go on. But if Rochester demanded it, he was prepared to make necessary adjustments, including further scaling down the number of stamps to be purchased. A smaller mill might be the way to start; its profits could be used to further the development of the company's lodes for the purpose of eventually supplying a larger mill with plenty of quartz. Ward was still stuck on a large mill for the sake of economies but was moderating his approach. "This plan is some[what] different from that contemplated at the commencement," he lamented, but he was prepared to admit that "it is the safer one in view of all circumstances."[32]

While waiting for the company to make up its mind, the professor constructed a small town of five buildings, which he named "Midasburg," on a narrow flat at the mouth of Pony Gulch, about a third of a mile above Sterling. Between Sterling and Midasburg were the mills of his competitors, Clark and Pratt. Sterling was now a town of at least thirty log cabins and several commercial houses and was serving as the temporary boarding place for Ward's labor force. His friend James Hodge, milling near Helena, had strongly recommended that Ward not board his own men, but the professor had weighed the pros and cons and decided to create his own town. This would be in effect a mini–company town in which he, as superintendent, could not only affect economies but could better control his workers. He was paying $2.30 per day to house and feed his workers in Sterling but believed he could better that by at least $0.80 a day by boarding them in Midasburg. And he could monitor their behavior. They could be roused from bed each morning on schedule, and Ward would have some leverage over their social habits—like carousing—which could impact the company's efficiency.[33]

Ward's determination to run a tight ship did not go unnoticed. The professor, one observer wrote, "scandalized the rough-and-ready miners by whitewashing all the buildings and by enforcing rules of sanitation."[34] When the company allowed the engineer assigned to the mill to bring his wife out to Montana, Ward, disturbed at the idea of a woman in a mining camp, built a mountainside cabin for the couple some distance from the workers' quarters. The observation that Midasburg was "more like an army post than a mining camp" was probably a fairly accurate description of Ward's company town.[35] But he was extremely proud of his community. And he was not acting out of the ordinary in designing a company town. After all, Midasburg was but a rough and scaled-down model built on long precedent in American history. During the Industrial Revolution that swept the United States in the early to mid–nineteenth century, company towns—textile company mill towns particularly, complete with basic facilities—had become established features of America's architectural and social landscape. Eventually, Ward arranged for mail to be forwarded directly to Midasburg rather than sent to Sterling.

Once he had made his decision to build Midasburg, Ward, in his accustomed way, would have nothing but the best. Having observed that Clark and Pratt had constructed inferior buildings with dirt roofs, unchinked walls, and dirt floors, all of which had to be replaced, Ward spent liberally, around $4,500—50 percent more than his competitors—to put up what he considered superior structures with "good roofs, good floors, tight walls and well-hewn logs." These buildings were five in number and included a home for himself, an office-storage facility, and a combination bunkhouse, kitchen, and cook's and housekeeper's living quarters. Ward was sure the bunkhouse—of which one third, 22 by 33 feet, or 726 square feet, was designed for sleeping—would easily suit the needs of thirty men! The two other buildings were a two-story barn and a combination carpenter's shop, toolroom, and blacksmith's shop.[36]

To compensate for the higher costs of construction, Ward cut wages by 20 percent, to $2.50 per day, which he further reduced by paying the men in greenbacks. He acknowledged that his workers were "disposed to revolt a little," but he felt the cutbacks were necessary adjustments to wages that were simply too high for the district. Although his competitors were paying higher wages, Ward was certain he could keep his men because he offered superior living facilities. Ward contemplated reducing wages even further as winter came on, to as low as a dollar a day for common laborers such as those who worked windlasses and other surface men. "First-class" laborers, men with experience, would be reduced to $1.75 per day.[37]

Reducing wages during slack periods was nothing new in the frontier mining business. It was a common policy among mill operators, and a laborer could do little during the difficult Montana winters to counter the practice. With transportation to the States seriously curtailed, workers were essentially stuck where they were at the outset of inclement weather. Ward figured that in this manner he could control wage levels until May 1 at least. The construction of the bunkhouse had been part of this cost-effective strategy, and he had bought all his food supplies, except fresh meat, before winter supply-and-demand factors forced a rise in prices.

Still, the costs had not been insignificant—in the month since his return to Montana, Henry Ward had run up bills of $11,500. This included his passage to Montana, Midasburg's buildings, furniture and stoves for his own residence, provisions, freight costs to Montana, and wages for the development of the company's lodes. He had also accumulated personal bills. Having been forced to the brink of borrowing from friends, Ward asked the directors in Rochester for an additional $2,500 to cover personal expenses.[38]

Ward's willingness to reduce the size of the quartz mill proved a relief to Samuel Selden and helped reduce opposition from others, but it did not satisfy everyone.[39] Those who still questioned Ward's policies saw as much more concrete the magnitude of the debt he was saddling the company with in preparation for a mill, the nature of which had not even been decided upon. George Mumford was particularly critical, finding many of Ward's expenditures highly questionable. Ward's use of the telegraph, for example, had in only weeks brought $150 in charges.

Historically, this bill had significance, for John Creighton had just linked Virginia City with the States by telegraphic wire, and Ward had quickly taken advantage of it. Creighton, who as a partner in the Herschel Mining Company had stakes in Hot Spring, had even talked of extending the service to Sterling. But trustees of the Midas Mining Company were not impressed. Henceforth, only messages that were absolutely necessary were to be sent in this manner, Mumford warned Ward, and they were to be "occasional & brief." On the other hand, Ward's mailed reports were not being submitted frequently enough, and his explanations of expenditures were inadequate. There was a feeling in Rochester that he was spending more freely than was necessary. He must henceforth exercise the "utmost economy" in every matter.[40]

For reasons Ward would later try to explain, the press of business kept him from responding immediately to the company's new directives, and it was mid-January before his next report was received in Rochester. This uncharacteristic lapse on Ward's part seriously damaged his credibility and threatened to jeopardize the company's entire Montana venture, for although the directors did not receive news from Ward in the interim, they did see his drafts on the company's accounts. By mid-December the drafts had tripled since Ward's report of late October—$34,000 in cash payments for salaries, freight, wages, board, construction costs, and so on. Ward, Mumford wrote, had taken with him to Montana a sum of almost $20,000 but had not provided the company with an accounting of its use. What had happened to it? Was he purchasing new mining properties? Mumford sincerely hoped not, as there was "great distrust" in Rochester regarding expenditures of this kind.[41]

To make their point clear, the directors decided to refuse to pay the latest of Ward's drafts. One of Ward's cousins, Joseph B. Ward, treasurer of Ward and Brothers, the family bank, was succinct in his remarks to Henry: "Mr Mumford and the other directors are quite offended, and the best interests of the Midas Co. are very much in jeopardy. . . . Confidence is the soul of all enterprises and the fact that you spend money so much faster than you lead us to expect, and refuse (or neglect—the result of which is the same) to report is taking the life out of the enterprise."[42]

However, Ward's belated report of December 18, received in Rochester in mid-January, helped assuage some of the directors' frustration and anger. He had been so absorbed in company business in Montana, Henry Ward said, that nothing had permitted him the time to report earlier:

> [M]y duties since I came to Sterling have been arduous and absorbing beyond all description. Have had to plan[,] provide material for, and oversee all the detail of extensive buildings; to locate miners at six or seven different places, over an area of three miles, furnish them with tools and visit each gang nearly every day; to arrange for all matters of board of some 30 men; to look up provisions and produce at the cheapest markets; together with the score or more of contracts which I have had to arrange with outside parties—bargaining for the terms and inspecting the execution. Steadily occupied while here at home I have had in addition a weekly trip to Virginia—30 miles & back,—and a daily ride of from ten to twenty miles on business to Ranches, Saw Mills, Lime-Kilns, Coal-pits, Woods, and other points. These things were of a nature which would positively admit of no postponing, and it is only now, in the final lull of work, that I am able to give you a letter which you must have expected . . . that I should have written a full month ago.[43]

As to the matter of costs, he assured the directors, they were radically different in Montana compared with Rochester. The Midasburg buildings, for example, had cost $7,500, whereas in Rochester they would have cost $4,000. And he had to draw on the company's accounts "so largely and so rapidly" because credit in Montana could not be obtained except at usurious rates—

5 percent per month, for example. Ready money, in fact, had enabled him to accomplish things he otherwise would have left undone. Ward was also vexed by the absence of coin and small bills, the result of which had been that prices were pegged to the denominations most available, often higher than real values (a circumstance common in western mining camps during the 1860s). In closing his report, Ward promised to submit further details soon.[44]

Thereafter, Ward's reports were sent off fast and furiously; two more were posted before the end of the year, a third on January 9, 1867, yet another on January 14. The most critical of these, that penned on December 22, turned the tide in Ward's favor and opened the way for the purchase of a new mill. This report reached Rochester on January 17, in very good time considering the season. It carried the news that much work had been performed on the Maltby, Empress, Good Omen, Old Mortality, and Helen lodes and that good depth had been reached on some of them. Indications were fair to good, Ward said, although it was still premature to predict their true value. Still, he now had a higher opinion of the company's prospects than he had envisioned in October, and he wanted to emphasize the promise the future held. "There is visible quartz enough within three or four miles around me," he argued, "to keep several mills running night and day." This meant quartz that showed gold right at the surface. Scores of such lodes existed in the district, and their owners yearned for a good mill to crush their ore for them. Ward was insistent that "the first good mill which is put up here will get it on almost any terms desired." With Clark's mill closed for alterations and Pratt's water-powered mill shut down for the winter, only Cope's steam-powered plant was running; and as inefficient as it was, it could not keep up with demand. In fact, a number of miners had erected arrastras as stopgaps. These primitive contraptions were a sure indication of how intent Hot Spring miners were to get results by any method. Ward offered these examples to demonstrate what could be done with proper machinery.[45]

The important lesson was that Hot Spring needed quartz mills. Those who responded with quality equipment would get the business. "I ask you now," Ward wrote, "and counsell [sic] it most earnestly . . . give me a 15-stamp mill at once." He insisted that this mill be purchased in California, for he had developed a strong bias against eastern machinery. Eastern-made mills, although cheaper, were not as durable and dependable as West Coast makes. He maintained that of seventy mills in the territory—a clear exaggeration—only ten were operating, the others having been forced to close for repairs that in some cases necessitated complete overhaul. Clark's situation was a perfect example. He had first sunk $40,000 into his eastern-built crusher and pulverizer;

now forced to replace them, he had committed a "second folly" by purchasing a used twenty-four-stamp model crafted east of Montana. Pratt's Brooklyn-made mill, presumably of much finer composition, had parts wear out in two months that should have lasted five years. Eaton's and Hodge's amalgamators, also Brooklyn-made, had proved impracticable. Hodge's eastern-made mill near Helena had defective separating tables. Although Ward agreed that the engine and boiler could be made effectively and economically in the East, the crushing, separating, and amalgamating machinery simply had to come from San Francisco, the leading producer of mills for the California mines. As for costs, Ward was certain that, if he personally attended to the purchase of the mill, it would run roughly $11,376. Freight from San Francisco to Sterling by way of Los Angeles would add $9,130; an engine and two boilers, $3,300; freight for same to Sterling up the Missouri River, $3,500; mill building, $8,000; belts and freight for same, $600; quicksilver and tools, $1,500. If payments were made in gold, the cost would be discounted. He set the total expense, with consideration given to the highest contingency, at $45,108.[46]

Ward was tired of waiting for commitments. He needed an immediate answer, as the time required to get freight through was fast fleeting. The month of April would be the last opportunity to ship a mill from the West Coast if it was to be put in operation the same season. Any delay would set the company's enterprise back another year. "I ought to hear from you at once," he all but demanded, "by telegraph . . . as soon as you form a conclusion of any kind, for all this needs planning far ahead."[47]

Ward soon got action from Rochester. On January 24 he was informed by telegraph from Mumford that his request for a fifteen-stamp mill had been approved.[48] The decision had not been arrived at easily, as Samuel Selden elaborated for his nephew in a letter of the same date. The directors had been divided on the merits of continuing a commitment to the Montana mining venture. Mumford and John H. Brewster had formed the opposition, which at first appeared to have the upper hand. But the matter had been tabled until Jonathan Watson, who had been out of town, could take part in the discussion. Upon his return, Watson had fortunately taken a strong supportive stand, particularly with respect to Ward's insistence that a mill be installed as soon as possible, but Watson alone had been willing to increase his subscription to help raise the additional $15,000 to $20,000 necessary to purchase a mill. The others had demurred, fearful of having already become committed to an "extra hazardous speculation" that might, on the one hand, "yield immense profits" but on the other "fail altogether." The latter view seemed to be gaining popularity: the latest subscription for $100,000 had been only 42 percent fulfilled. Faced with this stalemate, Selden, already deeper into it than anyone else but determined to save the enterprise, had pledged another $25,000 of his own money. This commitment had settled the question, and the immediate purchase of a mill was approved.[49]

Ward had to be delighted with this authorization, but there was little time for celebration. He now had imposing new responsibilities. With authorization had come unending requests for information. Ward put in an order to San Francisco for a mill, but he had recommended eastern manufacture of the engine and boiler (the directors were advising one boiler instead of two). With whom should the company contract for the engine and boiler? What horsepower did Ward desire? What height was suitable for the smokestack? What length of belting was required? How about shafting? How and when should all of this be shipped?[50]

Ward prided himself on his ability as a planner, but until he had seen the California mill firsthand he could answer few of these questions. He had equally important needs of his own to cope with. He had to get to California as soon as possible to be in on the design and making of the mill, and he had to make a final decision on how the mill would be shipped to Montana.

THE YEAR 1866 HAD BEEN ONE OF EXTRAORDINARY ACTIVITY FOR THE HOT SPRING MINING District. A whole new subdistrict, the Lower Hot Spring area, had been discovered and developed and had brought increased interest in Hot Spring's mineral prospects. An additional 226 discovery claims had been made throughout the entire district, and three new quartz milling enterprises had committed to the area. A town called Sterling had arisen in response to these developments. A small company town, Midasburg, had added to the population base. On the surface, the district's prospects looked good. Miners and mill operators alike continued to feel strongly that Hot Spring ranked among the territory's most promising gold districts.

Yet there were ample signs of difficulties already at hand or soon to be faced. Only one or two of the mill operators were nearly as optimistic in their estimates as they had been a year previous; the mills themselves had fallen short of expectations both in the efficiency of operations and in the values they had returned. A balance sheet of where these enterprises stood at the start of 1867, particularly with regard to the experience of the six quartz milling companies thus far committed to the area, puts the situation in perspective.

The Ragland, Cope, and Napton mill, which was steam-powered, was the only one at work during the winter of 1866–1867. Because it alone was operating, it had plenty of quartz on hand. And because it was the only mill in the Norwegian District, it was able to command that area with some effectiveness. But it was acknowledged that the mill's ability to achieve good returns was limited, and it stood to reason that it would be greatly disadvantaged if a more efficient mill commenced operating. Moreover, George Cope, the Missouri company's superintendent, was on notice that his partners, who held the majority of shares, clearly wanted to sell the mill whenever the opportunity arose.

Enfield Pratt, superintendent of the New York and Montana Mining and Discovery Company, had erected a sturdy mill on Hot Spring Creek, but he had lost his bet of a basket of champagne to Captain Maltby, having failed by several weeks to get his mill in operation by the Fourth of July. More seriously, Pratt had become painfully aware that the engineers who had built the mill's machinery had badly miscalculated the power required to work its turbine. The Meadow Creek water-diversion project had not been completed in time to assist in overcoming this handicap in the 1866 season. Because the absence of sufficient water had limited the mill's crushing capacity to two hours of work every other day, Pratt had decided to convert the plant to steam. As a water-driven operation it had been forced to close for the winter, and Pratt had gone to California in search of new machinery.

Over in Meadow Creek, the Golden Ore Mining and Prospecting Company had built a plant in preparation for a mill but so far had little more to offer than flowery platitudes from its superintendent, George Atkin. Nothing could be said in January 1867 as to whether his predictions of fabulous returns would materialize for the Brooklyn firm. Also in Meadow Creek the two partners, Andrew Hall and Don Spaulding, had gone on record as desiring to enter the quartz milling business, but they had not yet secured a mill for that purpose.

The Clark and Upson Mining Company of Hartford, Connecticut, less Gad Upson, who had died in early 1866, had, like the NY&MM&D Company, gotten off to a late start in 1866. Then the company's crushing and pulverizing machinery had proven unworthy of its reputation. In consequence, Clark had decided to rebuild his plant almost anew on Hot Spring Creek. But he had been in Montana for almost eighteen months and was shortly to return to Connecticut to check on his business there. On the way, he would stop in California to purchase new amalgamators and separators. In his absence, used eastern-made stamps were to be installed.

As for the Midas Mining Company of Rochester, New York, its directors had finally approved the construction of a quartz milling operation on Hot

Spring Creek with a California mill that would render obsolete the machinery of all its competitors. But as costs increased and the rosy prospects originally offered moderated, divisions had developed within the company over continuation of the enterprise. One man alone had kept this commitment alive; without Samuel Selden's continual personal backing, the company would have folded at the commencement of the new year. In short, the Hot Spring balance sheet for 1866 was at best mixed.

CHAPTER 6

The Midas Mining Company, 1867

"When you wish to laugh some rainy day, just compare your estimates with the amounts actually called for and spent."

—Joseph B. Ward

OR AT LEAST TWO MONTHS BEFORE DEPARTING FROM MIDASBURG FOR SAN FRANcisco, even before having received permission to acquire his new quartz mill, Henry Ward had given considerable thought to the route the machinery should take from California to Montana. Three routes were available to him. He could ship the mill directly east over the Sierra Nevada and the western Utah mountains, he could have it shipped south to Los Angeles and then up the Old Spanish Trail to Salt Lake City, or he could have it shipped south around the Baja Peninsula and up the Gulf of California and the Colorado River to Callville, Utah, from where it would be freighted to Salt Lake City. For good reason, Ward was inclined toward the southern routes, as they were cheaper than that over the Sierra. Southern routes would also be open far in advance of the California-Nevada mountain road, as the snowbound Sierra passes would be impenetrable until perhaps May. The winter of 1866–1867 had, in fact, commenced as one of California's fiercest, and Ward would have been privy to reports of paralyzing snowstorms hindering the efforts of the Central Pacific Railroad to penetrate the mountains.

The route around the Baja Peninsula was intriguing. Once the steamer had reached the mouth of the Colorado River, the freight would be transferred to smaller vessels for the passage up the river to Callville. This route had been tried experimentally in 1866.[1] But the shipper Ward consulted counseled against it because of a lack of the proper boats to make the difficult upstream run beyond Hardyville, or Fort Mojave, so far short of Callville as to make that alternative infeasible.[2]

Ward seemed to favor the Old Spanish Trail anyway. In Los Angeles oxen could be purchased quite reasonably—for as little as half of what they cost in Montana. This would be important, as Ward understood that freighters to Montana generally calculated their rates on what it would take to cover actual costs (oxen, wagons, wages, provisions, and the like), making their real profit on selling their outfits for inflated prices at journey's end. The lower the up-front costs to the freighter, the more he could turn a profit in Montana. Los Angeles offered both the Midas Company and the freighting company the best economies and the earliest arrival.[3]

On February 13, Ward left Midasburg on his faithful horse, Nellie, for Virginia City. Here he boarded the horse and, while waiting for the stage to Salt Lake, completed a sober report for George Mumford. Ward was uneasy about leaving his work behind; H. Roy Gilbert, his office manager, would do well, but there were uncertainties about the company's labor force. Just recently, twelve men had stampeded to the Salmon River diggings in Idaho Territory, and although they had been replaced, one couldn't vouch for the stability of the workforce. Day and night shifts had been more expensive than Ward had anticipated, but double shifts were necessary because he couldn't count on keeping his workers after May 1, that rough date when many of them—more than fifty were employed—could be expected to demand double or more their winter wages or they would "swarm"—take off to prospect on their own or move to presumably richer fields.

But these were minor matters. Far more serious was Ward's discouragement over "the slow uncertain yield" of the company's quartz properties. "Nothing could be more different," he reported, "than the expectations which we all had of our lodes in 1865 and the experience of digging on them in '66 & 67." Ward had great faith in the work of miners with California and Nevada experience, but even these men had failed, despite having found extraordinary values at the surface. Ward pointed out that most of the district's many lodes prospected "rich at the top, some of them immensely rich," but in 90 percent of cases the lodes would "pinch within the first twenty feet . . . and not open out again at any reasonable depth." This pinching induced "much uncertainty, and entail[ed] incessant search [for] instead of simple excavation of quartz." In 1865, before deep digging had taken place, Ward had thought with many others "that our lodes would furnish a steady yield from the very surface." Now he was convinced "that the upper part of the lodes will not meet our expectations."[4]

Ward's reluctant admission is critical to an understanding of Hot Spring's precious metals resources and the history of their development. It was becoming painfully apparent that the district's wealth in gold had been grossly overestimated. Ore values in Hot Spring had habitually been calculated from samples taken at or near the surface. Here oxidized ores, enriched and left in a more or less free state by exposure to weathering, paid handsome profits. Hot Spring surface values had been extraordinary. Many assays from the weathered zone had produced results unrivaled anywhere in Montana Territory, and in every instance the Hot Spring mills had been constructed on the expectation of unusually rich prospects. Moreover, many thought gold leads would increase in value with depth. As a standard guide to gold mining expressed it, the "superficial portion [of a lode] . . . is often less valuable than that below . . . and its treasures can only be won by penetrating into the earth to a great depth."[5]

Geologists and publicizers of national note confirmed the theory that vein mines increased in richness as they increased in depth. They pointed to the fabled Comstock Lode in Nevada, for example, which had quadrupled its surface values at depths of 400 feet and more. Other Nevada and California lodes had substantiated the hypothesis. Among the deeper-digging school was the nationally recognized Yale University geologist Benjamin Silliman Jr., whom Henry Ward knew personally. Secretary of the Interior John P. Usher advocated the same in his 1864 annual report.[6]

In Hot Spring, however, as the mines were deepened, values depreciated, veins pinched out, and gold—when found—was no longer free but in chemical combination with sulfides, which made recovery through simple amalgamation difficult. Miners had experienced similar problems in Colorado and Idaho, yet investors in Montana had ignored the warnings; and when the same patterns emerged in Hot Spring, the district's mill operators reacted at first with disbelief. These were aberrations, they said, interludes in a mining process in which the leads, however lacking in value at certain levels, would once again prove worthy at greater depth. No doubt the experience in Colorado and Idaho troubled them, but most observers—like editor Thomas Dimsdale, who addressed the issue in an article entitled "How Deep Will Quartz Mines Pay?"—wanted to believe the California and Nevada experience would prevail in Montana.[7]

Ward's painful conclusion that he had misread values in Hot Spring might have prompted him to halt operations and reevaluate his company's prospects. Here he stood, on the verge of purchasing and transporting a quartz mill and equipment from two shores thousands of miles apart at the cost of many tens of thousands of additional dollars he knew were being raised with great difficulty, and not without some hostility, back in Rochester. Wasn't this the time to admit failure and save the trustees and stockholders further loss? Perhaps, but Ward instead concluded that the company had to go on. Deeper digging was the only way, he argued, by which the company could prove whether it possessed a "permanent yield." Despite his great disappointment, his faith in Midas's holdings remained unchanged, "notwithstanding mistakes which I had made in judging from surface appearances, of the way in which the lodes would work." There was still hope. "We have," he believed, "among our 40 lodes . . . some that will prove persistent."[8]

Persisting himself, he had, he informed the directors, hired an experienced California millwright named Horace Countryman, who had recently arrived in Montana bringing several California master workmen whom the millwright would personally supervise in the erection of the Midas mill. The company's property and prospects would be in good hands.[9]

When Ward reached the Union Iron Works in San Francisco in mid-March, Enfield Pratt and William Clark had already been there. Pratt had been looking at steam-powered machinery to replace the New York and Montana Mining and Discovery (NY&MM&D) Company's water-powered turbine, and Clark had looked at new amalgamators and separators for the Clark and Upson mill. In their absence from Hot Spring, Pratt's mill had been shut down for the season, whereas Clark's was being outfitted with stamps from a used quartz mill brought into the territory by Charles Hendrie, the Iowa foundryman. Hendrie had Clark's mortars up in the Hot Spring mill by mid-March 1867, but lumber was hard to obtain because of foul weather, and the California separators and amalgamators were late in arriving from the West Coast. Development work on the mines of the Hartford and New York companies in Hot Spring lagged that winter season. Some men who earlier had worked for the New York companies were now among Ward's workers.

In the meantime, Asahel Eaton, one of the original spearheads of the NY&MM&D Company's Montana venture, was concentrating his interests in the Silver Star District on the Jefferson River and on the company's silver holdings in Beaverhead County. His younger brother Samuel—doctor, engineer, chemist, and Civil War veteran—had joined him in Montana. Although the company's primary holdings were now in Hot Spring, with the mill shut down for the winter the Eatons were looking after the firm's assets elsewhere.[10]

Some of Asahel Eaton's time was consumed by a new and unwelcome responsibility—a reminder that despite one's station in life, disorder and violence were constants on the mining frontier. Eaton's partner in the development and marketing of amalgamating and separating machinery, Professor James T. Hodge, superintendent of the Roosevelt Mining Company's mill at Oro Fino Gulch near Helena, had been charged with murder following a tragic confrontation over property ownership. A shootout had occurred in which one man was killed and Hodge and his son were badly wounded—Hodge almost died, and his son lost a hand and forearm to amputation. As the event had caused a heated controversy—it coincided with a trial of participants in a Confederate Gulch shootout over an alleged claim jumping in which one had died and four had been wounded—the Hodge case underwent a change of venue to Madison County. Hodge, too weak to survive incarceration in Virginia City's primitive jail, had been placed in Eaton's custody by the court, for which purpose Eaton had been deputized.[11] When the case was held over for the fall judicial session and Hodge was released on bail in March 1867, both Eatons headed east. Asahel did not return to Montana for four months.

Before Eaton showed up in New York, the NY&MM&D Company had made the decision to borrow $100,000 by issuing 200 bonds at $500 each at 12 percent annual interest. This the firm deemed necessary to finance the continuation of its Montana enterprise. To enhance or protect the agreement between the company and the bondholders, an attached provision stipulated that, if the company defaulted when the principal was due, the bondholders could take possession of the Montana property and dispose of it.[12]

The Golden Ore Mining and Prospecting Company of Brooklyn, New York, had been busy over the winter. At the start of the new year its superintendent, George Atkin, had purchased a twelve-stamp steam-powered mill from Charles Hendrie for $15,000 and was erecting it at the company's mill site north of Meadow Creek.[13] Atkin put down $10,000 as an initial payment, with the remaining $5,000 to be paid by agreement.[14] This mill would go into operation in May at the settlement now called "Atkinville."

The only mill crushing ore in Hot Spring District over the winter of 1866–1867 was that of Ragland, Cope, and Napton. Despite the reported inefficiency of its fifteen-stamp mill with combined Chilean arrastra and amalgamator, the absence of competition proved a boon to George Cope, who was running the mill on his own initiative, as Ragland and Napton had withdrawn from active participation. In mid-February the *Post* reported that a cleanup at the Canadian Gulch mill had produced a commendable 82.75 ounces of retort on just four-and-a-half tons of rock from the Galena Lode on Hot Spring Creek.[15] Under normal circumstances these Galena ores, because of their location, would have been processed by the mills of Clark and Pratt.

Whatever advantage Cope had was tempered, however, when the sad news of William Ragland's death reached Montana. Ragland, in ill health throughout the virtual entirety of his investment in mining, had died of a stroke in St. Louis on March 12, 1867.[16] Cope continued to crush ore, but it would be only a matter of time before the Ragland estate proceedings would force the sale of the mill.

WHILE HIS COMPETITORS DEALT WITH THEIR VARYING DIFFICULTIES IN LATE FEBRUARY 1867, Henry Ward was in Salt Lake City making arrangements for the carriage of his freight from Los Angeles to Montana. To his surprise and disappointment, he discovered that he could not secure a contract for an ox-drawn train, as it was already too late in the season to expect oxen to survive in the desert heat. He was therefore forced to contract with William S. Godbe, a well-known Mormon freighter, to send a train of 156 mules to Wilmington, the port servicing Los Angeles. The British-born Godbe had amassed a comfortable fortune freighting across the plains between St. Louis and Salt Lake City. Then, with the discovery of gold in Montana, he had developed successful commercial ties with the mountain territory, not in small part because he possessed some of the West's best mule teams.[17] For Ward's purposes, Godbe's train would leave Salt Lake essentially empty, carrying only the necessary supplies to sustain it plus extra grain that would be stored at various stations along the way as food for the mules on their return trip. The train would leave within the week and arrive at Wilmington on April 10. Ward expected the outfit to be loaded and on its way back to Salt Lake by the fifteenth, arriving in Sterling on or before July 10. As odd as it seemed to be contracting for freight before the goods had been purchased, Ward had no alternative if the train and the freight were to rendezvous at Wilmington.[18]

Ward arrived in San Francisco by the overland route from Salt Lake City in mid-March 1867. A thriving metropolis, San Francisco boasted a population of 125,000, the West Coast's most important port facilities, 17,000 buildings, and an impressive industrial capacity. Ward had first inspected quartz mills on the western slopes of the Sierra—particularly in Grass Valley—was excited by what he had encountered, and was convinced that in San Francisco he could secure a mill of such excellence and efficiency as to better any ever seen in Montana.[19] The quartz mill he had ordered was being constructed to his specifications at the Union Iron Works (UIW). UIW was a larger version of Woodruff and Beach's firm in Hartford. Organized in 1849 as a blacksmithing business, UIW had grown quickly and, following reorganization in 1866, had hit its stride. Although its major business was the manufacture of quartz mills and the equipment associated with them—stamps, mortars, pans, separators, screens, and such—it also produced railroad locomotives, railroad cars, large hoisting engines, boilers, pumps and pumping machines, and many tons of extra parts. It built sawmills, threshing machines, and gristmills and was proficient in steamboat repair. Three hundred workers labored to keep up with orders arriving faster than the foundry could handle them.[20]

Ward's order was nevertheless filled quickly: a custom-built fifteen-stamp mill with three Hendy concentrators, three Wheeler and Randall pans, and the necessary settlers. At this point Ward made a decision that committed the company even further—in addition to the fifteen-stamp quartz mill, he purchased a smaller six-stamp auxiliary mill, the engine for which had to be added to the shipment being assembled back east. On April 5, twenty-three tons of machinery in 282 boxes and fourteen tons of quicksilver in 160 flasks were moved to the San Francisco docks, where they were loaded onto a steamer bound for the port of Wilmington, just south of Los Angeles. William Godbe's mule-drawn wagon train was to have been waiting at dockside. But Godbe's train, wagon mastered by Crandall and Taylor, had not arrived when Ward's ship dropped anchor. Ward waited fruitlessly for several days. Nervous for want of time, he hastened back to San Francisco to make the trip to Montana by stagecoach over the mountains. Weather conditions on the Pacific slope of the Sierra were extreme, however, and it took him a fortnight to reach Salt Lake City. There he was informed that the Crandall and Taylor wagon train had only left Wilmington in the last days of April, passing through Los Angeles on May 1, and that it was struggling against terrible road conditions.[21]

The Old Spanish Trail, connecting Santa Fe, New Mexico, with Los Angeles, had first been used in the 1770s by Spanish traders. Looping far north from Santa Fe to avoid the scorching Arizona desert and confrontation with the hostile Apache Indians who occupied it, the trail wound northwest up through the mountains into central Utah and then followed the Santa Clara and Virgin rivers southwest, overland to Las Vegas, and then over the mountains and through the Mojave Desert to Los Angeles. In the 1850s it had become an important route for freighters, drovers, and immigrants, including Mormons who founded a colony in San Bernardino, roughly 65 miles east of Los Angeles. The road had been improved greatly over the years, but it still presented some extremely difficult terrain amid especially arid and unpredictable conditions.

Today, Interstate Highway 15 roughly parallels the western half of the trail employed by the Midas Mining Company's mule train on its trek from Los Angeles to Salt Lake City in May–July 1867. Although the initial several days of the journey would have been comparatively easy, once San Bernardino was reached the hard part began. Even today, the 3,000-foot ascent by automobile up Cajon Canyon north of San Bernardino to the Mojave Desert is arduous. Then came 400 grueling miles of desert, sandstorms, and sharp rocks, punctuated here and there by watering places of questionable purity.

Las Vegas provided a brief but welcome respite beside the bubbling waters of its renowned spring. What followed was one of the most difficult passages on the entire trip—50 waterless miles across the California Wash to the Virgin River, at best a three-day mule-train journey. In 1867 the Virgin River gorge was impenetrable. Although recently mastered by interstate road builders, it remains one of the wildest, steepest, and most awesome river canyons in the United States. Here, at the mouth of the Virgin River's 10-mile gorge, the wagon train swerved north, making a wide ascending arch up Utah Hill through the Beaver Dam Mountains to the valley of the Santa Clara River, passing through present-day Gunlock, Vejo, and Central and the site of the infamous 1857 Mountain Meadows massacre by Mormons of a wagon train of Arkansas immigrants.

The Crandall and Taylor train was now in snow country, even in late spring. It reached the site of what would become Cedar City, Utah, on June 4. North from Cedar City the train followed a high 4,000- to 5,000-foot plateau all the way to Provo, only 30 miles south of Salt Lake City.[22] After fighting through snowstorms and unusually heavy rains with wretched road conditions, the wagon train pulled into Salt Lake City on June 17.[23] There Ward's machinery was loaded onto a fresh train and sent on its way to Montana two days later. But the trek had been hard beyond imagination, and Godbe had to report to Ward, now in Montana, that the wagon masters, Crandall and Taylor, were demanding a larger payment, having made no profit because of the "extraordinarily bad weather and snow storms they had to go through and the hard usage their wagons have been subjected to in transporting such rough freight."[24]

But at least the wagon train, now under a different wagon master, was on its last leg north, and Ward fully expected it to reach Midasburg between the eighth and tenth of July. That expectation was dashed, however, when a flood washed out the Snake River bridge, delaying the train for a full three weeks, the river being too high to risk crossing the wagons on ferry.[25]

During these same weeks the other half of the Midas Company's machinery had been assembled in New York and shipped west for passage up the Missouri River to Fort Benton. These were the engines to run the two stamp mills and a boiler to assist both mills. Engines and a boiler, however, were only 3 items in the long list of 200 items Ward requested from the company, including shafting, belts, extra shoes for the stamps, quicksilver, and a variety of essential duplicate parts. Ward was very particular about what he needed. The engine, which was purchased in Utica, had to be constructed in such a manner as to fit the mill works being erected at Midasburg. The forged iron shoes for the stamps had to be cast in a certain way; they could be processed only in Pittsburgh. Tools that were very expensive in Montana came with this shipment from the East: picks, for example, and the right kind of handles for picks, hickory or ash—Ward's workers broke an average of three per day. They needed candles, too. Only the best nondripping variety was acceptable for working underground, as candle wax in quartz rock gave the amalgamators fits. Tobacco was obtainable in Montana, but Ward ordered a large stock of it anyway solely to prevent his miners from going into Sterling to buy it. Canned food was requested; it would be used not for the workers but for special occasions when visitors chanced by.

All of the machinery and supplies had to be packed with utmost care, as freight on the Missouri River frequently had to be unloaded and reloaded on lighter-draft vessels and, if behind in the season, freighted overland through hostile Indian country to Fort Benton. Then came 300 miles of rough roads between Fort Benton and Sterling. And it had to be freighted to Montana in the shortest time possible, for mills without engines, boilers, and parts were of absolutely no value to the company.[26]

Ward needed to assemble a team of men to work the big mill. No fewer than eight would be required: an amalgamator and his assistant, a battery feeder, two engineers, two stokers, and a clerk to assist Ward with the paperwork. Most of this group could be found in Montana, but the chief engineer had to come from the East; it would be better yet if he could bring a wife as cook. The clerk was needed to replace Roy Gilbert, who wanted to return to Rochester in late summer. The clerk would keep the books—a full-time job in itself—do errands for Ward, and mete out supplies to boardinghouses and

miners. Ward was very specific in instructing his directors as to the type of
person he wanted for the position: "The clerk whom you send must understand
accounting, be thoroughly honest, and not too lively, to stick seriously to his
business. He must be controllable from 6 A.M. (the miners' breakfast hour) to 8
P.M. although he will have many leisure moments in the interim. . . . With this
clerk to take Mr. Gilbert's place when he resigns, I can keep the office-work
up close."[27] Ward, in fact, had a particular person in mind—Peter V. Jackson,
a twenty-year-old schoolteacher from Irondequoit, New York, who had earlier
expressed an interest in joining Ward's western venture.[28]

Ward's concerns to coordinate the transportation of his mill and its accessories from two coasts almost 3,000 miles apart were complicated by anxious
communications from Samuel Selden. Previously, George Mumford—who,
had he had his choice, would have terminated the Hot Spring venture back
in the fall of 1866—had been the company's primary contact with Ward, but
Mumford was about to leave for San Francisco to look over the business of
the California State Telegraph Company, the western branch of Western
Union Telegraph's continental wire system. As a result of Mumford's temporary absence and his own increased stake in the enterprise, Selden was now
projected into the primary administrative position. He was greatly exercised
over rising costs of operation. He made clear to Ward that his $25,000 emer-
gency subscription, which had been necessary "to save our enterprise from
collapse," was to have been applied to the cost of the mill, not to operational
costs. But operational costs seemed on the verge of driving the company under. Wages, Selden understood, were incomprehensibly high, twice as high
as in California, yet it seemed to the judge that the costs of getting out quartz
for the mill were excessive and could bankrupt the company. He therefore
urged, almost demanded, that Ward close down the works on May 1 and
not reengage a mining crew until the mill was in place. Ward could keep one
mine open, no more.[29]

Then came Roy Gilbert's alarming report that the expected spring stampede for other diggings had begun, that fifteen or more men had quit, and
that wages had skyrocketed. Whereas Midas had been paying workers on
average less than $3 per day, including board, Clark's superintendent was
paying miners $6 per day, without board, in gold dust; windlass men drew
$5. Even without board factored in, the Hartford company was paying men
between $1 and $2 more per day than Midas was. Gilbert not only seriously
questioned whether he could keep his men at work, he questioned whether he
could even pay them, as he was "nearly out of money." March expenditures
at Midasburg had been in excess of $4,000.[30]

All of the company's costs had risen far beyond expectation. Purchase prices, freight, and insurance for the East Coast shipment had come to $35,600 alone. Then there had been the cost of freight from San Francisco to Sterling: $15,120. Without even knowing the West Coast costs, including the purchase of the two mills from the Union Iron Works, the company had expended over $50,000. And none of this freight had yet arrived in Montana. It was now feared total costs could reach $500,000.[31] Joseph B. Ward, treasurer of Ward and Brothers Banking House, could barely contain himself, penning frequent criticisms of his cousin's western venture: "How about the mill for $45,000!" he wrote in early May: "Oh, Henry, what a guesser you are!"[32] "When you wish to laugh some rainy day," he wrote on another occasion, "just compare your estimates with the amounts actually called for and spent. Nothing in known history will excel it save the estimate for the 'new Court House' in New York."[33] Just how strapped the company was for cash was apparent when William Godbe showed up in Rochester in late June to collect the balance of his freighting fee, only to be informed that the funds were not immediately available.[34]

It is hard not to be sympathetic to Henry Ward under these trying circumstances. He was desperately attempting to coordinate two shipments to Sterling, specifying their contents, expediting their arrivals, reporting dimmer and dimmer prospects from the company's mines, remaining unable to pay bills, and all the while being increasingly micromanaged from Rochester. With the company unwilling to pay charges for telegrams, communication was slow and dispatches crossed paths in transit. On top of it all, Ward had to suffer his cousin's constant barbs. Smaller men might have folded under like circumstances. Samuel Selden, the one man who now guaranteed support of the company, seems to have understood this better than most. "Let me say," he had written his nephew in late March,

> that however this enterprise may turn out, I shall not be disposed to cast any blame upon you. I know very well that you have exercised your best judgement from the beginning, & that you are straining every nerve to the utmost, and I fear even to the jeopardy of your health, to make it "a success." . . . I know too, that if constant vigilance, unremitting labor, & the most minute & painstaking attention to details, can make the affair "pay" it will be fine. This is all we can do, & we must patiently abide the results.[35]

Ward's return to Midasburg in mid-May did much to improve relations between Montana and Rochester. For one thing, communications were vastly improved. For another, Ward now agreed with his uncle that the continuation of deep digging was not producing the anticipated results. "Two days work very often digs a fine three-foot vein into a vein of less than one in thickness," he informed Selden. Lateral veins produced a similar irregularity, widening and narrowing suddenly "without any rule, logical or empirical which one can take for a guide." The irregular nature of the quartz veins had everybody vexed and had persuaded Ward to abandon the tactics of his competitors. He planned now to divert his operations to the custom crushing of quartz from mines independent of his—the holdings of miners looking for the best mill to give them the finest results.[36]

Ward had been impressed with the great number of new lodes discovered in the district—"unusual and unexpected"—on almost a daily basis and often found "directly under spots of ground which people have walked over un- suspectingly for three years past." These lodes were producing large amounts of quartz; he estimated that 1,000 tons were already out on the ground, with another 1,500 tons in sight. Ward had decided that it was to his advantage to start "foraging" for that quartz and to stop almost altogether the develop- ment of his own company's mines. Competition for milling was not strong. Observing the work of Clark, Pratt, and Cope had convinced Ward that their operations were greatly inferior and that once the Midas mill was erected, the company would "have an immense advantage over all the others." Lode owners everywhere in the district, including those with California experience, had echoed his confidence in the company's mill. Ward was convinced that if he applied this plan aggressively, he could gain complete control of the district's quartz. In relying on the abundance of surface quartz in the district, he would more than balance the uncertainty of the company's own lodes.[37]

Henry Ward had become quite optimistic. Once the mill was up and run- ning, he would ask for no additional support from Rochester, and he would be sending profits back soon thereafter. "Our enterprise is on the very eve of being a success," he concluded, "and a decided success."[38] "[We] possess a thorough foothold in this district," he told his uncle, "and [in] the value of the relations which we have established with the people. These relations, and the confidence following them, are such that we have . . . almost certain control of the quartz interest here." All that was necessary now was for the Rochester stockholders to stand strong behind the endeavor. Even though the original cost estimates had been greatly exceeded, Ward argued that it would be fool- ish to throw away fortunes already in reach merely because costs had risen.[39]

These positive reports and appeals had a strong influence on Rochester thinking. An additional $100,000 subscription was put successfully to the public, with Samuel Selden, now holding two-fifths of all stock, advancing another $25,000. Selden apologized for his previous criticisms of the venture and preached to his nephew a policy of market aggressiveness: "I, for one, wish you to act boldly & 'dash in' when you see a chance that looks to you very promising," he told Ward. From what he had heard, the place to "dash in" was the Lower Hot Spring District, in particular on the Boaz Lode.[40] The renewed energy in Rochester was infectious. Even Joseph Ward caught the changing spirit. Admitting to having given his cousin "some pretty hard rubs," Joseph hoped Henry had not taken it personally. "We will let the dead bury the dead," he wrote. "We will re-commence from now a new life as if the enterprise were just beginning & this news [were] my first letter."[41]

Virginia City, Montana, 1866.

Sterling, Montana, 1866. Clark and Upson Mill (background, center), *New York and Montana Mining and Discovery Company Mill* (foreground, right).

Sterling, Montana, 1997. From the same perspective as that in the 1866 photograph reproduced in the previous photo.

William Judson Clark, principal partner in the Clark and Upson Mining Company.
COURTESY, 100TH ANNIVERSARY, CLARK BROS. BOLT COMPANY, 1854–1954, P. 5

Samuel Woodruff, principal shareholder and trustee for the Clark and Upson Mining Company.
COURTESY, CONNECTICUT HISTORICAL SOCIETY MUSEUM, HARTFORD.

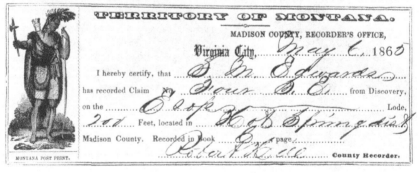

On November 1, 1865, William Clark purchased this claim on the Esop Lode from Stephen W. Edwards, a prospector. The Esop Lode was discovered on April 24, 1865, near Hot Spring Creek. Clark paid Edwards $5,000 for this and other claims.

COURTESY, AUTHOR

Henry A. Ward, 1865, superintendent for the Midas Mining Company.

Samuel L. Selden, trustee of the Midas Mining Company.

George Mumford, secretary of the Midas Mining Company.

Midasburg, 1867. The company town of the Midas Mining Company.

**COURTESY, DEPARTMENT OF RARE BOOKS AND SPECIAL COLLECTIONS,
UNIVERSITY OF ROCHESTER LIBRARY, ROCHESTER, NEW YORK**

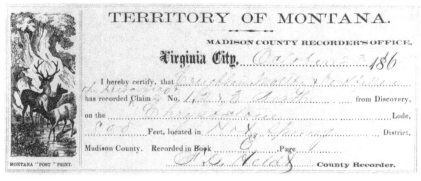

John Creighton, Captain Theodore Maltby, and John Rockfellow, partners in the Herschel Mining Company, headquartered in Sterling, claimed discovery on the Chrysostone Lode, located October 14, 1865, near Hot Spring Creek in the Hot Spring Mining District.

COURTESY, JOHN S. ROCKFELLOW PAPERS, SC 296, MONTANA HISTORICAL SOCIETY, HELENA

In early 1867 the New York and Montana Mining and Discovery Company sought to raise $100,000 through the sale of mortgage bonds. This certificate, dated March 9, 1867, records the sale of a $500 bond to James Emott, a trustee of the New York City company.

COURTESY, CLERK OF THE COURT, VIRGINIA CITY, MONTANA

John S. Rockfellow, a prominent Virginia City merchant and territorial treasurer, was heavily invested in Hot Spring gold mining. This stock certificate records his purchase of fifty shares of Midas Mining Company stock, dated June 26, 1867.

COURTESY, JOHN S. ROCKFELLOW PAPERS, SC 296, MONTANA HISTORICAL SOCIETY, HELENA

NO. 5.　　JACKSON STREET.　　NO. 5.

NO. 5.　　　　　　　　　　　　　　　NO. 5.

JOHN S. ROCKFELLOW,

WHOLESALE GROCER!

And Dealer in

SUGAR,　FLOUR,　LARD,　COFFEE,　BACON,
Candles　Tea,　　Hams,　　Soap,　　Molasses,

DRIED APPLES, PRUNES, SORGHUM, PEACHES,
Raisins,　Syrup,　Cherries. Candies,　Currants.
Tar.　Soda.　　Powder.　Nails.　Butts.

Shovels, Picks, Steel, and Mining Tools of all Kinds!

A full and complete stock of choice family groceries always on hand.

ALL GOODS SOLD GUARANTEED!

The only House in Virginia City that keeps a complete stock of the above goods the year 'round.

Orders for all Kinds of Goods
Accompanied by the Cash, promptly filled.

JACKSON ST., VIRGINIA CITY, MONTANA.

VIRGINIA CITY, MONTANA TERRITORY.

Groceries at Wholesale!

Greenbacks at Par!

John S. Rockfellow was arguably Virginia City's most prominent grocer.

COURTESY, MONTANA POST, DECEMBER 21, 1867

This impressive stone building, known as "Mountain Home," was constructed in 1867 in the Lower Hot Spring Mining District by James Isaacs, superintendent for the McAndrew and Wann Mining Company. It was built to serve as an office building and residence for Isaacs and the owners, but its size and expense became one of several contentious issues leading to Isaacs's dismissal in January 1868.

A view of Ward Peak and the Tobacco Root Mountains. Taken from the McAndrew and Wann mill site in Lower Hot Spring District.

All that remains today of the once-thriving gold camp of Sterling, Montana, are the ruins of the Midas Mining Company (foreground) *and the Clark and Upson Mining Company* (background) *quartz mills.*

CHAPTER 7

Increased Competition and Doubt, 1867

THE MCANDREW AND WANN MINING
COMPANY OF NEW YORK CITY, NEW YORK

"There is thousands of tons of rock out waiting for mills to crush."

—James P. Isaacs

ENRY WARD'S AND SAMUEL SELDEN'S NEW SENSE OF OPTIMISM MIGHT HAVE been tempered a bit had they known another competitor was about to locate in the very place on which they had begun to refocus their interest—the Lower Hot Spring District. That competitor was McAndrew and Wann of New York City, a company that would mount a strong and disharmonious challenge to the Rochester enterprise.

Alexander McAndrew and Samuel Wann were British-born naturalized citizens occupying offices in lower Manhattan as importers and as agents for the British-capitalized Atlantic and Great Western Railway. McAndrew, born in Scotland, settled in the New York area in the late 1840s. The Ireland-born

Wann came to New York a decade later and joined McAndrew in a partnership. In 1865 McAndrew was fifty-six years of age; Wann was forty-five. Their
success had been sufficient to enable them to acquire sizable estates on the
hill property of suburban Staten Island. There they enjoyed living as "squires"
in a peculiar sort of aristocracy. They and their neighbors were noted for the
lavishness of their properties and mansions and were attended to by numerous
servants. Samuel Cunard, of Cunard Steamship Company fame, possessed an
eighty-acre estate on the same ridge line, and the great railroad tycoon and
pioneer of steam navigation, Cornelius Vanderbilt, lived but one mile south
of McAndrew and Wann.[1]

Given their office location in lower Manhattan, McAndrew and Wann
could not have escaped the speculative environment that characterized New
York City in the 1850s and 1860s. "As this is the money center of the Western
Continent (as Paris and London are of the Eastern Continent)," a western correspondent noted in 1866, "it follows that most sharp men bring up in New
York. Each has his plans for the accumulation of a million. . . . Speculators have
captured us all."[2] During the mid-1860s, western ventures in transportation and
in all kinds of mining enterprise were pervasive components of New York's
investment scene. By 1865 downtown Manhattan had become infested with
small and large offices trumpeting the prospects of their respective businesses.
McAndrew and Wann was located just east of Broadway on the corner of Pine
and Nassau, directly across from the U.S. Customs House and convenient to
the London and Liverpool packet-line piers. Within the adjacent neighborhood were large numbers of speculative enterprises. Among these, mining
companies predominated. In 1866 *Trow's New York City Directory* contained 286
listings for mining companies alone. Many of these had offices on Broadway;
McAndrew and Wann would have had to pass the offices every day on their
way to and from the Staten Island Ferry. Perhaps they were familiar with the
occupants of 117 Broadway, where holders and traders of Montana properties
met daily at Tufts, Conner and Hagaman, unofficial headquarters for Montana
speculations.[3] Pine Street had its own conglomeration of mining companies—
at least 19 of them. Eight more were situated at two addresses around the
corner on Nassau Street. At 12 Pine, McAndrew and Wann shared quarters
with 4 more mining companies: the American Flag Gold Company, the Minnesota Mining Company, the Superior Mining Company, and the Wickopee
Copper Company.[4] It is hardly conceivable that McAndrew and Wann could
have entered or left their building or walked the neighboring streets without
brushing against someone caught up in the excitement surrounding America's
developing mineral industries.

McAndrew and Wann's work for the Atlantic and Great Western Railway (A&GWR) likely fed their interest in western investments. The A&GWR was one of the first railways to penetrate the oil regions of western Pennsylvania. Whether McAndrew and Wann speculated in oil is unknown, but that they were privy to the fortunes to be made in oil can hardly be denied. As agents for the A&GWR, McAndrew and Wann were familiar with the company's complete rail network, which started in New Jersey across from Manhattan on track leased from the Erie Railroad Company. The company's own lines began at Salamanca, a rail hub located on the border between New York and Pennsylvania. Here commenced the A&GWR rail network of 600 miles of lines in lower New York, northwestern Pennsylvania, and much of Ohio.[5]

But the Atlantic and Great Western Railway had interests beyond oil, and analogous to the goals of the Western Union Telegraph Company of Rochester, New York, the British railroad company aspired to tap the wealth of the old Northwest Territory by running a line through Dayton and Cincinnati to St. Louis.[6] This progressive movement west in all probability further encouraged the expanding interests of the two Scotch-Irish entrepreneurs, and soon after they became agents for the railroad, they began to invest in Montana gold mining.[7]

Initial indications of McAndrew and Wann's interests in Montana date from December 6, 1865, when Gilbert B. Weeks, a California-experienced Hot Spring quartz lode owner and ranking member of the Virginia City Mining Company—the Crawford brothers' company—struck an agreement with the partners in New York City.[8] Four months later the relationship was clarified when for $21,000 McAndrew and Wann purchased on approval from Weeks and John B. Wisenall, Weeks's prospecting partner, considerable mining property in Madison County, the majority of it in the Hot Spring District.[9] Weeks was amazed at his good fortune. Initially, he had experienced difficulty in finding a market for Montana gold properties, and once buyers were found he had felt it necessary to "sell very low." Moreover, he had been compelled to allow a 120-day grace period to enable the New York City partners to organize their company and send agents to Montana in order to verify the actual existence and legal authenticity of the lodes on which they had taken options. But prospects for completing the sale—and further sales—were prominent, Weeks assured Wisenall, as the purchasers were rich—"worth millions," as he put it.[10] On his overland return to Montana in early May, Weeks reassured Wisenall from Omaha that the contracts had been worked out with one of the "wealthiest firms in America," and that, although it had put him at great expense, he had not hesitated to agree that McAndrew and Wann, whom he deemed absolutely trustworthy, should have the right to check out the authenticity of their Montana lodes before closing the deal.[11]

Verification was to be accomplished in the person of James P. Isaacs, a forty-eight-year-old New York builder who accompanied Weeks to Montana as a one-man discovery team. Upon arrival, Isaacs went into the field with Weeks, Wisenall, and other members of the Crawford group; starting in early June 1866 he appears on a great number of their lode discoveries as either a discoverer or a claimant. Satisfied that the properties were indeed valuable, Isaacs bought out most of the claimants. He also preempted a quarter section in the Lower Hot Spring District—160 acres straddling Hot Spring Creek two miles east of the Asahel Eaton ranch and one mile north of the Boaz Lode.[12] No doubt Isaacs chose this location for its potential as a mill site.

But the company's interest in Hot Spring was diverted to Summit District, uppermost in Alder Gulch, when in August 1866 James Isaacs and the partners were able to purchase at a bargain price the quartz mill of the Seneca Falls Gold Mining Company of Seneca Falls, New York. This company had been the very first to install a steam-powered mill at Summit in 1865. Although Isaacs moved the mill to the Hot Spring District in 1867, for one year McAndrew and Wann concentrated their investments at Summit.[13]

James Isaacs, who had conducted the purchase of the mill as the field superintendent for McAndrew and Wann, immediately improved it, bringing in pans and amalgamators to increase the saving of gold. He spoke of sizably increasing the capacity of the mill, doubling its stamps, for instance.[14] Sometime during the fall of 1866, Isaacs had a gold brick made from ore crushed at the Summit mill and sent the brick to New York, where it was proudly displayed at the office of McAndrew and Wann.[15] The *Montana Post* readily adopted the new proprietors of the Seneca Falls mill, describing the company as a "heavy" firm representing "large monied interests in New York and Europe."[16] The *Post* understood that the company would erect a new thirty-stamp mill on a different site in the spring.[17]

In early February, back in New York, McAndrew and Wann brought Isaacs's wife, Maria Josephine Isaacs, into the company. For $10,000 McAndrew and Wann sold her one quarter of the company's Montana properties, including the Seneca Falls mill and the mill site in Lower Hot Spring. In the contract between Maria Josephine Isaacs and the company, her husband was designated general manager and superintendent, whereas she became a partner in the business.[18]

In early March 1867, Isaacs left by stagecoach for a brief visit to New York City to settle accounts, to arrange for his wife's transportation to Montana, and to secure a new contract with the owners. This contract granted him superintendency over all of the company's Montana properties, an annual salary of $4,000, and all expenses as a charge on the company for both him and his wife.[19] Having accomplished this business, Isaacs returned to Montana, arriving at the mill site between the fifteenth and twentieth of May. He had not returned alone; McAndrew and Wann had contracted James H. Gamble to serve as the company's financial agent in Montana. Gamble, a deeply religious and highly principled person, was the brother of Samuel Wann's wife, Jane. In the meantime, Maria Josephine Isaacs, preferring the comfort of water passage, had taken a single cabin on the Missouri River steamer *Abeona,* bound for Fort Benton.

Upon his return to Summit, Isaacs readied the mill for work and wrote to assure McAndrew and Wann that the company had on hand ample quartz of paying quality. To a newspaper reporter he remarked that the company was building another mill of thirty-stamp capacity in a location to be determined. In private, Isaacs revealed that he was leaning toward the site of the Alameda Lode, one of the Crawford brothers' major 1864 Fairweather District discoveries.[20] However, Isaacs had actually become less enthusiastic about Summit and, unbeknownst to McAndrew and Wann, had begun to focus on Hot Spring.

On June 2 Isaacs left Virginia City on the Wells, Fargo and Company stage for Helena and Fort Benton to meet his wife. Learning that the *Abeona* was running far behind schedule and unwilling to wait at Fort Benton, he took passage down the Missouri to intercept the vessel. He was all the way into Dakota Territory before his wife's steamer came into view. By the time he and Maria Josephine arrived at Fort Benton—on the Fourth of July—James Isaacs had spent almost four weeks on the river. He had left his mill site on June 1 and did not return to it until July 12. This represented a departure from his work of almost a month and a half at the height of the milling season.[21]

Isaacs then took another provocative step. Without consulting the owners, he made the decision to move the company's mill from Summit to the Lower Hot Spring District. Even knowing that McAndrew and Wann would not be pleased, Isaacs took a firm stand on his decision:

> Now I must say to you I have gone contrary to your wishes and I shall do so when I think—or I will say when I know—I am right . . . as I am here [I] must certainly know best although I won't wish to take too much on myself but in such matters you must let me be the Judge. . . . I know that you will say that we have plenty of quartz . . . and good quartz too but . . . not at the Summit. . . . Mr. Gamble and myself went to Hot Spring district to make an examination of our property which we find to be the best in the Country.[22]

Isaacs lauded the Lower Hot Spring location. All of the company's lodes there were situated uphill from the chosen mill site, facilitating easy passage down to the mill. The roads required for hauling were already there. The erection of a mill would give the company a significant advantage, as the miners in the

area were currently obliged to haul their ore six to eight miles to the mills at
Sterling and Norwegian, had to pay twenty dollars per ton for crushing, and
then weren't getting one-sixteenth part of the rock processed. Isaacs had made
up his mind: "I can now say to you that I shall most decidedly work our own
property for we will be where it is as we had not at Summit."[23]

Isaacs did not immediately move the mill but visited Hot Spring on several
occasions to strengthen his case. Each letter to McAndrew and Wann spoke
glowingly of the company's prospects there. The company did not own the
Boaz Lode, the district's richest, but the Truxton Lode, which the company did
hold title to, was an extension of the Boaz. On top of that, the opportunities
for profiting from custom crushing were bright: "There is thousands of tons
of rock out waiting for mills to crush at $20 per ton."[24] He continued to insist
on the wisdom of his decision to move the mill:

> As strange as it may appear to you and as badly as you may feel in refer-
> ence to our movement nevertheless it is right and we know it and we are
> the only ones to judge correctly. . . . [T]he greatest reason is that we have
> too many leads at Hot Spring. . . . When I was trying to get quartz at Sum-
> mit you would say why don't we work on our own quartz: the reason was
> as I have said in a former letter. We had none at that District.[25]

McAndrew and Wann may still have been fuming over Isaacs's absence from
the mill during June and July, but for Isaacs it was spilled milk: "My trip to
Benton was a great detriment, but that is past and gone."[26]

In just forty-six days, for $13,000, Isaacs had the old Seneca Falls mill at
Summit dismantled, freighted, and rebuilt at the new Lower Hot Spring site.
He also started four additional structures: an imposing two-story stone office
building and residence for him and his wife (and for McAndrew and Wann,
should they care to visit), a bunkhouse, a blacksmith shop, and an assay office—and the roads to service them.[27]

Isaacs might well have made a good decision to relocate the mill, but his
presumption in seizing the authority to do so was deeply resented in New
York. Previously, everything Isaacs had told McAndrew and Wann indicated
that quartz prospects in Summit were good and that rich ore was there for the
crushing. What was going on? Could they continue to trust his judgment? What
could they believe? As a consequence, there was no more talk of a second mill,
and McAndrew and Wann dispatched a second member of the Wann family,
William Hyndmann Wann, to serve as Isaacs's and the company's bookkeeper.
Simultaneously, they wrote James Gamble that they "had lost confidence" in
Isaacs, instructing him to convey that fact to their superintendent. When Gamble
carried the message to him, Isaacs was furious with the owners: "If you have

lost confidence in me let me know it," he snapped back, "for I cannot be connected with anyone that feels that way towards me."[28] It was the beginning of an increasingly acrimonious relationship: Isaacs's defiance and belligerence were now out in the open. The entire district would subsequently be impacted.

THAT THE MILLS IN THE DISTRICT WERE FAILING TO SAVE SUFFICIENT VALUES AND THAT THE costs of hauling ore to mills six to eight miles distant from Lower Hot Spring were prohibitive were important factors in Isaacs's determination that in placing a mill near the rich lodes of the lower district he could corner that trade. Henry Ward had made something of the same argument to his Rochester trustees in asking for a better mill that could produce better savings of gold. But by late August only one mill was operating in the district—the old Ragland, Cope, and Napton mill on Canadian Creek. This is remarkable when one considers that the middle months of a Montana year are the most important to the crushing and processing of quartz. Why was there such inaction?

For one thing, the Clark and Upson enterprise had ground to a halt. During William Clark's return to Connecticut in the late winter and early spring of 1867, Charles Hendrie had installed used mortars in the Hot Spring mill, but the California separators and amalgamators were late in arriving. As a result, the mill was delayed in operating, and when the machinery did arrive it proved as incapable as its predecessors of producing adequate results.[29] This was extremely disappointing for Clark, as he had believed improving his quartz mill would overcome previous difficulties.

In time, however, and certainly by early summer 1867, the realization dawned that rather than producing greater values, depth in Hot Spring mining was producing less value. When it became common knowledge among Hot Spring mill operators that the available machinery, whether crude or sophisticated, could not produce anticipated profits because of the declining values of the ores being processed, they moderated expectations and pared the margin between costs and profits, often drastically. The prime example of this had been the progressive reduction of Henry Ward's original euphoric predictions to estimates of modest and even meager return.

By June 1867, Clark, now back in Southington presiding over his bolt and nut factory, had become fully informed of these developments, but he did not accept the reality with grace. Labeling himself a failure, Clark confessed to being "dumbfounded" at the result of his mining experience, which was drawing ridicule not only in Montana but at home in Connecticut. He could not see how he had been "so wofully [sic] deceived" as to the value of Hot Spring's ores and blamed much of his difficulty on disingenuous lode owners who presented only the choicest ores for assay and then sold their quartz claims at great profit to unsuspecting operators like himself. Claiming he had been "badly sold," Clark was "chagrined to think I was ever duped to take charge of such a huge enterprise, of which I knew litterally [sic] nothing at the start." Perhaps Clark was thinking of the Nelson Mining Company, as he was certainly privy to the convictions of Woodruff and the other investors that Nelson had defrauded them. In October Clark intensified his attack on external forces, informing John Rockfellow that all of his mining investments were "going to the devil" because he had been deceived as to the quality of the ores, the extent of the mines, the large expense of starting such an enterprise, and unreasonably high taxation. Had he waited two or three years before starting up, Clark believed, the company might have profited from the experiences of its competitors and made a go of it.[30]

William Clark was disingenuous in laying blame so heavily on others. It is doubtful that he and Upson ever fully understood the complex issues facing them. From the start they had relied on seat-of-the-pants business instincts honed on eastern experience, on assayers who had little knowledge of the mineralogical issues involved in gold mining, and on the expertise of professors in the employ of their competitors. Further, they had not planned for the seasonal and transportation obstacles associated with Montana investments. To be sure, the company's choice of milling machinery played a significant role in its failure. The first milling outfit, purchased and transported at large expense, had been rushed pell-mell to Montana before the company had developed its mines or understood the exact value, size, and consistency of the ore deposits located there. For lack of such knowledge the mill machinery had failed, and its replacements had fared little better.

In mid-August 1867, Henry Ward reported to his trustees that Clark's "poorly managed" and "miserable worn-out" stamp mill had run daily for nearly three months and yielded an average of only $12.98 per ton. At best, this was less than half of what was needed to break even and dramatically less than the exorbitant figures predicted two years earlier. Later that autumn Ward noted that despite the overvaluing of the region's ores, as well as equipment alterations and new purchases, Clark's mill had never obtained two-thirds of what other mills in the district had secured from quartz drawn from the same lodes. Ward also observed that Clark had periodically overpaid his employees, sometimes hired inexperienced laborers at a cost to efficiency, and constructed inferior buildings, such as bunkhouses, that had to be rebuilt at additional expense. Of course, Ward was pointing to these things as justifications for the installation of his own superior machinery, but the implications for Clark's failure were clear.[31] Clark now understood all of this as well, and sometime in the summer of 1867 he made the decision to shut down operations. Although he informed John Rockfellow in Virginia City that he might yet "go to work [in Montana] and recover," his ardor for the mountains had cooled completely.[32]

THE GOLDEN ORE MINING AND PROSPECTING COMPANY OF BROOKLYN, NEW YORK, had also ceased operating. The mill had gone into operation in May and was reported by its superintendent, George Atkin, as having made good runs.[33] In June, letters from Atkin to his company in Brooklyn told in glowing terms the engineer's success in developing the George Atkin mine, which bid to "rival in auriferousness that of any of the old mines on this continent."[34] Atkin's use of the new and celebrated Wyckoff Process was given considerable attention in the eastern press, and the *Montana Post* paraphrased the reports:

> [I]n addition to that portion of the work accomplished in ordinary reduction, [the process] consists in boiling the pulp with chloride of sodium, for which purpose are used wooden barrels or cylinders suspended on axles, made to partly revolve, with a segment of the cylinder left open for the insertion of the pulp and the escape of steam. These cylinders are eight feet long and three feet in diameter. The pulp is placed therein in charges of 200 pounds. To this is added 100 pounds of mercury, thirty gallons of water, and the necessary quantity of chloride of sodium. The steam is turned on, giving the cylinders a rotary motion of 20 or 25 partial revolutions per minute, and a continual jet of steam entering and boiling the mass, accomplished the desulpherization [sic] and amalgamation.[35]

In introducing the Wyckoff Process, Atkin acknowledged what was being discovered about gold in Hot Spring—that at varying depths below the surface, ores were no longer free but existed in chemical combination with sulfides, which made recovery through simple amalgamation difficult.

Still, Atkin's milling process did not prove as successful as described. In June, after just three weeks of operation, he was forced to shut down his works as the result of mechanical failure. Whether this was a failure in elements of the Wyckoff Process is unclear. Two months later Atkin's mill was still out of operation, waiting for the arrival of replacement parts.[36] As the summer was no time for a mill to be out of work and the firm was being pressured to complete full payment of the original purchase price, the success of the Brooklyn firm had come into serious question.

The New York and Montana Mining and Discovery Company was in significant ways experiencing much of what had plagued William Clark. Accepting the inability of Hot Spring Creek to provide sufficient water power for its mill, the NY&MM&D Company had initially sought to increase its hydropower by building a three-and-a-half-mile diversion ditch from Meadow Creek, but the work had not been completed in time to support the company's quartz milling operation in the fall of 1866. Then the decision had been made to convert to steam. Enfield Pratt had gone to California in January 1867 to secure the desired machinery. From there he had gone on to New York, not returning to Montana until May. Between his return to Hot Spring and the arrival of the new machinery from California, Pratt ran the mill by its soon-to-be-replaced turbine, with mediocre results. Asahel K. Eaton arrived in Montana in early July but took little part in the company's work at Hot Spring, instead setting up a residence in Virginia City, converting a small portion of the Probate Court building into an assay office, and advertising himself as an "Analytical Chemist."[37] In the meantime, the company's decision to convert to steam was validated by the failure of the Meadow Creek ditch because of excessive leakage and repeated breakdowns.[38] That this ditch, attended to with such anticipation and with such effort and capital, proved a failure was a bitter pill not only to the New York company but also to John Rockfellow, who had financed it and banked so heavily on it; to Theodore Maltby, the partnership's field superintendent operating out of Sterling; and to the thirty to forty men who had labored on it for three months the previous autumn. On August 19 the NY&MM&D Company mill was shut down for two months to make the change from water power to steam.[39]

INASMUCH AS THE MIDAS MINING COMPANY AND MCANDREW AND WANN WERE EITHER constructing or relocating their mills in August and September, only George Cope in the Norwegian District was crushing Hot Spring ore at this time—but no longer under the name of Ragland, Cope, and Napton. Following the death of William Ragland earlier in the year, the administration of his estate and the interests of his heirs had made inevitable the breakup of the old mining company. In July, Napton and Cope had found a buyer, selling their combined $21/_{38}$ shares to the Upper Missouri Mining and Prospecting Company of New York.[40] Ragland's $17/_{38}$, ensnared in the red tape of probate court, was not conveyed. Cope, who received $5,789 for his share, stayed on as superintendent for the new majority owners.

The Upper Missouri Mining and Prospecting Company was not new to Montana, having been incorporated in 1865. The company's capital was set at $100,000; it was to be employed to discover, develop, and purchase valuable gold and silver mineral properties "believed to be worth millions." Composed of New York and New Jersey businessmen, the company maintained offices at the self-pronounced New York City headquarters for Montana investors—Tufts, Conner, and Hagaman.[41] Robert Hagaman and John Thomas Conner, along with Nathaniel J. and Charles M. Davis, became the company's discovery team—centering their work in Rattlesnake, Silver Star, Ruby Mountain, Alder Gulch, and other mining districts along the western slopes of the Tobacco Root Mountains. James Tufts, Conner, and Nathaniel Davis had subsequently become involved in the formation of the Montana Territory Society. Tufts had earlier been speaker of the house for the Idaho territorial legislature. Hagaman had been Madison County's first recorder, and Nathaniel Davis had become its first treasurer.

For reasons unapparent, the Upper Missouri Mining and Prospecting (UMM&P) Company seems to have lost some of its vigor during 1866, but in the spring of 1867 Tufts was appointed territorial secretary by the Andrew Johnson administration to replace deceased acting territorial governor General Thomas Francis Meagher. Whether coincidental or not, the UMM&P Company now acquired a new prominence in Montana. Conner and Nathaniel Davis had already arranged for the purchase of the Ragland mill and additional mining properties when Tufts arrived in Montana in early August to assume his appointed post.

The UMM&P made little or no change in the way George Cope had run the mill previously. With a skeleton crew— Cope and his engineer, Samuel Liddle—Cope did virtually every task related to the milling enterprise, adhering to no set number of hours and frequently working on Sundays and into the night. Liddle, who had formerly worked as an engineer for James Isaacs at the McAndrew and Wann mill at Summit, later argued that Isaacs had needed three men to do at Summit what Cope was achieving on Canadian Creek all by himself—superintending, keeping the books, amalgamating, running the engine, cleaning up, and watching over the mines. The UMM&P Company allowed Cope to function without supervision. "Tom" Conner stopped by infrequently, no more than two or three times, and seemed more interested in increasing his knowledge of the art than in conveying instructions.[42]

Conner's indifference toward Cope's superintendency extended to Cope's financial remuneration. The salary Cope would receive was never defined, and a controversy arose between the company and its superintendent over services, labor, and supplies Cope had provided out of his own pocket. Cope had used his own horse and his own teams at his own expense for the benefit of the company; he had fed those teams at his own expense; and he had supplied numerous items—such as tools, quicksilver, cooking equipment, even foodstuffs—for which he had received little or no compensation. There were also confrontations over the hauling and ownership of wood.[43] When Cope's grievances continued to be unaddressed, in early November he finally threw up his hands and resigned.

Cope's resignation brought operations at the old Ragland mill to a complete close. It is unlikely that his competitors were surprised by the closure, for Cope's operation, although by far the most consistent in the Hot Spring District, had survived at least in part because of the peculiar difficulties faced by its competitors. Some had wondered how he had managed to stay operative. Henry Ward had long looked with a jaundiced eye on Cope's mill. He had judged it inferior from the start and had wondered, in fact, if Cope hadn't quoted inflated values in his prospectus to the UMM&P Company. No other owners on the same leads had saved half of what Cope claimed. "There is something wrong here," Ward concluded.[44] But all of this became academic when George Cope's Canadian Creek operation closed down.[45]

CHAPTER **8**

The Mood in the District, Autumn 1867

"Nothing on earth is more fickle or uncertain than is a mine."

—Henry Augustus Ward

I**N MID-JULY 1867, HOT SPRING DISTRICT QUARTZ LODE DISCOVERIES WENT INTO AN** abrupt decline. Up to that point rates of discovery had been good. With the breaking of winter in early April, many miners had come out of hibernation or left the employ of their companies for the customary rush into the hills and gulches. After April 6, claimants on new discoveries in the Hot Spring District appeared before the Madison County recorder on a regular basis, more than one every other day. Between that date and July 19, fifty-eight discoveries were recorded—the large majority for leads in the Lower Hot Spring District, with the Boaz Lode the most frequent geographic reference. Then discoveries dropped off markedly. Only four were recorded for all of August and only nineteen more for the remainder of the year. This dramatic decline was not an 1867 aberration. In 1868 only four discovery claims were recorded for the Hot Spring District. The number increased slightly to seven in 1869 but receded to only one in 1870. This development was not unique to the Hot Spring District; mineral districts throughout the county were experiencing similar trends. Such change might have generated considerable public comment. Since the spring of 1864 the recording of discovery claims in Madison County had become an established and frequent routine. The sudden cessation of discoveries does not appear to have attracted attention, however. The press paid little notice, and the records of the quartz milling companies working the district carry no comment on the lack of new claims.

Had another stampede diverted the attention of the press? One of the standard causes of diminished prospecting activity had always been the proclivity of miners, at the slightest hint of advantage, to head for new diggings. The Salmon River mines of Idaho Territory had attracted many from Madison County earlier in the year; Henry Ward had lost a dozen workers to that stampede. Later in the spring a stampede took place to Radersburg and the Crow Creek mines on the Missouri River to the north. Although this strike soon leveled out, some Hot Spring miners and prospectors joined the migration to these diggings. Other prospectors might have left to follow up on news of new discoveries in Wyoming; the Sweetwater mines at South Pass lured one of the original Boaz boys. Another of the Boaz's discoverers joined the outmigration to the States, and yet others were engaged in the Indian campaign during the spring and summer of 1867—twenty-five men, including miners, enlisted at Sterling.

Some prospectors no doubt turned their attention to developing old discoveries. Henry Ward noted that one of the remarkable events of the summer of 1867 was the "rediscovery" of a significant number of previously recorded lodes that had been abandoned or left dormant—that is, they had not had periodic "assessment work" performed on them according to law. One of these had been rediscovered in the yard of the Rochester company's compound at Midasburg.[1] Unworked or abandoned claims represented golden—and often the only—opportunities in a district as heavily prospected as the Hot Spring District, especially for newcomers.

It is also obvious that good numbers of miners and prospectors around Sterling turned to laboring for the new mills—assisting in their construction and reconversion or putting in time on the building of roads and the erection of outbuildings. Others diverted their energies from prospecting to mining, getting out ore from their leads to satisfy the mill owners' insatiable demand for quartz. That demand, Ward estimated, had "set many score of prospectors to work to furnish the supply."[2]

What is certain is that the cessation of discoveries appears to have caused no alarm in any quarter. Ward did not seem perplexed or bothered by it, and nothing in the Clark, Cope, and Atkin records suggests that a dramatic diminution in new claims played any part in their decision to cease operations. Neither does this phenomenon appear to have impacted the decision making of the companies still operating. The press, moreover, seemed perfectly insensitive to the fact that any change had taken place at all. As one enthusiastic observer expressed more than three months after the decline began:

> Take Sterling as a center and Meadow Creek as a radius, describe a circle, and anywhere inside the circumference it would be dangerous, I assure you, to venture out any distance during a dark night without running a risk of losing one's position on this mundane sphere by falling into some one of the numerous perforations which have been made during the past season in pursuit of the precious metal.[3]

This exaggerated the impact the fewer than 100 discoveries in 1867 would make on the topography, but taken altogether the sum of those recorded between April 1864 and July 19, 1867—715 in all—could well have justified such an alert.[4] There was plenty of quartz, demand for labor was high, and wages were competitive. Why worry about a decline in discoveries when hundreds of them, many yet to be developed or rediscovered, were present in every direction? Instead of foreboding, excitement was in the air. The Hot Spring District was developing rapidly, and new and improved mills promised to make short work of the ore bodies already on hand.

THE FIRM OF MCANDREW AND WANN WAS THE FIRST OF THE THREE REMAINING COMPANies to get its mill in operation. To supply it with ore, James Isaacs, whose relations with the owners had become seriously strained, managed to increase their alienation further by taking yet another unauthorized step. "Now I shall tell you of something I have done and it is contrary to your wish and also Mr. Gamble's," he wrote New York, "but I must differ with you all. . . . I have leased the Red Bluff Lead." Isaacs knew full well that McAndrew, Wann, and Gamble preferred to work the company's own lodes and did not care to incur the expense of working those of others. But Isaacs had become discouraged with the company's lodes, most of which, contrary to his earlier assurance, had not been worked out sufficiently to provide an adequate supply of quartz. Consequently, he had leased footage on the Red Bluff Lode. "[W]hen I can get hold of rich quartz on leads that are fully developed and at a nominal figure," he informed McAndrew and Wann, "it is [my] policy to take hold of all such chances." Such a move would not prevent the company from continuing to work its own property, but the important thing was to keep the mill working and, just as important if not more so, to acquire positions on lodes to prevent competitors from getting on them first. "The mill men are doing all they can to get such chances and I shall not let them pass me," he wrote, meaning, of course, Ward and Pratt at their upstream locations.[5]

In mid-October Isaacs had the old Seneca Falls mill running. Located on Hot Spring Creek in the lower district, it was situated on the north bank just above where the stream enters its lower canyon. On that foundation, forty-two by forty-five feet in size, was a wooden superstructure. Within it were fifteen stamps in addition to tables, blankets, riffles, sluices, two arrastras, a crusher, and a settler. A sixty-horsepower engine operated the stamps. The mill site was considered a favorable one, as it was situated directly adjacent to the Virginia City–Gallatin Valley road, was located easterly enough from the Tobacco Roots to escape heavy snows, and promised to have perpetual use of water because of the warming of Hot Spring Creek by the spring of similar name located two miles upstream.[6]

Visitors were equally impressed with the company's other buildings. They included a twenty-by-fifty-foot stone boardinghouse; a blacksmith shop, twenty by thirty feet, also of stone; an assay office; a sixteen-by-thirty-five-foot warehouse for ore; and an imposing two-story stone residence for Isaacs and his wife. This latter structure, named "Mountain Home" for its magnificent views of the Tobacco Roots, was one of the most impressive in the entire territory.[7]

Isaacs's concern that his company's lodes would not produce ore rich enough or sufficient to keep his mill running was shortly vindicated, for by early December he had failed on all ores except those coming from the Red Bluff Lode. But even that source of custom ore was insufficient to keep his mill operating on a constant basis, and he determined that if he hoped to succeed, he would have to get in on the Boaz Lode.[8] This brought him into confrontation with Henry Ward, who had determined to corner the same mine. This confrontation, which came to a nasty head in late December, was caused to some degree by a clash in personalities but even more by the clash of identical work agendas, as both superintendents had determined to forgo work on their own lodes for the ores of others.

AS THE MIDAS MILL SITE WAS BEING IMPROVED IN JULY AND AUGUST AND THE DATE FOR commencing operations neared, Henry Ward and the company's directors and stockholders had a positive, upbeat view of their prospects. Ward promised to have the mill, which he deemed the most efficient in Montana, running by September 25 at the latest, with ore processed and values determined by October 1. To the skeptical George Mumford, the prospect of finally seeing light at the end of the tunnel was a huge relief; he could hardly believe the moment had finally arrived when the "delectable land of dividends will soon be plain before our rejoicing eyes."[9] Rochesterians who had hastened to buy shares in Midas discovered to their disappointment an absence of stock on the market and no one inclined to sell. An elated company informed its stockholders, "[T]here will be no need of any more care for Montana, but money will thence come to us."[10] Ward was even bolder in his prognostications. As far as he could see, the mill was perfect in every way; it would not only succeed in returning profits to its stockholders but would have the advantage over every other quartz enterprise in the district, indeed throughout the territory.[11]

Samuel Selden rejoiced at this kind of talk. He sensed that the company had achieved an extraordinary position within the Montana economic community, and he wanted to press the advantage at once. His monetary commitment to the company added to his sense of urgency; as the largest stockholder by far, he stood the greatest chance of losing his investment. "I have so entirely exhausted my present pecuniary resources in my efforts to keep our enterprise from collapsing," he wrote Ward, "that I shall greatly need to realize something from the earnings of our mill, sometime in the course of the autumn."[12] Selden's claim to destitution was overstated, but he was making a point—impressing upon his nephew the opportunities to be gained by moving aggressively to control the entire Hot Spring District and to gain for the Midas the reputation as the leading territorial mining company: "If there are rich mines anywhere in the Hot Spring district we want an interest in them; & I do not see that this can be secured by any degree of astuteness or principles." Selden was determined that his company "take a leading position among the Mining Companies of Montana." To do this Ward would have to increase the company's mining properties substantially.[13]

Selden began to bombard Ward with instructions on how to accomplish this. Acquiring control over the properties of the Clark and Upson Mining Company was one of his early thoughts. Increasing the company's ownership in quartz properties was another. Ward had once owned footage on the Red Bluff but had sold it. Then he had had a chance to buy in on the Boaz and Galena lodes but had decided against it. Selden regretted both moves: "I would sell nothing, but would grasp after & cling to, every mine in the District, as far as means will allow, & especially those what [sic] have abundant specimens of rich quartz." Profits from custom work were to be applied to deep digging on the company's own leads, "below the extreme fluctuations which prevail near the top." Selden was not asking Ward to carry out his recommendations, he was insisting that he do so.[14]

Ward was caught between two rocks. His enthusiasm had been translated by Selden into a policy quite contrary to that held by the other directors. Selden wanted Ward to act aggressively—to increase the company's holdings, to dominate the district and the territory, and to adopt what the judge called the entrepreneurial "wide, far-seeing course." Other directors, in contrast, had demanded that Ward restrain himself to the absolute lowest rate of expenditure. But these courses of action were incompatible. "The two things will not go together," Ward complained to his uncle; he simply couldn't meet such contrasting expectations. His inclination was to "turn a deaf ear" to Selden's grasping policy and to maintain one of austerity.[15]

Selden would accept none of this. He expressed "great anxiety" to increase the company's interests in the district's lodes and continued to regret Ward's failure to secure such interests at lower prices earlier in the game. Having come up with yet another $25,000 for the enterprise, Selden rejoiced that recent fund-raising had gotten the company "out of the woods" financially, but only to the extent of covering expenses and paying bills. As there was no surplus cash, Selden asked Ward to consider working on lode owners to turn their properties over to the Midas Company in exchange for stock. Ward had told him that one of the owners of the Galena Lode was "poor"; perhaps in his needy condition he would take stock in lieu of cash.[16]

Ward didn't warm to the stock exchange tactic but agreed with the logic of taking advantage of the miners. "Our lode-owners here are, almost without exception," he wrote,

> miners and prospectors with small means, who dig over the hills on their own account during the five months of summer and work for wages, or hole up in their cabins during the winter months. Much of the time these men are quite independent, and talk big figures for their ground, but the time of the year for going home to "the States," and the winter, when they lack grub, and have no money, are periods when they can be bought out for measly low rates.[17]

Ward explained how he had utilized these conditions to wrangle lodes out of some owners for a pittance of their real worth and to secure "lay outs" from others, where for the sinking of a shaft on the lode Ward was able to acquire desirable quantities of quartz. In this manner, he pointed out, he had built up the company's ownership to over 32,000 feet on seventy-eight different lodes. He proposed to continue to expand. There were, he noted, a "thousand spur, thread, & outcrop lodes" in the Hot Spring District, and he aimed to secure at least a few feet on every one of these to cover the possibility that one or more would produce and to control them in the face of competition.[18]

Not unexpectedly, George Mumford took this expansionist policy to task. He expressed delight that "the end of the road" had been reached with respect to assessing the stockholders, but he criticized Ward and Selden's policy of purchasing additional properties, expressing the stockholders' concerns that, with the exception of the Boaz Lode, the company should not take on custom work and should not purchase additional lodes but should stick entirely to the development of its own.[19] Samuel Selden strongly disagreed with this view-point and explained the different points of view to his nephew. The trustees, he said, "will, for the most part . . . be content with such a temporary success as will enable them to dispose of their stock at a large advance over cash. I[,] however, am anxious to build up a permanent business . . . & [I am] pretty sure, an extensive business also."[20]

Hardly satisfied with the current operation alone, Selden contemplated enlarging the mill by an additional fifteen stamps and thought to add a second and even a third mill in Montana—one in the Lower Hot Spring District, the other on the company's leads in the Wisconsin District. Selden was thinking big: with its superior machinery the company had a chance to extensively monopolize these districts. "This may look a little visionary," he informed Ward, "but it is not nearly as utopian as was the conception . . . of making the Western Union Telegraph company absorb all other Companies, & ultimately monopolize the whole telegraphing of the United States." Selden could not agree with those who would limit the company's work to its own lodes. He was not high on custom work either, viewing it as a temporary expedient only, as competition for custom work was ensured for the future. Ownership on as many paying lodes as possible was the policy to be adopted: "Our safety lies in the extent of our ownership," he emphasized. Selden took this view to the trustees, putting before them a proposal to raise another $100,000 for the purchase of Hot Spring lodes.[21]

In the meantime, Selden had come to some startling conclusions about deep mining. He had initially accepted as a matter of course that veins of gold-bearing quartz grew both "broader & richer as they were followed down to great depths." His reading of an account of a year in the Rockies by Colonel Alexander K. McClure, an eastern editor and politician who had a stake in an Alder Gulch quartz mill, had strengthened his commitment to deep mining.

But now new and apparently better-informed authorities were taking this concept to task. As a result, Selden had been converted to the understanding that there was no sure thing in deep digging—that reliance on it had no basis in truth or fact. Confessing his change of mind to Ward, Selden urged his nephew to purchase everything that appeared rich "at or near the surface," particularly, if possible, on the Boaz, Red Bluff, and Galena lodes.[22]

This debate between Selden and the trustees, with their superintendent caught in the middle, was exacerbated in large part by Ward's failure to get his mill into operation by September 25, the date first set. For reasons entirely out of Ward's control, one problem after another set back the agenda. To start with, the consignment of freight up the Missouri on the steamer *Little Rock* had fallen behind schedule. Moreover, several important pumps and a two-and-a-half-ton engine lathe shipped from New York had missed connections and had to be shipped on a later boat. A party of three from the company had taken passage on the *Little Rock*—the chosen engineer, Cyrus A. Prouty, and his wife and young Peter V. Jackson, on his way to Montana to replace Roy Gilbert as Ward's clerk. Their lateness would not help speed the start-up.

Soon Ward had pushed the start-up date back two weeks to October 6, blaming labor difficulties in addition to the tardy arrival of supplies. His effort to build a mill in a polished and professional manner was complicated by his inability to get good mechanics and by a highly contested territorial political campaign. The latter had distracted his workforce and stirred them into a "fever heat." The task of producing quality work under such circumstances, Ward lamented, was extreme. The uselessness of Prouty's wife had added to his displeasure. Presumably, she had been sent out not only as a companion to the company's engineer but to serve the enterprise by doing "woman's work." However, although she was a "pleasant agreeable lady," she was "far *too* much a lady," unable to "help us about cooking, sewing, or any other thing by which to be of one single dollar of service to the Co.," Ward complained. He had spent an unbudgeted $1,500 building and furnishing the Proutys with their own exclusive cabin, valuable cash that could have been applied to other, needier causes had Prouty left his wife at home.[23] That Ward had left behind in Rochester a wife of his own, in addition to young children, undoubtedly contributed to his pique.

Then it was discovered that one of the main steam pipes, necessary to connect the boiler to the engine, had not arrived. A substitute of copper was worked in, but the equipment on hand to properly fashion copper was lacking, and the results were uncertain. Next, an elbow to connect everything had to be fashioned. Now the commencement of operations was set back to October 16 or 17, with another five days necessary to get everything working smoothly before ore could be processed.[24] When the jerry-built steam pipe failed, one of cast iron had to be ordered from Helena. Then the fittings for the steam and water pipes in the engine room and mill failed, as, at roughly the same time, did the boiler wall, which had to be reconstructed.[25]

To add to Ward's problems, a new quartz milling company had arrived in Hot Spring. The wagon train of the Hot Spring Gold and Silver Mining Company, organized in Wheeling, West Virginia, arrived at Sterling from Fort Benton in early October with a fifteen-stamp mill. Lewis W. Borton, James G. Spratt, and Samuel Word—Virginia City lawyers—had watched Hot Spring's development with interest, had purchased sizable footage on a number of leads there, and in the winter of 1866 had gone east to organize a company with which to develop these properties.[26] But Ward had come on hard to the company's superintendent, T. F. Hardy, convincing Hardy there was no room in Hot Spring for yet another mill. Consequently, Hardy had been persuaded to wait out the winter season and to assess the success of the Midas Company before commencing construction in Hot Spring. Ward, greatly relieved, had allowed the company to store its machinery on Midas property.[27]

Finally, the long-awaited news arrived in Rochester: the Midas mill had commenced operations on November 15, and, with the exception of the Lord's Day, had run steadily and satisfactorily ever since. But it proved a hollow victory. Although it was Ward's pleasure to report the start-up, the costs had been severe and the delays worse. One by one, Ward had seen the lots of ore promised him go to Pratt and Isaacs's mill, as the prospectors had been forced to patronize his competitor's services to secure revenue for their winter supplies. Even worse, Ward, with great reluctance, had to report extremely disappointing initial results for the yields of the quartz he had thus far processed. He had crushed 118 tons of ore, composed of eight lots, and not one of the lots had reached expectations. Only one, 4 tons from the Boaz, had paid for itself. Ward was bewildered by this outcome and by the disparity between the perceived values of the amalgam and the retort produced from it. Mill operators employed a rule of thumb to determine values by first observing the bulk of the amalgam and, on that basis, obtaining reasonable estimates of what the retort would bring. Ward's ores were not following that rule. Alarmed, he sent his retort to Professor Eaton in Virginia City for assaying.[28]

Conditions did not improve after two more weeks of operation. After sending a brief telegraph to Rochester to prepare the company for his full explanation, Ward wrote a long report to George Mumford on December 2, 1867. "It is a very sad task for me to have to tell you," he informed Mumford, "that these results are most unfavorable. The perfect, excellent and economically working of our mill is entirely overshadowed by the totally unexpected poor yield of our quartz." Since his report of mid-November, Ward had crushed an additional 300 tons of ore, with a yield of only $1,561. That amounted to only $5 per ton in gold. Out of fifteen lodes tested, only the Boaz gave a paying yield. "I am completely overwhelmed by this failure in our quartz," Ward confessed, "and hardly know how to undertake its explanation." There was absolutely no logic to it. For example, earlier in the year Ward had sent ore from the Housel Lode, considered one of the company's best Norwegian holdings, to the United States Assaying Office in New York City. There it had been valued at $300 per ton. But at the Midas mill in November, Housel ore had yielded $.24 per ton!

The Boaz Lode had also failed to live up to expectations; although it paid expenses, it had yielded only a small percentage of its assay. Ward had tested many lodes by periodic pannings, a primitive system by every standard but much less expensive than assays. These had invariably revealed values of from $15 to $50 a ton. Now they too had been proven wrong. Ward simply could not understand why values he had calculated at the bottom of his pan weren't duplicated at the mill. He had concluded that impurities masquerading as gold, such as gold-copper alloys, seemed to have become indistinguishable constituents of the amalgam, thus skewing the results. Ward had also found that the shoes on the mill's stamps, in addition to other surfaces engaged in grinding the quartz, had "filled the amalgam with a fine flour of iron, which greatly increased its bulk," thereby creating false impressions of its true worth. "I must admit it," Ward confessed, "the poor quality of our gold has . . . entirely escaped me in the past, and has now become most painfully apparent."[29]

Ward did not hold himself entirely blameless. Like William Clark before him, he was convinced that the miners were in part culpable. They must have presented ore from the richer portion of their mines as evidence of its total worth while withholding ores of poorer quality and later selling these off to the mills. Ward realized now that he had probably been victimized in this manner with ore taken from the Red Bluff. His lot from the Red Bluff had assayed poorly, whereas the ore brought to the mill for custom work by other owners on the same lode had assayed well. These men had proclaimed their innocence, but Ward was skeptical. Out of curiosity, if not necessity, Ward queried Enfield Pratt as to how the NY&MM&D Company had managed to get better values than the Midas had. Pratt, previously tight-lipped about such matters, confessed, now that Ward had experienced poor results with a superior mill, to having reported far higher yields from his mill than were actually produced. Concerned that his mill, like Clark and Upson's, was inadequate to the task, Pratt had lied to his company out of fear that a revelation of poor yields would cause him to lose work to his competitors and prompt the company's investors to withdraw their support. Ward now was certain that George Cope had employed similar tactics, for it was not logical that the Missourian could have reported such good results from a substandard mill. As each mill commonly assessed its own results on a comparative basis, Pratt's and Cope's practice had misled everybody.[30]

Pratt was now willing to elaborate on his failure. In fact, this had been the situation at his mill for many months. The Thermopylae Lode, considered the NY&MM&D Company's crown jewel and for which the company had once been offered $10,000, had been worked for many months with a yield of only a dollar per ton. The Red Bluff Lode ore Pratt had purchased for $20 per ton had produced a yield of $2. He and the men who provided the quartz had first concluded that mill wastage was the cause; now they knew better. In the wake of Pratt's confession, James Isaacs told Ward that his mill, too, had failed him.[31]

Some miners were slowly beginning to appreciate these new realities. Gilbert Weeks, who with John Wisenall had sold at substantial profit to McAndrew and Wann the previous year, had run through all of his money and was reduced to prospecting for placer gold on Willow Creek. "I would not stop to dig on a quartz lode an hour," he wrote Wisenall, "for they are of no worth whatever."[32] At one time Weeks's and Wisenall's claims on the Armenia Lode, located in the vicinity of the Midas Mill, had made a great show of gold in the pan. Convinced of its wealth and unable to wait for Ward's mill to open, the two men had entrusted it to Pratt, who crushed sixty tons for them but got only fifty cents to the ton. Incensed, they had rented an arrastra four miles downstream and were hauling their ore to it. But this alternative had failed as well.[33] Wisenall, disillusioned, left the territory. Weeks stayed behind, but he doubted he could get twenty-five cents a foot on the sale of his claims. "It is hard to fall so low," he confessed to his departed partner. "Oh that God may help us to be faithful and save us in heaven at last is my prayer."[34] Ward could commiserate. He went on to cite for the directors back in Rochester numerous other failures of ores from lodes along Hot Spring Creek that up to this time had been considered sure things: they had assayed out at good values but were yielding discouraging results.[35]

These outcomes left Ward in a state of serious depression. "I would almost give my life to have this enterprise [be] a success," he wrote. "It may take it . . . if it is a failure." Attitudes in Sterling were not helping his mental state; many residents were convinced he was playing a freeze-out game designed to depreciate quartz property in an effort to monopolize the district. Ward understood their anxieties; he knew that a considerable amount of Montana money had been staked on the success of the Midas Company.[36]

Despite this litany of failures, Ward was not yet willing to give up: "All is too new, and facts come from all sides too suddenly," he reported to Rochester that December. One course was certain: "We must go forward." He cut expenses in every way possible, reduced the size of his labor force, and worked the men on a smaller scale. For December he ran the mill only during the day while continuing to test the company's remaining lots of quartz. He did not doubt that sooner or later he would be able to pay the cost of hauling and crushing. He concentrated on certain lodes. The Galena was one; he expected to hit its pay streak at 60 to 70 feet, and he was already down to 40. He had eight men at work on the Galena day and night, averaging a foot a day in the tough granite. Another eight men were working day and night shifts on a shaft intended to hit the Red Bluff Lode at 100 feet. Experiencing less resistance than found at the Galena site, this crew was averaging 9 feet per week. That was on property Ward had purchased recently from Thomas Dunn, who ran a stable at Sterling. Ward had once offered Dunn $1,000 for his share of the Red Bluff, only to be refused. But Dunn, impulsive, as Ward believed most miners were, and wanting "to get off on a spree," had suddenly sold Ward for $200 nearly 2,000 feet of quartz property—including his half of the Red Bluff—in addition to half of a ranch. Whereas work proceeded on the Galena and the Red Bluff, Ward was not working the Boaz because he hadn't been able to get one of its owners, Joseph Arnold, to sign an agreement. He still hoped to finalize the matter, although he feared James Isaacs would beat him to it.[37]

His fears aside, Ward did not want to create undue skepticism in Rochester. This was not the time to back off the experiment, he told Mumford. Although Midas may have met a severe setback, this was no time to quit. A pledge had been made to the stockholders and trustees, and as long as there was a possibility of rich quartz being found in the district, the company had to persevere. Although Ward's contract with the Midas was slated to expire on January 25, he assured Mumford he would remain in Montana as long as Rochester wanted him to. But Roy Gilbert, who had stayed on at Ward's pleading, was returning east, "quite broken down in health and spirit," Ward said, from the "temporary failure of things."[38]

Ward's full report, written on December 2, did not reach Rochester for three weeks. In the interim, with only a cryptic telegraph message in hand, Samuel Selden was greatly disturbed: "[M]y confidence & composure I must confess," he wrote Ward, "have been somewhat rudely shaken by the results of your milling thus far." His immediate inclination was to believe that Ward's machinery wasn't being utilized efficiently. Even so, he was heartened by the results on the Boaz, even if it meant only $24-per-ton yields. Although the stockholders, "who have been expecting very large returns from a very small investment," wouldn't like it, Selden, with much larger interests, could manage on a small profit over the long haul. Selden fixed on the Boaz, the one lode that seemed capable of paying for itself. Gone was his insistence that Ward grasp hold of every lode in the district: "After ascertaining beyond question, that your separating machinery is, or is not, perfect, I would for the time, abandon everything else & go to work upon the Boaz." Selden's calculations, done at long distance and based entirely on remarks in Ward's periodic reports, led the judge to believe the first 100 feet of the Boaz, along its 1,000-foot eastern extension, would provide enough quartz for four years. Ward was not to abandon the enterprise as long as there was any hope it could be made self-sustaining.[39]

As the year came to a close, Selden adopted a more positive approach. Perhaps it was good the district's mines were not paying across the board, he decided. Had everything been rosy, fierce competition would have been inevitable. The Midas Company had the advantage of being on the spot and could ascertain the district's true values. More important, the company appeared to have a hold on the Boaz, which would enable Ward to pay expenses "until we can grasp upon some of the paying veins that are certainly there."[40] Although little hope was now expressed by company stockholders and directors, Selden was not willing to accept failure. He was certain there were rich mines in Montana and in Hot Spring and that others would develop them if the Midas failed to find and work them first.[41]

However, when Ward's December 2 report reached Rochester, the trustees gathered in emergency session. All were astounded that Ward and the other mill operators had been so badly misled by the inexplicable poor quality of Hot Spring's quartz. Forecasting a "general crash" in Rochester if the Midas failed, Selden directed Ward to suspend at once all work on the Red Bluff and Galena lodes and "put all hands upon the Boaz" to "settle the question in the shortest time possible whether that lode can be made to pay by mere surface mining."[42]

WARD HARDLY NEEDED SELDEN'S COUNSEL TO UNDERSTAND THE SIGNIFICANCE OF THE Boaz Lode to the company's success. Long before, he had moved aggressively to obtain a hold on the Boaz. His concern, bolstered by that of his uncle, that he beat James Isaacs to the lode had created a storm in the Lower Hot Spring District during much of December 1867. The controversy might have been settled at the outset on reasonable terms, but conflicting claims were involved and neither man would budge.

The dispute began in early December. Ward and Jordan Hyde, an old-timer and original settler at Sterling, jointly owned claims Nos. 1 and 2 East of

Discovery, and Joseph Arnold owned No. 1 West. In between lay the Discovery claim itself, owned undivided by Arnold, Watson Forst, and James S. Watson, the so-called Boaz boys. Arnold had leased his No. 1 West to Isaacs. Isaacs—knowing, in what was common knowledge, that the most valuable quartz thus far located on the Boaz was in the Discovery claim—had staked the ground he had leased from Arnold seventy feet farther east than was understood to be proper, thereby giving him seventy feet on discovery. Ward had tried to convince Isaacs of his mistake, but Isaacs had refused to make the adjustment, stating that he would commence working his claims at once. Ward took Isaacs for his word. Acting under the caveat that "possession is everything in Montana," Ward roused his hands at 3:00 the next morning and with nine men and two teams took possession of the disputed property before Isaacs's men arrived at 7:00. Finding themselves outnumbered and hardly prepared for a fight, Isaacs's men had reported back to their superintendent, who hastened to Virginia City to seek an injunction against Ward. While in the capital, Isaacs spread false and exaggerated rumors of an armed confrontation. When Ward got wind of Isaacs's allegations, he had his own rendition of what happened published in the *Montana Tri-Weekly Post*.[43] He argued that his men had been armed only with picks and shovels and that no force had been used, as the lode had been unoccupied. Isaacs, Ward asserted, was guilty of circulating false statements with malignant intent.

> [N]ot one man of my little party had any gun, pistol, sword, lance, spear, cannon, club, bomb, rocket or other weapon of offense, or defense, with him on the occasion. This is a thing which I would positively have forbidden. I note this with some emphasis and feeling. Has not the moral sense of our Montana community been too often and too rudely shocked of late by heart-sickening rencontres and murders which have followed the free display of fire-arms, and their use in endeavoring to conquer—by "brute force, rights" which the law ever stands ready to vindicate. God forbid that I should add the influence of one man towards countenancing these procedures. My business as agent of the Midas Mining Company is mining. At present I am working the discovery claim on the Boaz Lode.[44]

Isaacs's rejoinder, published in the *Montana Post*, alleged that Ward, "armed with his revolver," had taken forcible possession of land he had no title to, working under orders from his company to "[h]old the ground at all hazards against any force except law."[45] The *Post* wanted no part of the matter. "There is no possibility of such controversy being decided by newspaper discussion," wrote its editor. "It will only grow more bitter and give unpleasant publicity to matters of a private business nature, or lead to personalities." The *Post* hoped Ward and Isaacs would cease burdening the paper with this "unpleasant correspondence."[46]

Ward, loathing the idea of a lawsuit, which would be long and costly, proposed arbitration; and both parties signed an agreement to abide by it. Each party chose a referee. Truman C. Everts, territorial assessor and owner of a ranch on Meadow Creek, served for Isaacs. Ward chose Andrew C. Hall, postmaster and mercantilist at Sterling. Hall and Everts then chose as umpire Colonel Alexander K. McClure, who promised to come over from his mill up Alder Gulch. The site for the arbitration was the Boaz Lode. On the date set for the meeting, the day before Christmas, a blizzard appeared but McClure did not. The referees chose a new umpire from the attending group, Colonel Wilbur Fisk Sanders—the territory's ranking republican, noted vigilante, and nephew of former territorial governor Sidney Edgerton. Witnesses were put under oath and, according to Ward, "swore for me and for [Isaacs] with the most complete recklessness." Sanders, whom Ward later discovered was once Everts's business partner, decided in favor of Isaacs, granting McAndrew and Wann's superintendent forty-seven feet of discovery—in effect, pushing Ward's and Hyde's claims forty-seven feet to the east. As Hyde expressed it, "[T]he man with the longest pole got the persimmons." No sooner had the arbitration concluded than Isaacs purchased Joseph Arnold's one-third share of discovery for $5,000. Further efforts by Ward to negotiate a solution failing, Ward filed his own injunction against Isaacs.[47]

The impasse was finally broken when Ward secured the aid of James Gamble, who was living in Virginia City but acting, at the request of McAndrew and Wann, as a kind of overseer of Isaacs's superintendency. Gamble was no friend of Isaacs's; in later testimony he described him as "imperious and im-pudent" with the public, "unpopular" with his workmen at Hot Spring, and disingenuous and dishonorable in his dealings with both him and McAndrew and Wann. Gamble gladly agreed to assist Ward in forcing better terms from Isaacs. Isaacs had at first been loath to make any adjustment, but Gamble's influence with the owners (he was Wann's brother-in-law) carried the day, and Isaacs assented to reduce the forty-seven feet he had secured on discovery to thirty-three-and-a-third feet.[48]

Isaacs's unreasonable, confrontational, and possibly unlawful role in this affair cost him his job—but not without a fight. When Gamble, on instructions from McAndrew and Wann, fired Isaacs, the superintendent refused to leave the mill and his elegant home at Lower Hot Spring. Gamble then posted notice that Isaacs had been relieved of his duties.[49] Isaacs responded by inserting a notice in the *Montana Post* that he alone was general agent and that authority over the company's mill and mining property remained solely his.[50] Henry Ward reported to his superiors that the heated struggle between Gamble and Isaacs had "convulsed" operations at Lower Hot Spring.[51] Gamble became terribly exercised over the conflict and began to pack a loaded revolver.[52] The case was taken to court, which twice changed its opinion with the introduction of new evidence. In the meantime, McAndrew and Wann had dispatched another member of the family, William Dempsey Wann, to assume the superintendency.[53]

Finally, in early February 1868, Isaacs, under threat of being removed by force, left "Mountain Home" with his wife to take up residency in Virginia City. Henry Ward could now rejoice that his nemesis, a "very coarse, low-lived, quarrelsome man," had been removed, for Isaacs's successor, William D. Wann, was agreeable to a more just alignment of the Boaz claim boundaries.[54] Ward benefited in another way; during the controversy his competitor's mill in Lower Hot Spring had worked only sporadically. It finally shut down on January 8 of the new year.

WARD, TOO, HAD DECIDED TO CLOSE HIS WORKS. AN INTENSE COLD WAVE, WITH TEMPERA-tures falling to as much as thirty degrees below zero, had made the operation of the mill in early January extremely difficult and had terminated Ward's supply of quartz because the miners were unable to work on the surface under such conditions. But his hands could labor beneath the surface, and he assigned them to the Boaz, Galena, and Rising Sun lodes. The Boaz was drawing most of his attention; Ward had been able to buy out Jordan Hyde's ownership.[55] But the "Boaz boys," having discounted the long-range future of the mine, had neglected to keep it in good repair. Ward spent the first two-and-a-half months of the new year getting it into shape, sinking a shaft from the top and, as the Boaz was situated on the side of a steep hill, running a level, hoping to hit the main vein from two directions.[56]

For Ward, this would be his final effort before admitting defeat. He went to great lengths to remind the directors and stockholders that in gold mining, change was a constant from week to week and month to month and that a mill operator had to modify his plans incessantly to meet new and unpredictable developments. "Nothing on earth is more fickle or uncertain than is a mine," he wrote Rochester. Given these realities, the stockholders would have to expect far more moderate returns than previously anticipated. Patience was called for above all: "We have too much looked on Montana as an extraordinary and exceptional country," he reported, "and have forgotten the time-honored Mexican proverb, 'Dos años hacer una Mina'—It takes two years to make a mine."[57]

CHAPTER 9
Decline of the District, 1868

"Like the blind following the blind [we] all stumble into the
same gulf, baited by a 'color' of gold to a mountain of granite."
—William J. Clark

ENRY WARD WAS ALWAYS QUICK TO POINT OUT TO HIS DIRECTORS THAT MINING
was unpredictable. Yet his and Samuel Selden's strategies on how to
pursue success in the field were often as unpredictable as mining itself.
One matter the two vacillated on for months was the issue of deep digging. In
early 1867 both had been of a mind that deep digging in Montana, as it had
evolved in California and Nevada, would produce values considerably superior
to those on the surface. However, when Hot Spring's deeper veins showed
much pinching and capping and expert opinion seemed to corroborate their
growing skepticism about deep digging, uncle and nephew launched a plan
to secure as much surface footage as possible, but that plan, too, had failed to

return yields. Thus, in the lull of winter 1867–1868, while the Midas mill sat idle awaiting its reopening in March, Ward and Selden once again adjusted their reasoning and came full circle, reverting to a philosophy of deep digging.

Ward opened the dialogue in January with a discourse on the "strange and uncertain distribution" of gold in the district. He reasoned that some kind of natural law was responsible. Sooner or later this would be revealed, but in any event he had once again become convinced that surface values, however rich, were deceptively superficial and that deeper digging would produce the greatest values. He was of the opinion that many valuable ore deposits might show no surface indications at all but would be revealed only after persistent digging.[1] "Do our lodes widen out, and become rich, at considerable depth below the surface," he asked rhetorically. "Until this fact is settled by one or two experiments, we do not know what mining property in Hot Spring is worth." He was even tempted to work with the New York and Montana Mining and Discovery (NY&MM&D) Company in a joint effort to get down to the 300- to 400-foot depths he thought would yield the values he sought.[2]

Selden had come to the same conclusion. That Professor James Hodge had stopped in Rochester on his way back from Montana following the successful conclusion of his murder trial and had confided to Selden his own doubts about the efficacy of surface mining helped sway the judge. During the stampede to the Lower Hot Spring District in the summer of 1866, Hodge had purchased 5,200 feet of surface-rich lodes, a compulsive acquisition he had come to regret.[3] Then Theodore Maltby had written Selden favoring the strategy of deep digging. As a subscriber to the *Montana Post*, Selden would have been privy as well to Asahel Eaton's report to Governor Green Clay Smith:

> That which has proven one of the most serious obstacles to successful mining in the Territory has been the profusion of gold bearing veins showing temptingly at the surface. Nature is never so lavish as she . . . in this case appears, and in the light of general mining experience, we have no right to expect more than a small percentage of true, strong, and uniformly rich veins from this great surface display. Thus it is that several failures may precede one great success in the development of mines. There can be no doubt in the mind of any one making the country a careful study, of the boundless wealth that is hidden in its bosom. Indefatigable energy, and untiring perseverance will alone reveal its true magnitude.[4]

Selden weighed these opinions and those of his nephew and informed Ward that he, too, had abandoned the concept of surface mining. Applying his own intuitive geologic rationalization, the judge developed a theory that explained the thousand outcroppings as emanations from "one or only a few central sources" located somewhere below the surface at some unknown but substantial depth. This source or sources would be reached by tracking the surface features down. Just how far down was the question, but that this "reunion" of outcroppings would eventually take place was the centerpiece of his theorem. In due time the Hot Spring District would vindicate this judgment, but only by those who possessed the energy and faith to pursue it. The big question now was whether the Midas would reach this subterranean mother lode before others did.[5] Selden's theorem strengthened the determination of both men to go down—deep down—on the Boaz, Galena, and Rising Sun.

Ward knew the Midas Company's experience was not unique; other companies in the territory were suffering the same lack of success. From the superintendent of a mill working ore from the Kennett Lode near Virginia City, he learned that despite its fabulous assays and the efforts of the mill men there, the lode was not paying. The Kennett's superintendent was as mystified as Ward in trying to explain the discrepancies between assays and retorts. The Kennett and the Midas, moreover, were only two examples of countywide failures. Of the fifteen to eighteen mills of Madison County, not one was running, Ward advised his trustees in early February 1868, adding that this applied as well to mills throughout the territory.[6] The decline of Madison County mining that had begun in 1866 with the play-out of its placer diggings had now spread to hard-rock mining. Hot Spring's experience was a part of the whole.

This was certainly true for the mills in the Hot Spring District. Three of these mills were not only closed for the season, they had closed shop permanently. The Golden Ore Mining and Prospecting Company had crushed ore briefly in the spring and summer of 1867 in a mill produced by Charles Hendrie. For this George Atkin, the company's superintendent, had paid $10,000 on delivery, with a second payment of $5,000 due shortly thereafter. Unfortunately, Atkin had experienced poor results with both the mill and its celebrated Wyckoff separating and amalgamating system. When these investments failed to produce paying values, he had not only closed the mill, he refused to make good on the remainder of his debt. He also reneged on a personal loan he had taken out for $2,517 with interest. To meet expenses, Atkin sold his Wyckoff machinery and equipment to John T. Conner for use in the Golden Gate Company's quartz mill in Brown's Gulch.[7] Atkin had then gone back to New York City.

Both parties to whom Atkin owed money sued the Golden Ore Company. In each case the company lost, and to cover debts and damages the court ordered Madison County sheriff David McCranor to attach the mill and its property and present both for public auction. On February 11, 1868, the mill, boiler, engine, stamps, buildings, and ground were sold for the paltry sum of just under $900.[8] This did not end the matter entirely, as Atkin subsequently sued Conner for not paying him for the Wyckoff equipment, and Conner countersued, contending that the Wyckoff Process had failed in his Brown's Gulch mill, contrary to Atkin's promise. Conner, in fact, was in much the same boat as Atkin, as the Golden Gate Company's Brown's Gulch operation had also failed; the supposed inadequacy of its machinery was the alleged cause.[9] Finally, on August 8, 1868, the Montana territorial court ordered a judgment against the Golden Ore Mining Company for $5,708.78—the sum owed Charles Hendrie on the final payment for the mill—plus 10 percent interest per annum from March 1, 1867.[10] There is no record that this judgment was satisfied. In any event, thus ended the short and undistinguished career of George Atkin and his Brooklyn mining company.

The old Ragland, Cope, and Napton Company's mill on Canadian Creek in Norwegian, now owned by the Upper Missouri Mining and Prospecting (UMM&P) Company, had been closed in early November when its superintendent, George Cope, resigned. With winter on hand, the mill was not reopened. In late spring Cope decided to sue the UMM&P Company for damages. As the depositions—uniformly unflattering to the company's interests—were being taken, Henry K. Bull and Joseph Morse, president and secretary-treasurer, respectively, of the New York company, appeared in Sterling to assess their property and gauge its prospects. They decided against continuing their investment, abandoned the mill and the company's property in Norwegian, and returned to the States.[11] Cope managed to purchase the mill at a sheriff's sale but did nothing with it. Eventually, he shifted into ranching on Meadow Creek and placer mining at Washington Bar.[12]

The Clark and Upson mill had lain idle since the previous summer. William Clark had never quite recovered from his failed Montana enterprise. Although in October 1867 he had informed John Rockfellow in Virginia City that he might yet "go to work [in Montana] and recover," his ardor for the mountains had cooled considerably. "To continue the struggle in its present shape is useless," he concluded,[13] and he wrote Henry Ward that his work in Southington had put him in such a state that he didn't know which was worse, "Suicide or Montana."[14] A vituperative, long-distance, two-year exchange with Madison County officials over the settling of Gad Upson's estate rankled him, as did his similarly extended suit with the Copelin Steamship Company. "I am about tired of the thankless task of trying to do any business in your Territory, for your own development, or my friend[']s profit," he informed a difficult probate judge in May 1868.[15] Once settled, Upson's estate brought his heirs practically nothing; in fact, it cost Clark almost $1,500 to send one of Upson's brothers to Montana to represent the family. Losing his suit with Copelin and unwilling to pay the $2,700 in damages, Clark essentially abandoned his mill and property at Sterling, leaving behind only a skeleton caretaking crew. In 1871, at age forty-six, Clark resigned as president of his prosperous Southington bolt and nut business and retired to a life of politics and Prohibition. He did not resume an industrial career.[16]

William Clark was not the only loser in this venture to make Connecticut capital work in Montana's goldfields. Earlier, Colonel John Nelson and the Nelson Mining Company had failed. Employees of the two companies suffered, and the stockholders lost virtually everything. But the biggest loser may have been Samuel Woodruff. From the moment he became entangled in operations foreign to the iron trade, Woodruff encountered difficulties. In June 1865, only weeks after he had helped organize the two Montana mining companies, Woodruff had been elected president of the Putnam Fire Insurance Company of Hartford. From the outset of his presidency the firm ran a deficit, and in 1868 he was acrimoniously forced out, one of the charges against him being that between 1865 and 1868 he had diverted company revenues into "a variety of outside schemes" into which he had been "willingly allured."[17] Woodruff's speculations affected his ironworks fortunes as well. As Woodruff continued to engage himself in operations unrelated to the iron trade, his relationship with his partner, Henry Beach, grew strained. The company became disorganized and lost its preeminence in the trade. In 1871 the company declared bankruptcy and went into receivership. In time the firm's reputation was reestablished, but it was Beach, not Woodruff, who regained ownership, the latter's business acumen having been thoroughly discredited.[18]

Whereas all of the aforementioned companies had abandoned their works, the New York and Montana Mining and Discovery Company and McAndrew and Wann hung on—barely. Asahel K. Eaton, pretty much removed from the New York company's operations in the Hot Spring District, left for the East in early January 1868 with A. K. McClure and John Creighton. To all extents and purposes, Eaton's affiliation with the Hot Spring enterprise was terminated. With his departure Montana lost an important personage. The *Post* seemed to sense that; the paper lamented Eaton's departure and applauded his role as a publicizer, investor, and developer of the territory, expressing hope that he would return with his family and make Montana his home.[19] But Eaton did not return to the territory. Although that fall he wrote the 1869 report on Montana mineral resources and mining for the U.S. Interior Department, Eaton's connections with the territory were fading, and in 1871 and 1872 he sold off what he could of his Montana gold claims. Thereafter he seems to have abjured any further in-the-field relationship with mining and to have settled into his laboratory work as a chemist.

Shortly after Eaton's departure, Enfield Pratt, superintendent of the NY&MM&D Company, also left Montana. He might have left sooner, but he had obligated himself as a bondsman for William Clark in the latter's difficulties with the district probate court over Gad Upson's estate.[20] He was also detained by a suit brought against the New York company by two former miners whose case seemed to be carrying the day in district court. Like William Clark and the heirs of William Ragland, Pratt was coming to understand that a company's chances in court were reduced significantly upon its decline. "The fact is," he wrote Henry Ward, "we have injured every poor man who hoped to make money out of our companies by not making money to spend among them and our Courts and Judges seem to be in league against the Mining Companies."[21] Eaton's and Pratt's departures signaled the end of the New York company's on-site management of its quartz mill operation in the Hot Spring District, and the NY&MM&D Company never again resumed operations.

The Herschel Mining Company, with headquarters at Sterling, was also experiencing difficulty in 1868. Theodore Maltby, who managed the company's leads in Hot Spring and ran its offices, stables, and blacksmith shop in Sterling, was struggling. When Maltby failed to make payment on a $2,400 loan to Andrew J. Davis, an agent for mining companies, he was obliged to relinquish his collateral to Davis: ten head of cattle, four wagons, about a ton of flour, and all of his stock of iron and woodwork in his Sterling shops.[22] Simultaneously, Maltby sold Davis his one-third interest in the Herschel Mining Company, embracing "all houses, stables, [and] property of every description."[23]

The Herschel Mining Company was fast losing its dynamism. John Creighton went east after the first of the year, and Maltby, because of his financial difficulties, dropped out. Perhaps most serious, John Rockfellow, the Virginia City merchant who had been such a vital element in the company's activities, had fallen critically ill. Rockfellow had experienced a year of triumph and tragedy in 1867. Valued as one of Virginia City's leading citizens and most successful and trusted businessmen, Rockfellow was completing his second year as territorial treasurer. Earlier in the year, his marriage to Mollie McNeill had been one of the county's most notable social events.[24] The seven-room home Rockfellow had built on Cover Street for his comely bride—the house still graces Virginia City—featured hot and cold running water and was touted as similar to the "country seat of a retired banker" and "superior to any dwelling in the Territory."[25]

But in the fall of 1867 Rockfellow had contracted cancer of the palate, a debilitating condition that necessitated constant medical attention and at least two surgeries performed by Dr. Livinus Daems, who was also the city's mayor. In late December Rockfellow was compelled to resign his public offices and take to his bed. In March, reconciled to his impending death, Rockfellow put his store, its goods, his house, its furnishings, and its grounds up for sale and left for his family home in New Jersey.[26] After insufferable delays caused by severe cold and snow, he and his wife arrived in Salt Lake City, where Rockfellow's palate was amputated on March 28.[27] The operation failed, and Rockfellow, only twenty-eight, died in Salt Lake on April 11. With his departure and subsequent death, Virginia City lost one of its most esteemed citizens, and the Herschel Mining Company, for all intents and purposes, ceased to exist.

Theodore Maltby, in the meantime, had gotten a new leg on life when the NY&MM&D Company decided to lease its mill and machinery to him for one year. The captain jumped at the opportunity and soon earned Sterling's plaudits for his energies in developing leads and crushing custom ores at rates considerably below those formerly charged by the lessors and other Hot Spring District companies. Maltby, a popular favorite wherever he resided, was particularly liked in Sterling—not only for his experience, resourcefulness, and self-reliance but also as a champion of the community's working and commercial classes, who were suffering from the loss of several former sources of employment. Maltby, it was reported, planned to make significant changes in the NY&MM&D Company's crushing process, emulating the Midas method by shortening and quickening the stroke of the stamps.[28]

Maltby's decision to maintain his operation in Hot Spring was not the course followed by McAndrew and Wann. After the squabbling between James Gamble and James Isaacs had subsided, William Dempsey Wann had replaced Isaacs as superintendent for the New York firm. In mid-March 1868, Wann started up the mill in the Lower Hot Spring District, working on ore from the Boaz Lode, but with no success.[29] Deciding to shift the company's focus elsewhere, Wann began purchasing sizable quartz property for the company on the Watseka Lode in Rochester Gulch, west of where the Beaverhead and Big Hole rivers meet at present-day Twin Bridges.[30] When he had the mill machinery moved in July, it was the company's second relocation within a year. Rochester was fifty miles west of Sterling and at that time was a smaller version of the Hot Spring mining camp, with a population of 200 people, three saloons, two grocery stores, two blacksmith shops, and a doctor.[31] Of course, as was the custom for every new district, Rochester was "conceded to be the best quartz camp in Montana."[32] At one time the Hot Spring District had been accorded similar accolades. As for the company's impressive "Mountain Home" back on Hot Spring Creek, it now stood vacant, boarded up for security.

Henry Augustus Ward's decision to close his own mill struck the greatest blow to the aspirations of those who hoped for big things in Hot Spring gold. During January and February Ward had also worked on the Boaz, but in early March the lode had pinched in on the level and in the shaft. Ward laid off his miners. On March 9, 1868, he started up his mill, crushing thirty-nine tons of Boaz ore. The reporter the *Democrat* sent to check on progress was exhilarated by the "cheering sound" and "full blast" of the Midas mill, describing it as a "monument" to Ward's "genius, skill and practical ability." Interviews with Sterling's citizens were upbeat. As yet uninformed of Ward's real plans, they regarded the upcoming summer "as the period of their long anticipated success."[33]

But the Boaz ore was of poor quality, yielding only $12.75 per ton—far short of paying costs. This failure represented the last straw. Ward cleaned up the mill, had its machinery oiled, and prepared to leave Montana. To young Peter Jackson, only twenty-one years of age, he entrusted full power to act as agent and superintendent for the company.[34] Passing through Virginia City, Ward stopped at the *Montana Democrat* to advertise the company's desire to accept bids for the relocation of the mill anywhere in the territory.[35] To a Virginia City clergyman he confided that Hot Spring was "played out."[36] So ended the active life of the Midas mill, arguably the territory's finest.

Samuel Selden beseeched his nephew to stay, predicting the ignominy of failure he and Ward would have to endure if the professor did not come home a success.[37] But Henry Ward had made up his mind; he left Montana in late March for Salt Lake City, where he delayed for eight days as a courtesy to John and Mollie Rockfellow, who were sadly anticipating John's impending death. When Ward arrived in Rochester on April 27, he found that Midas stock had dropped as low as ten cents a share, Ward and Brothers was in a state of bankruptcy, and the Rochester banking community—as Selden had predicted if the mining venture failed—was in crisis. Although Ward and Brothers' collapse was not solely a result of the failure of the Midas—the firm closed because of its inability to pay a 25 percent dividend on notes taken out two years previously to remedy an earlier banking crisis—the mining company's failure, with its fortunes so closely linked to the Ward banking family, definitely exacerbated matters. The failure of Ward and Brothers was not limited to that firm alone; its bankruptcy had ramifications throughout Rochester's banking circles and resulted in two additional closures.[38] Reverberations were actually felt throughout the Northeast. Not surprisingly, when Henry Ward checked in with the directors of the Midas Company, he found them "very flat, with no disposition to do any further work at present."[39]

Selden could not contest his nephew's desire to return to Rochester and his young family after an absence of nearly two years. But he did not intend for it to mark the end of the Midas Company's mining endeavors. Within ten days of Ward's return to Rochester, Selden sent him on a mission to attempt a reorganization of the company with backing from the Hartford and two New York City companies. In exchange for subscribing dollars, Ward was to offer the companies as many seats on the board of directors as they desired.[40] In New York City, Ward enjoyed immensely his visits with Asahel Eaton, Alexander McAndrew, and Samuel Wann. He was greatly impressed with Wann's "palatial" Staten Island home.[41] But he accomplished nothing. Ward and Selden had placed big hopes on the Hartford company, but in keeping with their soured expectations, Clark, Woodruff, and the trustees rejected the proposal to organize a partnership. Shortly thereafter, when a California mining expert hired to evaluate Clark's Hot Spring properties turned in an adverse report, Woodruff and the trustees prevailed upon Clark to "wind up affairs," recall their employees from Montana, and accept the venture for what it had become—a hopeless enterprise. Clark summarized matters succinctly: the old mining district was no longer Hot Spring District but "Hot Water District," he told Ward.[42]

Disgusted, Samuel Selden turned to reorganizing the Midas Mining Company on his own initiative. "We can carry out the project without them," he told his nephew.[43] When Ward proposed a trip to western Pennsylvania in an effort to drum up support from oil interests, Selden turned him down; it would waste valuable time, time needed to get Ward back on the road to Montana. Selden was simply not done with it; he was now high on promising discoveries reported from the Flint Creek area—over the divide west of Deer Lodge.[44]

For all Selden's newfound optimism, Ward's trip to Montana did not materialize. It is clear that Ward had lost his enthusiasm for the territory, and when it became apparent that most of the directors would not support another Montana endeavor, Ward was content to more or less play his uncle and the directors against each other.[45] Selden was deeply disturbed by his nephew's intransigence. When Ward informed his uncle of his uncertainty about returning to Montana, Selden responded, "You no doubt understand that an utter & final failure of this enterprise, is substantially the end of life with me. It is too late for me to retrieve my losses." Selden could not afford to give up until there was absolutely no other recourse: "All I ask of you is, to see the enterprise through, i.e., to a point, where it seems to be left without any chance which can be seen, of resuscitation." The directors had no right, he pointed out, to prevent Ward from returning to Montana. Even if the directors should decide against Ward going, Selden insisted, "you must still go for me."[46]

But Selden's reorganization and ascendancy to the presidency of the company failed to procure from the trustees the necessary moneys. Some directors would have sold off everything for any price, whereas others preferred total inaction. When Selden called a meeting of the company and its stockholders, only three of the latter showed up, and the judge reluctantly concluded that any effort to start the mill up again in 1868 was fruitless.[47] In October the Midas Mining Company announced to its stockholders that it had ceased operations for 1868 and issued a pro rata assessment on the company's outstanding debt of $15,000.[48]

But the president and some of the directors still harbored hopes of future profits, for a spur of the transcontinental railroad was sure to reach Montana, new territorial discoveries were certain, and the company still possessed the finest mill and machinery east of California. With these givens, the optimists hoped not only to pay off debts "but to pay a dividend to the stockholders also, and justify at last the name of our company, by turning the rocks into gold for many years to come."[49] It was not Henry Ward who penned these words. Ward had lost his heart for it; he would never return to Montana. Save for a brief assessment of auriferous properties in South Carolina, Ward ceased work as a mining engineer and devoted the remainder of his life to collecting in the fields of paleontology, geology, and zoology and to pioneering the development of museums to house and display his specimens. Ward's reputation for improving museum technology received international acclaim. Indeed, Ward's devotion to science earned him recognition as one of the founders of the nation's nineteenth-century natural history museum movement.[50]

In effect, when the Midas Mining Company made the decision to cease operations for 1868, it put the lie to Henry Ward's many arguments that success would come only to the firm that had superior machinery. If anything had been learned in Hot Spring, it was that Ward's mill, no matter how efficient in operation, had been built at a price so excessive that its costs of production negated its ability to turn a profit—much less earn its way—in an environment in which the abundance of high-grade ore had been greatly overrated. The decisions of other firms—the Golden Ore, Clark and Upson, and

New York and Montana Mining and Discovery companies, for instance—to upgrade their technical capabilities at large expense had also proved unwise; no mill operation in the district had been able to cover costs.

THIS HAD NOT BEEN LOST ON THE CITIZENS OF THE HOT SPRING DISTRICT, AND IN 1868 some sought to make good on the failure of the better-equipped and bigger mills by implementing strategies of simplicity. Andrew Hall and Don Spaulding opened a small water-powered overshot mill on Meadow Creek, Carroll T. Hobart erected an even smaller one just downstream from Sterling, and Theodore Maltby attempted to simplify and economize at the old NY&MM&D Company mill just above Sterling. These efforts produced mixed results, certainly nothing in the way of riches.

Andrew Hall and Don Spaulding had come close to erecting a steam-powered mill in 1866 but had postponed the project when the Hosmer Mining Company, which was to supply the machinery, rejected Meadow Creek for Ramshorn Gulch. Then the Golden Ore steam-powered mill, utilizing the presumably advanced but expensive Wyckoff Process, had been positioned to treat ores from this area. The subsequent demise of the Golden Ore mill in late 1867 encouraged Hall and Spaulding to expand their own ranching, mining, and sawmilling work into the processing of quartz. Spurning steam power, Hall and Spaulding constructed a water-powered ten-stamp mill fitted with Chicago machinery on a site just northeast of where the road to Gallatin County crossed Meadow Creek. The mill commenced operations on August 25 but could not have succeeded, as whatever work it carried on subsequently attracted little public interest.[51]

Even less successful but initiated on the same principles was the mill erected just below Sterling in 1868 by Carroll T. Hobart. Hobart had moved to Sterling in 1867. During the summer of 1868, believing the Hot Spring mills had failed because of their elaborateness, he constructed a simple, eighteen-foot, overshot wheel-driven five-stamp operation in a frame building about a quarter of a mile below the mining camp on the south side of Hot Spring Creek. Although it was as rudimentary a mill as could be built, the *Montana Post* wanted to believe with Hobart that a more simplistic test of Hot Spring's ores would restore the district's former reputation.[52] It did not. From the outset, Hobart lacked the resources to make it profitable. At year's end the mill lay closed because of winter conditions, and Hobart was struggling to come up with overdue payments on loans and workers' salaries and was casting his eye on what he thought were more promising prospects in Lander County, Nevada.[53]

Theodore Maltby's efforts to make a go of the New York and Montana Mining and Discovery Company's mill came closer than any to redeeming Hot Spring's reputation. When Maltby took the mill on lease in early 1868, he did not initially operate on steam but went back to using the mill's fifteen-inch turbine waterwheel. This plan was cost-effective; after Ward's shutdown in mid-March, Maltby had almost exclusive use of Hot Spring Creek water and could thus run the mill at a large reduction in expense, particularly with respect to fuel. Although Maltby could drive only ten of the mill's twenty stamps in this manner, he was able to operate the mill largely on his own effort and expertise, eliminating the necessity for engineers and amalgamators and thereby saving substantially on labor costs.[54] Only when water ran out in July did Maltby convert to steam and to the mill's full twenty-stamp capability.

Maltby's effort to resuscitate Sterling as a viable mining camp was observed closely and applauded whenever it showed any degree of promise. Maltby ran the mill, but it took dozens of men to supply the ore for it. This need for a labor force, now that Midas Mining had closed shop, kept up Sterling's hopes. That Maltby took ore from up and down Hot Spring Creek and from lodes up on Gold Field to the south gave him a broad range of influence. During the summer Maltby did reasonably well on ore from the Red Bluff Lode, even as he converted by necessity to the more expensive steam-powered machinery. He also worked ore out of the Galena and received permission from others to work their ores at no cost. As Maltby's crew on the Galena alone numbered ten, one can assume he had as many as three dozen or more miners in his employ, in addition to teamsters, sawyers, carpenters, and blacksmiths. One report estimated his workforce at no fewer than sixty men.[55] His men were not lodged or fed at the mill but resided in their own cabins or utilized boardinghouses and hotels in Sterling. During his weeks of profit, Maltby was the toast of the town—"one of the best fellows in the country," as he himself put it. The citizens of Sterling were understandably grateful for his work in keeping the camp alive and feted him with a ceremony at which they gave him a $250 gold watch.[56]

But the deeper Maltby dug, the poorer the Red Bluff produced. Soon Red Bluff ore was worth less than nine dollars a ton. Declining values and rising water finally compelled him to abandon the mine. Running at a loss, Maltby couldn't pay his workers.[57] Grand jury duty in Virginia City took him away from Sterling for a week.[58] Then, revisited by his old Mexican War wounds, he was prostrated by rheumatism the better part of November. While he lay immobilized in bed, some of his workforce, certain he could not pay them, broke into the mill and blacksmith shop and stole everything they figured they could get a dollar for, including all of Maltby's quicksilver.[59] Maltby borrowed money from Peter Jackson but, failing to meet his payment, forfeited a heavy wagon and his only span of horses.[60] Penniless, Maltby was forced to shut down the mill, lay off his entire workforce, and leave Sterling for Virginia City, thereby depriving the Hot Spring District of one of its earliest and most dedicated pioneers.

Maltby's subsequent life paralleled the decline of Hot Spring. On the verge of accepting an offer to put up a steam stamp mill near Helena, he received news that his wife had become critically ill back in Louisiana. Returning to New Orleans, he tended to his wife's needs and took employment as an agent for several Texas newspapers. But the newspaper chain failed, and Maltby, who could not leave his wife, was reduced to subsistence farming—he had, as he put it, "thrown down the shovel & the pick and taken up the shovel and the hoe."[61] But Maltby's health was as fragile as his wife's, and within the year he was dead; his spouse, left penniless, was reduced to begging for financial assistance from his old Montana friends.[62] Even before Maltby died, Henry Ward left this memorial—and commentary on Hot Spring's demise—to the troubled Louisianan: "I feel *very* sorry for Capt. Maltby. It is too bad for an old man, who needs the comforts as well as the necessaries of life, to find himself at Captain's advanced years, without his old age provided for. How firm was his faith in Mines, and how sadly it has deceived him."[63]

With Maltby's departure Hot Spring became a shell of its former self, and the town of Sterling, like countless other quartz camps, embarked on the road to obsolescence. City lots that had sold for as much as $500 in 1866 were now available for as little as a dollar.[64] A traveler passing through found Sterling "almost deserted."[65] Only a handful of diehards remained.

THE FAILURE OF HOT SPRING QUARTZ MINING REMAINED A FOCUS POINT OF ATTENTION for many months. Time and time again the collapse came up as an example of one of many disappointments in the territory's quartz milling experience. In the Hot Spring District itself second-guessing had commenced as early as 1867 when the Clark and Upson and the Golden Ore enterprises had faltered, but the closure and then failure in 1868 of the district's flagship company, the Midas, brought criticisms into full voice. When it became clear in March 1868 that Ward would cease operations, a correspondent for the *Post* did not fault Ward, who had done all he could to succeed, but mocked the company that had failed to live up to the legendary "alchymistic power of the 'long-eared King'" for whom it had been named. As for all those unoccupied buildings at Midasburg, they might as well be converted to a territorial prison or a home for the aged as ever hope to make a dollar mining.[66] Surely, Benjamin Dittes, the new owner of the *Montana Post,* opined, the Midas was "the greatest and most beautiful monument of misplaced confidence in a quartz camp" in county history.[67] Another critical attack called Hot Spring the site of "Lavish Expenditures" but incommensurate results.[68] In an unjust and snide remark leveled against Henry Ward, the *Democrat* applauded Theodore Maltby for "exemplifying the difference between Professorships and honest hard-working practical knowledge" when the captain arrived in Virginia City with several small gold bricks.[69]

Criticisms weren't limited to newspaper columns. Peter Jackson became painfully aware of this as he was forced to endure the disapprobation of Sterling's rank and file. Previously, the company's strict employment policies had kept grumbling and dissatisfaction in check, but now that the mill was closed, a number of former employees were poisoning the air with ridicule of the company and its record.[70]

Criticism was not restricted to the failure of the Rochester company, of course, as all the mills erected in Hot Spring had closed—or were performing questionably, if not poorly—by late 1868. In September and October, when the territorial surveyor, John Corbett—who owned claims in Hot Spring and stood to lose without their development—laid out his chains in the district, he snorted at what he saw, labeling the empty mills "monuments of misman-agement and folly."[71]

Some of the condemnations heaped upon Hot Spring's failure stemmed from sheer disappointment as well as cynicism. By 1868 the placer mines of Alder Gulch were in serious decline, and Madison County's prospects for any kind of continued prosperity were increasingly linked to quartz. But quartz mining and milling countywide were also failing, and it stood to reason that these shortcomings would be subjected to close and critical scrutiny. That Helena, which was Virginia City's rival and was bidding to replace it as ter-ritorial capital, was, by comparison, thriving added fuel to the complaints of those dependent on the industry.[72]

Whatever the causes, all those who looked at Hot Spring's history could not help but regard its demise with astonishment and remorse. Only two years prior, one resident of Sterling observed, the proposition that the district could have degenerated into such a state of quiescence "would have been regarded by the most doubtful minds as almost an impossibility."[73] But now, as someone who had visited the Midas noted, "grass grows in the great yard and bats are flitting at night through the offices."[74] Twenty-two years later, Montana's first inspector of mines, G. C. Swallow, nostalgically remembered his visits to the mining camps of the 1860s, including Sterling. Where "in olden times the steam whistle aroused the miner to his daily toil or called him from labor to refreshment," Sterling now was ruled by "the silence of dead works," including the Ward mill, which had "lost its machinery"; the Pratt mill, which had been "despoiled"; and the Hobart mill, which had "disappeared."[75] Today, at the former site of Sterling, the NY&MM&D Company mill is entirely gone, and the only remnants of what was once a small but vigorous 1860s boom-bust mining camp are the ragged stone silhouettes of the Midas and the Clark and Upson quartz mills.

Many sought to understand what had gone wrong. One view was expressed in the *Montana Democrat*, which blasted the superintendents as a "Kid Glove fraternity" that fastened itself on eastern capital and operated from unlimited resources. Instead of making profitable investments, these men had "with but few exceptions, squandered the money of their principals, and through ignorance of machinery, mining and in many cases of ordinary business transactions . . . destroyed the confidence of Eastern capitalists in the value of our ores."[76] Although it is not possible to apply this criticism specifically to any single Hot Spring quartz milling enterprise, it does remind one of William Clark's admission that he had entered the business with scant knowledge of what he was getting into and that his ignorance had doomed his Hartford enterprise.

Another assessment of cause and effect came from a Sterling resident who argued that the closed mills should be regarded "not as monuments of man's folly, but as monuments of misguided capital." This view held that the mill superintendents had been sincere and competent in their work but were hamstrung by ignorant directors, trustees, and stockholders who, having but "faint theoretical knowledge of the business," attempted to micromanage the enterprises from distances of thousands of miles. Once the mills were erected, the assessment went, the directors withheld the funds necessary to develop the mines while at the same time demanding instant dividends sufficient to enable the owners of stock to take early retirements.[77] This analysis describes quite succinctly some of the problems associated with the Midas effort; it might also describe difficulties faced by others of whom we have lesser knowledge. The *Post* elaborated this theory with some objectivity:

> We have ascertained to a certainty, that the richness of our quartz was greatly overestimated by the first discoverers, and that thereby the people of the Territory, and foreign capitalists, were misled by exaggerated statements, and as a consequence, deceived in results. The character of both country and people suffered greatly on this account—foreign capitalists believed themselves swindled—and what was really a mistake, has in their estimation, taken the form of crime. Many who invested largely have abandoned their interests, amounting to many thousands, in disgust—and

others, who intended to invest, have refrained from doing so, upon the supposition that the story of our wealth was a myth, concocted for mercenary purposes.[78]

In referencing the overestimation of the richness of Montana quartz, the *Post* was touching on yet another cause for failure: the milling companies' total reliance on the availability of high-grade ores. Once faced with the finite nature of the district's rich surface values, no Hot Spring quartz mills, not even the advanced Midas Company model, stood a chance, so crude were their milling capabilities. Further, these primitive mills could not have captured accessory base metals with which to reduce the cost of mining.[79]

There is no question that the capitalists who invested their money in Hot Spring did so on the naive, if not absurd, belief that expensive machinery could be installed and made profitable all in the same season with only scant understanding of what it took to succeed in a territory thousands of miles distant. Moreover, these companies ventured resources without knowledge of the real value of what they were developing. "Perhaps no district in the Territory showed stronger indications of rich auriferous deposits than this when first examined," reported U.S. commissioner for mining statistics J. Ross Browne in 1868, but because Hot Spring's mills were erected "previous to any considerable development of the lodes upon which the hopes of the proprietors were based," they had uniformly failed.[80] The territory's *Statistical Almanac for 1869* agreed: the "disastrous policy of the past" might have been avoided had the lodes "been so far developed before machinery [was] erected as to furnish the strongest presumptive evidence of permanency and pay." The book's compilers also singled out the inferior quality of the machinery initially brought into the territory, machinery that had been "better adapted to crushing the hopes of owners than ore." In addition, capital brought into and controlled in Montana by eastern capitalists had too often been accompanied by inexperience and had "in most cases proven at present non-productive, and in some a total loss."[81] Asahel K. Eaton had concluded as much in a survey of Hot Spring's mills in November 1867:

> A large number of mills for the working of gold ores, have been erected in the territory, and few of them with more than partial success. . . . The principal difficulty . . . has been the imperfect management of these different enterprises, arising sometimes from the incapacity of agents, but more frequently from the impossibility of anticipating in a country, new and undeveloped, the exact requirements of the case. One great error has been made by almost all. It has arisen from the over sanguine belief that quartz could be mined in quantity without preliminary expense in development. The mills are erected, the money and patience of the proprietors

exhausted, and with untold wealth the machinery is left to rust and rot for want of ore.[82]

This development was hardly unique to Montana. Only a few years prior, Colorado had gone through a similar experience—poor management by inexperienced men, the installation of inferior machinery purchased at high cost, and the erection of expensive buildings before the profitability of the lodes had been determined. Similar mistakes had been made in California a decade earlier. But these precedents were ignored in Montana, as they had been in Colorado.[83]

The real cost of mining in Montana was also frequently misunderstood. Here the California experience serves as a measure. Ore values in California were barely more significant than those in Montana, but the costs of operation were considerably lower. California mining enterprises, in close proximity to a major industrial and supply center—San Francisco—and contiguous to one of the world's most fertile valleys, could be kept alive at a fraction of what it cost in Montana to purchase machinery, tools, clothing, and groceries. Consequently, ore that brought only twenty dollars to the ton in California cost perhaps ten to fifteen dollars to process, whereas twenty-dollar ore in Montana usually cost that much to process, rendering any profit negligible.[84] Wages were also considerably higher in Montana than in California. It took a lot to induce a miner to stay in a territory where the winters were so cruel and long and where basic social amenities were minimal. Henry Ward's letters to his directors in 1866–1867 were perpetual litanies of complaints and reminders of the costs of keeping and maintaining an active work crew. Ward had also urged patience—patience above all. A mine could not be developed in a day, a week, or even a month or a year, he said, but he was never able to convey that reality to his company in Rochester.

The stockholders and trustees were not only ignorant of these factors; the corporate mining failure in Montana illustrates how insensitive these companies were to the formidable impediments presented by the territory's geography and climate. Montana's isolation made procuring proper information difficult and adept management from eastern boardrooms impracticable. The vast distances also made transportation costly; both the overland and river routes were long, arduous, and dangerous. Operations so far removed from their source of supplies were inherently handicapped. Moreover, Montana's alpine climate effectively limited the working year to eight, even seven, months rather than twelve.

The failure of these mining companies serves as a reminder that relatively few people ever got rich from gold mining and that the majority of the capitalists who ventured their resources in it, not only in Montana but throughout the West, received more injury than benefit from their speculations. Very little of the capital invested ever returned to its source.

Despite the odds against success and despite all the warnings that profitable mining was an illusive objective, in the flush years of the Civil War—and even later—some entrepreneurs were willing to take a chance. Usual tendencies toward caution evaporated when capitalists were tempted with prospects of handsome, even enormous, returns on relatively modest investments. The image of gold heightened expectations and fostered speculation. As William Clark lamented, it seemed "'foreordained' [that] we all fail and like the blind following the blind all stumble into the same gulf, baited by a 'color' of gold to a mountain of granite."[85]

Epilogue

IN CONTRAST TO PLACER MINING, WHICH CONTINUED AT THE WASHINGTON BAR AND Norwegian sites throughout the late nineteenth century and beyond, Hot Spring quartz lode mining, as well as hard-rock mining throughout Madison County, did not fare well in the 1870s and early 1880s and was only revitalized when the recovery of gold from low-grade ores and inefficiently milled tailings was made possible by the arrival of railroads and the application of chemical solutions—in this case, cyanide. During the 1890s the Hot Spring District attracted much attention. Most of the work was concentrated up on Revenue Flats (formerly called Gold Field) and in the Lower Hot Spring District, with the Revenue, Boaz, and Red Bluff lodes in the forefront. Sterling, however, continued to decline; its demise was certified when it lost its post office in 1880.

Two new, albeit small, communities quickly rose to eclipse Sterling. Red Bluff was located on the site of the former McAndrew and Wann enterprise in Lower Hot Spring. Norris, located at the epicenter of the entire Hot Spring District, just west of the district's namesake, was the response to the Sappington-to-Norris spur of the Northern Pacific Railroad, constructed in 1890 and the surest indication that industrialists saw the area as commercially viable. The inducements for a branch line were stated effusively; there were expectations of making the Hot Spring and Pony districts "the largest mining operation in Montana," capable of producing 1,000 to 2,000 tons of ore per day.[1]

Following a setback in the district's prospects after the turn of the twentieth century—marked by the demise of the town of Red Bluff—Hot Spring mining took an upward turn during the Great Depression, attracting capital and many miners from the state's mineral centers. This activity declined only when the federal government restricted the mining of gold in 1942 and redirected those energies into the extraction of raw materials more essential to the war effort.

But as the price of gold rose in the postwar years and as improvements were made in extraction and processing, efforts to make Hot Spring and Madison County ores pay were renewed. They have continued to this day. So far, none has met expectations, but hardly a day goes by without discussion of some company, from within or outside the United States, purchasing or selling lode property; without the sight of company rigs drilling test holes; without the sound of helicopters whirring overhead with torpedolike sensing devices suspended below to pinpoint promising leads.

In fact, in many ways things have changed remarkably little from those speculative years of the 1860s. In 1902, Montana's inspector of mines, although forecasting that the future wealth of the state would "rest on its mineral lodes," also enumerated the many false beliefs that held, and continued to hold, back the mining industry. Absentee ownership, the inability of stockholders to understand and support true costs of management and labor, and the unwillingness of the same subscribers to exercise patience in the development of their investments headed his list of impediments to successful extraction of gold in Montana.[2]

Eighty years later I personally experienced the effects of these impediments. In 1982, Resources America, a mining firm based in Winter Park, Florida, commenced operations in the Lower Hot Spring District. By summer 1983 it had reopened the Grubstake Lode, was building a sophisticated indoor cyanide separating system, was expanding into the Boaz, and had begun negotiating for rights to work the tailings of other abandoned mines, including the Red Bluff. On July 22, 1983, I accompanied an old-timer, John Willis, who had worked at the Boaz and Revenue mines in the 1930s and early 1940s and was serving as a consultant for Resources America, on a visit to the company's superintendent at the Grubstake. The superintendent was on the phone, talking with company headquarters in Florida. John and I waited just outside the open door to his office, and we overheard a conversation that in remarkable ways paralleled much of what one would get from reading correspondence in the 1860s between Henry Ward and the Midas Mining Company. Resources America had expected to commence working ores on August 1, but operations were several weeks or more behind, as only one of three cyanide vats had been installed, and the entire crushing and conveyance system—from the mine shaft through the crusher over the belts to the cyanide separation equipment—had not been put in place. The superintendent, on the defensive because of this delay, was clearly out of patience, barely able to contain his exasperation in explaining the state of operations to Winter Park people and allaying their fears as to the soundness of their investment. Over and over he urged the need for patience; this kind of enterprise could not turn profits overnight, he said. Once off the phone, he lamented the stinginess with which the company had underwritten operations, having advanced money sufficient for the mill to be built and the Grubstake reopened but reluctant to venture further capital until the capabilities of the machinery and the value of the ores to be processed were authenticated. Predictably, the company ceased operations within a year, having expended, according to locals, something in excess of $1 million in a failed effort.

Despite that failure, optimism for the future still abounds. In 1988 I purchased for a token twenty dollars a number of shares in the long-defunct Revenue Mine Developing Group, Inc. Francis Niven, an elderly stockholder, didn't want to take any money for the shares, but I insisted on it as a kind of ritual entrance into the fraternity of Hot Spring's aspirants. The transfer of this stock from Francis to me was accompanied by an impassioned explanation of why the company had failed and how an enterprising chap like myself could really make a go of it if only I would follow his directions, for the company had failed to understand the drift of the lode. There were, Francis insisted, untold millions down there if only the right methods could be brought to bear. And so it goes and assuredly will continue to do so, not only for Hot Spring but for Montana and for the entire western mining scene, as long as any signs of the precious metal persist.

Notes

PROLOGUE

1. Quoted in Paula Mitchell Marks, *Precious Gold: The American Gold Rush Era, 1848–1900* (New York, 1994), 152.

2. Elizabeth Jameson, *All That Glitters: Class, Conflict, and Community in Cripple Creek* (Urbana, 1998); Sally Zanjani, *A Mine of Her Own: Women Prospectors in the American West, 1850–1950* (Lincoln, 1997); Linda Peavy and Ursula Smith, *The Gold Rush Widows of Little Falls* (St. Paul, 1990); Linda Peavy and Ursula Smith, *Women in Waiting in the Western Movement: Life on the Home Frontier* (Norman, 1994); Malcolm J. Rohrbough, *Aspen: The History of a Silver Mining Town, 1879–1893* (New York, 1986); Malcolm J. Rohrbough, *Days of Gold: The California Gold Rush and the American Nation* (Berkeley, 1997); Rodman Wilson Paul, *Mining Frontiers of the Far West, 1848–1880* (rev., expanded ed. by Elliott West, Albuquerque, 2001). See also Robert V. Hine and John Mack Faragher, "Mining Frontiers," in Hine and Faragher, *The American West: A New Interpretative History* (New Haven, 2000), 234–273.

3. Henry A. Ward to John Creighton, September 7, 1897, Henry A. Ward Papers, Department of Rare Books and Special Collections, University of Rochester Library. Hereafter cited as WP.

4. See, for example, Dick Pace, *Golden Gulch: The Story of Montana's Fabulous Alder Gulch* (Virginia City, MT, 1962); Larry Barsness, *Gold Camp: Alder Gulch and Virginia City, Montana* (New York, 1962).

5. Duane A. Smith, *Rocky Mountain Mining Camps: The Urban Frontier* (Bloomington, 1967), 256. In *Gold Rushes and Mining Camps of the Early American West* (Caldwell, ID, 1990), Vardis Fisher and Opal Laurel Holmes find much distortion and misrepresentation accompanying the story of all of the Old West.

6. Alexander K. McClure, *Three Thousand Miles Through the Rocky Mountains* (Philadelphia, 1869), 91–92, 214–215.

7. Joseph E. King, *A Mine to Make a Mine: Financing the Colorado Mining Industry, 1859–1902* (College Station, TX, 1977); Harvey N. Gardiner, *Mining Among the Clouds: The Mosquito Range and the Origins of Colorado's Silver Boom* (Denver, 2002); Merle W. Wells, *Gold Camps and Silver Cities: Nineteenth Century Mining in Central and Southern Idaho*, 2nd ed. (Moscow, ID, 1983); Paul Fatout, *Meadow Lake Gold Town* (Lincoln, 1974).

8. W. Turrentine Jackson, *Treasure Hill: Portrait of a Silver Mining Camp* (Tucson, 1963), 1.

CHAPTER 1

1. William Y. Lovell, "Hot Spring District and Surroundings," *Montana Post*, November 9, 1867.

2. Franklin Luther Kirkaldie to his wife, March 18, 1866, Letters of Franklin Luther Kirkaldie, May 1, 1864–March 30, 1869, Collection 43, Special Collections, Renne Library, Montana State University, Bozeman, Montana. Hereafter cited as MSUSC.

3. *Montana Post,* November 26, 1864. See also issues of August 17, September 3, 1864. A guide to the Idaho mines put it this way: "All cannot mine. . . . Simply digging gold or other precious metals is a lottery in which there are many prizes but very many blanks; and I doubt whether there is a class of people in the world who succeed generally so well in life as the mechanic and the industrious farmer, especially when these vocations are followed in the vicinity of productive mines." J. L. Campbell, *Idaho: Six Months in the New Gold Diggings: The Emigrant's Guide Overland* (New York, 1864), 39.

4. Quotation from the *Concise Dictionary of American History* (New York, 1962), 433; Everett Dick, *The Lure of the Land: A Social History of the Public Lands from the Articles of Confederation to the New Deal* (Lincoln, 1970), 139. Another provision denied entitlement of a homestead to anyone who had borne arms against the U.S. government, but there is no record that this was ever enforced in Montana. With numerous modifications, the basic features of the law are in force today. In subsequent years, variations of the Homestead Act enabled larger preemptions and preemptions for other reasons, including lands designated for timber culture and for the agriculturalization of desert lands.

5. Richard White, *"It's Your Misfortune and None of My Own": A New History of the American West* (Norman, 1991), 139.

6. William Joseph Trimble, *The Mining Advance into the Inland Empire* (Madison, WI, 1914), 224; Merrill G. Burlingame, *The Montana Frontier* (Bozeman, MT, 1942), 347–348; Dick, *The Lure of the Land,* 55–56.

7. Preemptions for agricultural land and mineral discoveries are contained in "Record Books" located in the Madison County Clerk and Recorder's Office, Virginia City, Montana.

8. Abram H. Vorhees Diary, Entry of August 8, 1864, Microfilm 460, Montana State Historical Society Archives, Helena. Hereafter cited as MHSA.

9. Richard Owen Diaries, 1864–1865, Entry of September 5, 1864, SC 613, MHSA.

10. John S. Hackney Diary, Entry of September 4, 1864, printed in Susan Badger Doyle (ed.), *Journeys to the Land of Gold: Emigrant Diaries from the Bozeman Trail, 1863–1866,* 2 vols. (Helena, 2000), I:314.

11. Robert A. Chadwick, "Investigations of the Geology and Ore Deposits of the Red Bluff–Norris Area, Madison County, Montana," unpublished manuscript, 1984; Hugh D. Safford, "Outline of the Geology and Ore Deposits at the Hot Spring Mining District, Madison County, MT," unpublished manuscript, 1993.

12. Lovell, "Hot Spring District and Surroundings."

13. Ibid.

14. Record Book A, pages 92 and 94, Clerk and Recorder's Office, Madison County Courthouse, Virginia City, Montana. Hereafter cited as book plus page, MCC.

15. This description is taken from a discovery made between the forks of Meadow Creek on December 23, 1865; E/704, MCC. This is a rare instance when the county recorder took the time and effort to incorporate this language in the record book.

16. Otis E. Young Jr., *Western Mining: An Informal Account of Precious-Metals Prospecting, Placering, Lode Mining, and Milling on the American Frontier from Spanish Times to 1893* (Norman, 1970), 108–118, 121–124; Trimble, *Mining Advance into the Inland Empire,* 82.

17. Elliott West, *Contested Plains: Indians, Goldseekers, and the Rush to Colorado* (Lawrence, KS, 1998), 106.

18. Otis E. Young Jr., "The Craft of the Prospector," *Montana: The Magazine of Western History* 20 (Winter 1970), 31; Young, *Western Mining,* 3–32.

19. *Montana Post,* January 26, 1867.

20. Chadwick, "Investigations"; Safford, "Outline." William Y. Lovell and Ferdinand V. Hayden remarked, respectively, on the "bright red ochre" and "bright red jasper" coloration found in Hot Spring gold-bearing ores. See Lovell, "Hot Spring District and Surroundings"; Hayden, *Preliminary Report of the United States Geologic Survey of Montana and Portions of Adjacent Territories, Being a Fifth Annual Report of Progress* (Washington, DC, 1872), 172.

21. Young, "The Craft of the Prospector," 28–39.

22. Ibid.

23. A/152, MCC.

24. A/99, MCC.

25. A/252, 310, MCC.

26. B/236, MCC. Author's emphasis.

27. The Rev. E. J. Stanley, *Life of Rev. L. B. Stateler, or Sixty-Five Years on the Frontier* (Nashville, 1907), 184–186.

28. "Diary of James H. Morley," entry of June 10, 1864, James Henry Morley Papers, SC 644, MHSA.

29. William Emory Atchison, "Excerpts from the Personal Diary of the Late William Emory Atchison in 1864," mimeographed, published by J. E. Haynes and Charles H. Ramsdell, Haynes Papers, Collection 1504, MSUSC.

30. Charles W. Baker Diary, April 21, 1864–September 1867, SC 1275, MHSA. If Baker filed any claims at this time, they are not officially recorded.

31. Benjamin W. Ryan, "The Bozeman Trail to Virginia City," *Annals of Wyoming* 19, 2 (July 1947), 94.

32. B/17–19, MCC.

33. A/483, MCC.

34. A/191, MCC.

35. A/97, MCC.

36. Speech of February 6, 1867, Lyman Ezra Munson Papers, 1865–1899, SC 553, MHSA.

37. Edward B. Nealley to Hezekiah L. Hosmer, May 7, 1865, Hosmer MSS, Beinecke Rare Book and Manuscripts Library, Yale University, New Haven, Connecticut.

38. B/457–458, MCC.

39. From the Journal of William Y. Pemberton, Entry of December 5, 1864, William Y. Pemberton Papers, SC 629, MHSA.

40. C/263, MCC.

41. For an excellent description of the relationship between prospecting and company patronage, see "Montana," address given by Chief Justice Hezekiah L. Hosmer before the Traveller's Club, New York City, 1866, Rare Books Collection, Library of Congress, Washington, DC.

42. Richard Owen Diaries, Entry of September 6, 1864.

43. Stanley, *Life of Rev. L. B. Stateler*, 188.

44. Poll Lists for the Montana Territorial Election of 1864, Records of the Montana Territory, Secretary, 1864, Record Series 160, MHSA.

CHAPTER 2

1. S. P. Bassett and Joseph Magee (comps.), *Statistical Almanac for 1869 and Year Book of Facts Showing the Material Resources of Montana* (Helena, 1869), 7.

2. In 1868, U.S. commissioner of mining J. Ross Browne lamented that the wastage caused by such methods and tendencies had resulted in a loss to the country of

not less than $300 million in gold alone and immeasurable additional losses of other mineral values. J. Ross Browne, *Mineral Resources of the United States* (Washington, DC, 1868), 9.

3. Randall E. Rohe, "Hydraulicking in the American West: The Development and Diffusion of a Mining Technique," *Montana: The Magazine of Western History* 35 (Spring 1985), 18–35.

4. Trimble, *Mining Advance into the Inland Empire*, 97.

5. B/333, MCC.

6. B/454–455, MCC.

7. James U. Sanders (ed.), *Society of Montana Pioneers: Constitution, Members, and Officers, with Portraits and Maps*, vol. I (Helena, 1899), 47.

8. Adobetown Justice of the Peace Records, July 7, 1864, SC 267, MHSA.

9. William Barclay Napton, *Over the Santa Fe Trail* (Santa Fe, NM, 1964 [1905]).

10. Ibid.

11. William Barclay Napton, *Past and Present of Saline County, Missouri* (Indianapolis, 1910), 899–900.

12. National Historical Company, *History of Howard and Cooper Counties, Missouri* (St. Louis, 1883), 1157–1158; Estate of William N. Ragland, Probate Files, MCC. For accounts of the war around Boonville, see Michael Fellman, *Inside War: The Guerrilla Conflict in Missouri During the Civil War* (New York, 1989); Thomas Goodrich, *Black Flag: Guerrilla Warfare on the Western Border, 1861–1865* (Bloomington, 1995).

13. William B. Napton to Henry A. Ward, August 4, 1866, WP.

14. *Montana Post*, May 27, 1865.

15. A/556, MCC.

16. A comprehensive list of Oro Fino Mining Company shareholders does not exist. But transfers of property and company agreements with Ragland, Cope, and Napton provide helpful information. See, for example, B/520–523, 541; H/237–238, 583–586, MCC.

17. *Montana Post*, July 1, 1865; H/583–586, MCC.

18. H/583–586, MCC.

19. Napton to Ward, August 4, 1866, WP.

20. Entry of August 24, 1865, Henry Hauser Diary, 1865–1869, SC 986, MHSA.

21. F/729, MCC.

22. H/345–348, MCC.

23. H/306–307, I/26, 217, MCC.

24. *Montana Post*, August 26, 1865.

25. George Rogers Taylor, *The Transportation Revolution, 1815–1860* (New York, 1951), 396–398; Robert Greenhalgh Albion, *The Rise of the Port of New York, 1815–1860* (New York, 1939), 386; Edward K. Spann, *The New Metropolis: New York City, 1840–1857* (New York, 1981), 401–427; Sven Beckert, *The Monied Metropolis: New York City and the Consolidation of the American Bourgeoisie, 1850–1896* (New York, 2001), 135–137, 146–148. Surplus capital wasn't confined to New York alone. As Rodman Paul noted, during the war years "the speculative impulse was strong throughout America" and proved easy to tap for the capital development of western mining. See Paul, *Mining Frontiers of the Far West*, 120. See also Victor S. Clark, *History of Manufactures in the United States* (New York, 1949), 36; Emerson David Fite, *Social and Industrial Conditions in the North During the Civil War* (New York, 1930), 84.

26. Edwin G. Burrows and Mike Wallace, *Gotham: A History of New York City to 1898* (New York, 1999), 906–908; Taylor, *Transportation Revolution*, 398; Beckert, *Monied Metropolis*, 151–153; *Trow's New York City Directories*, 1864–1866.

27. Edwin Ruthven Purple, *Perilous Passage: A Narrative of the Montana Goldrush, 1862–1863*, ed. Kenneth N. Owens (Helena, 1995), introduction.

28. *Montana Post*, November 19, 1864.

29. Ibid.

30. B/487; C/125, 126, MCC.

31. *Montana Post*, November 19, 1864.

32. This is the prospectus of the Northwestern Mining and Exploring (NM&E) Company, organized in New York City in early 1865, SC 585, MHSA. Simultaneously, James Tufts, a trustee of the NM&E Company and presider over a Broadway agency specializing in Montana mining speculations, published a glowing tract on Montana and the unquestioned potential of its economic resources. See Tufts, *A Tract Descriptive of Montana Territory, with a Sketch of Its Mineral and Agricultural Resources* (New York, 1865).

33. NM&E Company Prospectus.

34. William Worthington Fowler, *Ten Years in Wall Street* (Hartford, 1879), 299–300.

35. I/145–148, MCC.

36. *New York Evening Post*, January 17, 1865.

37. Robert L. Spude, "To Test by Fire: The Assayer in the American Mining West, 1848–1920," unpublished Ph.D. diss. (University of Illinois, 1989), 55–66.

38. *Cleveland Herald*, published in the *Rochester Evening Express*, April 30, 1866.

39. Despite Eaton's scientific prominence during the 1860s, he has passed into anonymity. As Clark Spence observes in his work on mining engineers in the late nineteenth century, many of these early-day "jack-of-all-trades" practitioners "have remained shadowy and relatively obscure historical figures," eclipsed by other, more colorful western figures and developments. See Spence, *Mining Engineers and the American West: The Lace-Boot Brigade, 1849–1933* (New Haven, 1970), 1–2.

40. New York and Montana Mining and Discovery Company "Circular" to its stockholders, January 28, 1866, WP.

41. Ibid.

42. Ibid.

43. NY&MM&D Company "Journal," May 10, 1865–February 29, 1868, Jackson Family Papers, Madison County, Montana. Hereafter cited as JP.

44. Daniel Jones and Three Sons, Field, Albert, and Alfred B. Jones, "Travels Across the Plains" (1865), Western Historical Manuscript Collection, Missouri State Historical Society, Columbia, Missouri. See also David Bailey Diary; Joseph Culton Walker Reminiscence, SC 962, MHSA. Walker's train left West Point, Iowa, on May 1, 1865, arriving in Virginia City on September 17.

45. See, for example, the advice of Colonel J. A. Martin, dated April 29, 1865, published in the *Atchison Daily Champion*, May 6, 1865. Martin had just completed a journey across the plains to Denver.

46. Dorothy M. Johnson, *The Bloody Bozeman: The Perilous Trail to Montana's Gold* (Missoula, 1983).

47. The wind here must have been truly fierce; on my own journey over this entire route in 1992, the wind, which began in Virginia Dale, Colorado, was incessant all the way to the divide; and had it been present in 1865, which from accounts was undoubtedly the case, it must have been a great burden to the wagon train.

48. Dr. Wade Howard Journal, "A Journey from Tipton, Mo. to Virginia City, Mont. T. April 23, to Sept. 1865," Western Historical Manuscript Collection, Missouri State Historical Society, Columbia, Missouri, 20. The previously cited reminiscence of

Joseph Culton Walker, who wagon-trained through here at approximately the same time, is equally graphic. For other vivid accounts, see *Montana Post,* January 5, 1867, January 11, 1868.

49. NY&MM&D Company Circular, WP, and Journal, JP.

50. Henry A. Ward to "Doctor," July 11, 1865, WP.

51. "Report of Prof. A. K. Eaton," January 18, 1866, NY&MM&D Company Circular, WP; sale of 480 acres to Eaton on August 21, 1865, F/687–686, MCC.

52. Eaton Report, NY&MM&D Company Circular, January 18, 1866, WP.

53. Jones and sons, "Travels Across the Plains." "Oh, what a lonely, dark and desolate place," journaled another traveler. "These mountains ever remain in the hands of the savage or be the haunt of wild beasts." S. Lyman Tyler (ed.), *The Montana Gold Rush Diary of Kate Dunlap* (Salt Lake City, 1969), entry of July 16, 1864.

54. NY&MM&D Company Journal, JP; *Montana Post,* November 25, 1865.

55. NY&MM&D Company Journal, JP.

56. NY&MM&D Company Circular, WP.

CHAPTER 3

1. The Rev. Heman R. Timlow, *Ecclesiastical and Other Sketches of Southington, Conn.* (Hartford, 1875), 542–543; Service Record of Gad E. Upson, Company E, First Mississippi Infantry (Riflemen), Mexican War, Record Group 94, Records of the Office of the Adjutant General, National Archives, Washington, DC (hereafter NA); Gad E. Upson, *Report of the Commissioner of Indian Affairs, 1864,* in Burlingame, *The Montana Frontier, 39.*

2. Upson to William T. Dole, November 10, December 25, 1863, Letters Received by the Office of Indian Affairs, 1824–1880, Blackfeet Agency, Record Group 48, Records of the Office of the Secretary of the Interior, Indian Division, NA.

3. A/440, 504, 557, 589; C/60, 99, MCC.

4. William R. Wilbur, *History of the Bolt and Nut Industry of America* (Cleveland, 1905), 69–75; Francis Atwater (comp.), *History of Southington, Conn.* (New Haven, 1924), 51–57; *Hartford Daily Courant,* October 30, 1909.

5. Wilbur, *History of the Bolt and Nut Industry,* 70–73; *100th Anniversary: Clark Bros. Bolt Company, 1854–1954* (Milldale, CT, 1954); Connecticut State Census, 1866, State Historical Society, 2:2,329.

6. "Incorporating the Clark and Upson Mining Company," Special Acts of the General Assembly, May 1867, 264–266, State of Connecticut, vol. 6, Office of the Secretary of State, Hartford. On May 13, 1865, the *Connecticut Courant* (Hartford) announced formation of the company and listed its stockholders.

7. *Geer's Hartford City Directory, 1865–1866* (Hartford: Elihu Geer, 1866), 350; Atwater, *History of Southington,* 53; Timlow, *Ecclesiastical and Other Sketches,* 543–544; *Montana Post,* November 18, 1865, January 13, 1866; P. Henry Woodward, "The Manufacturing Interests of Hartford," in William T. Davis (ed.), *The New England States: Their Constitutional, Judicial, Educational, Commercial, Professional and Industrial History* (Boston, 1897), 2:815–862; William John Niven Jr., "The Time of the Whirlwind: A Study of the Political, Social, and Economic History of Connecticut from 1861 to 1875," unpublished Ph.D. diss. (Columbia University, 1954), 168.

8. Deposition of William J. Clark, November 2, 1868, Hartford, Conn., in *John G. Copelin v. Clark & Upson Mining Company,* File no. 739, Civil Cases, Records of the Clerk of the Court, MCC.

9. *Montana Post*, October 15, 1864; Deposition of John A. Nelson, January 13, 1867, in *John A. Nelson v. Nelson Mining Co.* (hereafter *Nelson v. Nelson*), File no. 578, Civil Cases, MCC; Charles W. Burpee, *History of Hartford County, Connecticut, 1633–1928*, 3 vols. (Chicago, 1928), I:424; Service Record of John A. Nelson, Colonel, Tenth United States Colored Infantry, Union, Record Group 94, NA.

10. *Montana Post*, October 1, December 24, 1864.

11. See, for example, Andrew Rolle (ed.), *The Road to Virginia City: The Diary of James Knox Polk Miller* (Norman, 1960), 94.

12. For Nelson's sale of Leviathan Hall, see D/250, MCC. A February 4, 1865, consignment of two claims to Nelson, which he deeded over to the Hartford company, is located in D/217, MCC.

13. Nelson deposition, January 13, 1867, *Nelson v. Nelson*, Exhibit A, dated April 29, 1865, lists the claims Nelson presented to the group as under his control. This list was also recorded in the Madison County Clerk and Recorder's Office on December 11, 1865, Record Book J/175. The results of the tests made at the U.S. Assay Office in New York are contained in *Nelson v. Nelson*, MCC.

14. A recent analysis of Colorado's silver rush underlines this observation. See Gardiner, *Mining Among the Clouds*, 28.

15. Nelson deposition, January 13, 1867, *Nelson v. Nelson*, MCC.

16. The origins and development of hydraulic mining in California are described in Robert K. Kelley, *Gold vs. Grain: The Hydraulic Mining Controversy in California's Sacramento Valley* (Glendale, 1959), 23–29. For Nevada, see Eliot Lord, *Comstock Mining and Miners* (1883; reprint, Berkeley, 1959), 222. See also Rohe, "Hydraulicking in the American West."

17. Woodruff to Nelson, June 11, 1865; Porter to Nelson, July 2, 1865; Beach to Nelson, May 24, 1865, in *Nelson v. Nelson*, MCC.

18. Clark deposition, November 2, 1868, *Copelin v. Clark & Upson*, MCC.

19. Ibid.

20. Ibid.; Deposition of Jesse Williams, October 19, 1868, *Copelin v. Clark & Upson*, MCC.

21. Clark deposition, *Copelin v. Clark & Upson*, MCC.

22. Clark and Williams depositions, *Copelin v. Clark & Upson*, MCC; G/90, I/76–78, 81–82, MCC.

23. Nelson deposition, *Nelson v. Nelson*, MCC.

24. Ibid.; Depositions of Matthew Hort, January 2, 1868, and Edward W. Moore, November 27, 1867, *Nelson v. Nelson*, MCC; *Montana Post*, August 19, September 23, 30, 1865 (quotation from September 30, 1865).

25. *Montana Post*, November 11, December 2, 1865.

26. Ibid., December 2, 1865.

27. Ibid.

28. Nelson deposition, *Nelson v. Nelson*, MCC.

29. Robert Hedge to Jester Hedge, December 4, 1865, SC 816, MHSA; *Montana Post*, December 9, 1865.

30. Clark deposition, *Copelin v. Clark & Upson*, MCC. Not only did Clark's freight arrive late, but several items were missing, including an irreplaceable cookstove.

31. *Montana Post*, January 13, 1866; J/367, MCC; *Sacramento Daily Union*, March 31, 1866, reprinted in *Montana Post*, April 21, 1866.

32. Theodore D. Maltby to Henry A. Ward, April 7, 1866, WP; Napton to Ward, August 4, 1866, WP.

33. Eaton Report, January 18, 1866, WP.

CHAPTER 4

1. First public mention of the name is documented in a mortgage taken out on January 6, 1866, by the New York company, J/284, MCC.

2. Benjamin Dailey Diary, 1866, entry of September 7, 1866, SC 2074, MHSA.

3. This letter, dated November 4, 1867, was printed in the *Montana Post Tri-Weekly*, date unknown, WP.

4. State of Montana, Business License Receipts, etc., Collection no. 72, Mansfield Library Archives, University of Montana, Missoula, Montana.

5. Ward to Mumford, February 20, 1867, WP.

6. John L. Corbett, "Field Notes of the Exterior Boundaries of Townships One-Two-Three-Four and Five South, Range One West of the Principal Meridian in the Territory of Montana," entry of October 10, 1868, Bureau of Land Management, Billings, Montana.

7. *Report of J. Ross Browne on the Mineral Resources of the States and Territories West of the Rocky Mountains* (Washington, DC, 1868), 487. Population figures for the territory fluctuate wildly, generally on the side of excess, and are often unreliable. Still, 310 Hot Spring men voted in the September 2, 1867, territorial elections.

8. See, for example, William S. Greever, *The Bonanza West: The Story of the Western Mining Rushes, 1848–1900* (Norman, 1963), 71; Rohrbough, *Days of Gold*, 220–229; Marks, *Precious Dust*, 280–282.

9. *Montana Post*, May 18, 1867.

10. Ibid., April 20, 1867. On a verdict of self-defense, the miner wasn't even arraigned.

11. Ward to Mumford, September 6, 1867, WP. Ward was including New Englanders who had migrated to Montana through the Midwest.

12. See Rohe, "Hydraulicking in the American West."

13. Langford to James W. Taylor, May 20, 1866, printed in Michael Kennedy (ed.), "Infernal Collector," *Montana: The Magazine of Western History* 4 (Spring 1954), 13–23.

14. Hosmer address "Montana," delivered before the Traveller's Club, New York City, January 1866, Rare Books Collection, Library of Congress, Washington, DC.

15. H/37–39, MCC.

16. A/486, 505, MCC.

17. Patrick Aloysius Mullens, S.J., *Creighton: Biographical Sketches of Edward Creighton, John A. Creighton, Mary Lucretia Creighton, Sarah Emily Creighton* (Omaha, 1901), 1–54; Raymond P. Nelson, "Edward Creighton and the Pacific Telegraph," *Mid-America* 24 (1942), 61–74. Creighton University is named for John Creighton, a major benefactor.

18. A/505, MCC.

19. *Montana Post*, advertisements of September 10, 1864, January 14, 1865.

20. H/37–39, MCC.

21. Betty M. and Brigham D. Madsen, *North to Montana: Jehus, Bullwhackers, and Mule Skinners on the Montana Trail* (Salt Lake City, 1980), 78.

22. Maltby's background is discussed in Mary J. Maltby to Henry Ward, November 26, 1871, WP.

23. Maltby was a man accustomed to hard work, hard play, and hard drinking. Although his forte was in the field, he was well-known in Virginia City for his addiction to bowling, cards, and billiards. See Rolle, *Road to Virginia City*, 85, 86, 88, 97.

24. A/486, MCC.

25. The metes and bounds are described in part in N/145, MCC.

26. Ibid.

27. J/82–83, MCC.

28. M/152, MCC.

29. H/506, MCC.

30. G/219, MCC. Rockfellow made claim to the waters and the right to construct the ditch on January 24, 1866; ibid.

31. Deposition of Elijah W. Moore, September 17, 1866, *Elijah W. Moore v. Nelson Mining Co.* (hereafter *Moore v. Nelson*), File no. 409, Civil Cases, MCC; Deposition of Edward J. Murphy, *Nelson v. Nelson*, MCC.

32. Depositions of William A. Mitchell, January 4, 1868, and of Matthew Hort, January 2, 1868, *Nelson v. Nelson*, MCC; *Montana Post*, April 7, 1866.

33. J/533–534, MCC.

34. *Montana Post*, May 19, 26, August 4, November 24, 1866 (quotation from May 19, 1866); Elijah W. Moore deposition, *Moore v. Nelson*; Edward J. Murphy deposition, *Nelson v. Nelson*, MCC.

35. Isaac Irvine Moore to Col. John H. Moore, September 14, 1866, Isaac Irvine Moore Letter, SC 517, MHSA.

36. *Montana Post*, July 29, 1865; Deposition of J. H. Pfeill, January 17, 1868, *Nelson v. Nelson*, MCC. The legal battle between Nelson and the Hartford trustees remained alive for many months. After Nelson had moved to diggings farther north, the courts deliberated over two suits—Nelson's against the company for damages and wages and the company's countersuit—and ordered numerous long-lasting delays. The suits were finally settled in March 1868 when the court issued a verdict in Nelson's favor. There was no way to secure the judgment in cash, so the court ordered the county sheriff to take possession of the company's Alder Gulch property for public auction. It did not bring a big price—only $1,928.98—with the court taking roughly 20 percent for costs. See Judgment by the Court, March 16, 1868, in *Nelson v. Nelson*, MCC; *Montana Post*, March 21, 1868; *Montana Democrat*, April 16, 1868. After winning his case, Nelson engaged in hydraulicking near Helena and then left Montana in 1871 for prospects in Park City, Utah, where he worked for nine years with better success. In October 1880 Nelson caught a cold and, after a short illness, died of pneumonia, leaving a widow and seven children. His funeral in Park City attracted "the largest turn out ever seen in that camp." See *Salt Lake Daily Tribune*, October 28, 30, 1880.

37. In Ovando J. Hollister, *The Mines of Colorado* (New York, 1974 [1867]), 221–222, the author describes the workings of a Gardner Thunderbolt crusher–based milling operation in Colorado in the mid-1860s.

38. Ward to Mumford, October 28, 1866, WP.

39. *Montana Post*, June 9, 1866.

40. Maltby to Ward, July 15, 1866; James T. Hodge to Ward, August 5, 1866; Ward to Mumford, October 28, 1866, WP. The Howland pulverizer appears to have had a history of underperforming with hard materials. See Henry Louis, *The Dressing of Minerals* (New York, 1909), 194–195.

41. Ward to Mumford, October 28, 1866, WP; *Montana Post*, January 5, February 2, 1867.

42. Napton to Ward, August 4, 1866, WP; J/497, MCC.

43. *Montana Post*, June 1, 1867.

44. Ward to Mumford, December 16, 1866, WP.

45. *Montana Post*, January 26, 1867.

46. J/241–265, 268, MCC.

47. NY&MM&D Company Circular, January 18, 1866, WP.

48. Ibid.

49. *Cleveland Herald,* reprinted in the *Rochester Evening Press,* April 30, 1866.

50. N/27, MCC.

51. This description is the product of two newspaper accounts published in the *Montana Post* on June 16, 1866, and November 30, 1867; the company's journal; one photograph; and my personal acquaintance with the site. The mill's foundation can still be observed.

52. Louis C. Hunter, "Waterpower in the Century of the Steam Engine," in Brooke Hindle (ed.), *America's Wooden Age: Aspects of Its Early Technology* (Tarrytown, NY, 1985), 160–190.

53. E/588, 687, MCC.

54. *Montana Post,* February 3, 1866. The map, drawn by Walter de Lacy, has not survived.

55. NY&MM&D Company Journal, JP.

56. *Montana Post,* October 20, 1866.

57. Ibid., August 4, 1866; Atkin to the Golden Ore Mining & Prospecting Company, reprinted in the *Brooklyn Daily Union,* September 15, 1866.

58. Atkin's letters reprinted in the *Brooklyn Daily Union,* September 15, November 15, 1866. Quotation from September 15, 1866, letter. The letters were also printed in the *Montana Post* on October 13, December 15, 1866. However, the *Post* not only omitted portions of the letters, it also changed wording.

59. *Brooklyn Daily Union,* September 15, November 15, 1866.

60. Ward to Mumford, December 22, 1866, WP.

61. *Montana Post,* December 29, 1866.

62. Ibid., August 4, 1866.

63. *Hezekiah L. Hosmer v. the Hosmer Gold & Silver Mining Company,* File no. 510, Civil Cases, MCC.

CHAPTER 5

1. Undated report of Henry A. Ward, Fall 1867, WP; George A. Bruffey, *Eighty-One Years in the West* (Butte, 1925), 45.

2. K/138, MCC. The name Boaz, which carries biblical significance connoting charitability, was attached to discoveries in numerous mining districts throughout the West.

3. K/133, 280, MCC.

4. K/271, MCC.

5. Ward, *Henry A. Ward*; Blake McKelvey, *Rochester: The Flower City, 1855–1890* (Cambridge, MA, 1949), 41–42.

6. "Memorandum of Agreement," February 13, 1865, WP; H/486, MCC.

7. Ward to Francis Gorton, July 4, 1865, WP.

8. *Montana Post,* May 13, 1865.

9. Ward to Francis Gorton, July 4, 1865, WP.

10. Ward, *Henry A. Ward,* 143.

11. Ward to Hiram Sibley, July 12, 1865, WP.

12. Ibid.

13. Samuel Selden to Ward, August 31, 1865, WP.

14. Blake McKelvey, *Rochester: The Water-Power City, 1812–1854* (Cambridge, MA, 1945), 296.

15. Robert L. Thompson, *Wiring a Continent: The History of the Telegraph Industry in the United States, 1832–1866* (Princeton, 1947), 370–371.

16. McKelvey, *Rochester: The Water-Power City*, 71; McKelvey, *Rochester: The Flower City*, 6–7, 98–105.

17. Lockwood R. Doty (ed.), *History of the Genesee Country* (Chicago, 1925), 705.

18. Ward to Gorton, September 6, 1865, WP.

19. Agreement Between W. J. Clark, G. E. Upson, Henry A. Ward, and John G. Gill, August 10, 1865, WP.

20. *Montana Post*, June 17, 1865.

21. Ward to Selden, November 10, 1865, WP. The recording of this transaction lists a figure of $12,000. H/506, 535, MCC.

22. Ibid.

23. Ward to Selden, November 10, 1865, WP.

24. Ward, *Henry A. Ward*, 145–147. Ward's investigations of Nevada mining investments were not productive. Ward to Selden, December 6, 1865, WP.

25. Midas Mining Company to Its Stockholders, February 9, 1866, including "Report of Henry A. Ward to the President and Directors of the Midas Mining Company," February 8, 1866, WP.

26. Ward Report, February 8, 1866, WP.

27. Ibid.

28. Ibid.

29. Theodore Maltby to Ward, April 7, 1866, WP.

30. Selden to Ward, September 18, 1866, WP.

31. Ward to Mumford, October 28, 1866, WP.

32. Ibid.

33. Ibid.

34. Ward, *Henry A. Ward*, 150.

35. Quoted in ibid.

36. Ward to Mumford, October 28, 1866, WP.

37. Ibid.

38. Ward, *Henry A. Ward*, 150.

39. Selden to Ward, November 25, 1866, WP.

40. Mumford to Ward, November 4, 1866, WP.

41. Mumford to Ward, December 14, 1866, WP.

42. J. B. Ward to Ward, December 18, 1866, WP.

43. Ward to Mumford, December 18, 1866, WP.

44. Ibid.

45. Ward to Mumford, December 22, 1866, WP.

46. Ibid.

47. Ibid.

48. Mumford to Ward, January 24, 1867, WP.

49. Selden to Ward, January 24, 1867, WP; J. B. Ward to Ward, February 22, 1867, WP.

50. Mumford to Ward, January 24, 1867, WP; J. B. Ward to Ward, January 25, 1867, WP.

CHAPTER 6

1. *Sacramento Bee*, March 31, 1866.

2. A. E. Eldridge to Ward, February 7, 1867, WP.

3. Ward to Mumford, December 22, 1866, WP.

4. Ward to Mumford, February 12, 1867, WP.

5. J. Silversmith (comp.), *The Miner's Companion and Guide: A Compendium of Most Valuable Information for the Prospector, Miner, Geologist, Mineralogist and Assayer Together with a Comprehensive Glossary of Technical Phrases Used in the Work* (San Francisco, 1861), 51.

6. Both quoted in the prospectus of the New York–based Harmony Gold and Silver Mining Company of Nevada, Bancroft Library, University of California–Berkeley.

7. *Montana Post*, September 29, 1865. For the Colorado experience, see King, *A Mine to Make a Mine*, 42–43.

8. Ward to Mumford, February 12, 1867, WP.

9. Ward to Mumford, February 23, 1867, WP.

10. N/126, 129, 131, 133, 138, 357, 617, MCC.

11. *Montana Post*, February 2, 1867. In the November trial, both Hodges were declared not guilty.

12. P/283–288, MCC.

13. *Montana Post*, January 5, 1867.

14. *Chandler J. Dow v. the Gold Ore Mining Company*, File no. 743, Civil Cases, MCC.

15. *Montana Post*, February 16, 1867.

16. Ibid., April 13, 1867.

17. William S. Godbe biography, Hampton Godbe Papers, MS 664, Special Collections, Marriott Library, University of Utah.

18. Ward to Mumford, February 28, 1867, WP.

19. Ward to Mumford, March 30, 1867, WP.

20. Lewis Publishiing Co., *The Bay of San Francisco: A History* (Chicago: Lewis Publishing Co., 1892), I:660–666; *Polk's San Francisco City Directory, 1865–1866*, (San Francisco: R. L. Polk & Co., 1866), lviii.

21. Ward to Mumford, May 5, 1867, WP; Godbe to Ward, May 15, 1867, WP.

22. C. Gregory Crampton and Steven K. Madsen provide superb maps of the trail in their account, *In Search of the Spanish Trail: Santa Fe to Los Angeles, 1829–1848* (Layton, 1994).

23. *Deseret News*, Salt Lake City, June 15, 18, 19, 1867.

24. Godbe to Ward, June 20, 1867, WP; *Deseret News*, June 15, 18, 19, 1867.

25. Ward to Mumford, July 1, August 1, 1867, WP.

26. Ward to Mumford, February 27, 1867, WP.

27. Ibid.

28. Ward to Peter V. Jackson, March 1, 1867, WP; "Memorandum of Agreement" between Midas Mining Company and Peter V. Jackson, April 8, 1867, WP.

29. Selden to Ward, March 31, April 9, 1867, WP.

30. Gilbert to Mumford, April 7, 1867, WP. Gilbert's worries about holding on to his laborers were exacerbated by the Indian campaign of May–September 1867. Sterling raised a company of twenty-five volunteers who trained in the Hot Spring District. Some of the rank and file of the mining workforce in Sterling enlisted in this company; others joined companies outfitted in Virginia City. The drain of men throughout the county, whether for military purposes or as a result of stampeding, impacted the supply and demand for labor—and helped inflate wages.

31. J. B. Ward to Ward, May 23, 1867, WP.

32. J. B. Ward to Ward, May 1, 1867, WP.

33. J. B. Ward to Ward, June 27, 1867, WP. J. B. Ward's reference to the "new Court House" in New York City parallel warrants an explanation. Although the 1858 enact-

ment law for the courthouse set a construction limit of $250,000 (including furnishings), by the time the building was completed in 1871 the cost had skyrocketed to over $9 million! See Alexander B. Callow Jr., *The Tweed Ring* (Oxford, 1965), 198–206.

34. Godbe waited several weeks before the company was able to raise the money.

35. Selden to Ward, March 31, 1867, WP.

36. Ward to Mumford, June 10, 1867, WP.

37. Ibid.

38. Ibid.

39. Ward to Selden, June 17, 1867, WP.

40. Selden to Ward, July 26, 1867, WP.

41. J. B. Ward to Ward, July 18, 1867, WP.

CHAPTER 7

1. Charles W. Leng and William T. Davis, *Staten Island and Its People: A History, 1609–1929*, 2 vols. (New York, 1930), I. Today, the Wann grounds and the McAndrew grounds are occupied by the Richmond County Country Club.

2. *Montana Post*, June 2, 1866.

3. Ibid., January 27, 1866.

4. *Trow's New York City Directory for Year Ending May 1, 1865*, (New York: J. S. Trow, 1865).

5. *Prospectus of the Atlantic and Great Western Railway of Pennsylvania and Ohio* (N.c., 1858); Patrick Barry, *Over the Atlantic & Great Western Railway* (London, 1866).

6. The A&GWR eventually proved a failure. Its inability to acquire a terminal in New York City put it in an isolated position. Its financial conditions suffered greatly in the late 1860s, and in 1880 it was sold to the New York, Pennsylvania, and Ohio Railroad.

7. Others may have joined in financing the enterprise, but this is difficult to document. British late-nineteenth-century investments in the mineral fields of the West were extensive. See Clark C. Spence, *British Investments and the American Mining Frontier, 1860–1901* (Ithaca, NY, 1958).

8. This agreement is known only through reference in a later understanding. Weeks was acting independently of the VCMC.

9. L/121, J/557, MCC. Wisenall subsequently offered McAndrew and Wann additional properties of his own, asking the remarkable sum of $200,000: $10,000 on delivery of the deeds with the balance to be paid within one or two years. See "Montana Misc. Records," Manuscript Division, New York Historical Society, New York City. There is no record of a sale.

10. Weeks to Wisenall, April 21, 1866, John B. Wisenall Papers, Collection 2462, MSUSC.

11. Weeks to Wisenall, May [1866], ibid. The numerological dates are missing because of a tear in the page. In this letter Weeks mentioned a down-payment in stock as well as in money. Perhaps this was stock issued by McAndrew and Wann in lieu of cash.

12. L/65–66, 68, G/325, MCC.

13. The Seneca Falls Gold Mining Company was formed in the spring of 1865. Organized as a unit, thirty men from the Seneca Falls area pooled their money, purchased a mill, transported it to Montana over the plains, and had it erected and working in Summit District in early December. The venture commenced with optimism but soon ran into difficulty because of the inferiority of the mill and the company's inability to obtain sufficient ores with which to operate it. Despairing of making a profit, the

company abruptly sold out to McAndrew and Wann at a 40 percent loss on its original investment. See Seneca Falls Gold Mining Company file, Seneca Falls Historical Society, Seneca Falls, New York. The *Seneca Falls Reveille, Seneca County Courier,* and *Montana Post* commented periodically on the company's Montana gold milling venture.

14. *Montana Post,* August 25, 1866.

15. *Isaacs v. McAndrew & Wann,* File no. 830, Civil Cases, MCC.

16. *Montana Post,* August 25, 1866.

17. Ibid., January 26, 1867.

18. P/183–188, 194–196, MCC.

19. McAndrew and Wann to Isaacs, March 9, 1867, *Isaacs v. McAndrew & Wann,* MCC.

20. Isaacs to McAndrew & Wann, May 20, July 13, 1867, *Isaacs v. McAndrew & Wann,* MCC; *Montana Post,* May 25, 1867.

21. Deposition of S. S. Huntley and James Gamble, *Isaacs v. McAndrew & Wann,* MCC.

22. Isaacs to McAndrew & Wann, July 13, 1867, *Isaacs v. McAndrew & Wann,* MCC.

23. Ibid.

24. Isaacs to McAndrew & Wann, August 9, 1867, *Isaacs v. McAndrew & Wann,* MCC.

25. Isaacs to McAndrew & Wann, August 11, 1867, *Isaacs v. McAndrew & Wann,* MCC.

26. Ibid.

27. *Montana Post,* December 27, 1867; Isaacs testimony, *Isaacs v. McAndrew & Wann,* MCC.

28. Isaacs to McAndrew & Wann, August 27, 1867, *Isaacs v. McAndrew & Wann,* MCC.

29. H. Roy Gilbert to Ward, March 17, 1867, WP.

30. Clark to Ward, July 20, 1867, WP; Clark to Rockfellow, undated, but October 1867, WP.

31. Ward to Mumford, August 18, 1867, and Ward to Mumford, undated (fall 1867), WP.

32. Clark to Rockfellow, undated, but October 1867, WP.

33. *Montana Post,* June 1, 1867.

34. *Brooklyn Daily Union,* June 25, 1867.

35. *Montana Post,* July 27, 1867.

36. Ward to Mumford, August 1, 18, 1867, WP.

37. *Montana Post,* August 17, 24, 1867.

38. Ibid., November 30, 1867.

39. Ward to Mumford, August 18, 1867, WP.

40. R/116–126, MCC.

41. "Prospectus of the Upper Missouri Mining and Prospecting Company," William Robertson Coe Collection, Beinecke Library, Yale University, New Haven, Connecticut.

42. Deposition of Samuel Liddle, June 11, 1868, *George Cope v. Upper Missouri Mining & Prospecting Company,* File no. 746, Civil Cases, MCC; Deposition of James B. Percy, July 13, 1868, *George Cope v. Upper Missouri Mining & Prospecting Company,* MCC.

43. Deposition of Samuel Liddle, June 11, 1868, *George Cope v. Upper Missouri Mining & Prospecting Company,* File no. 746, Civil Cases, MCC; Deposition of George Cope, July 8, 1868, File no. 746, Civil Cases, MCC.

44. Ward to Mumford, August 18, 1867, WP.

45. Cope was able to purchase the mill when it was sold at auction later that year, but he never reopened it. Subsequently, Cope moved to Virginia City and won a seat in the territorial assembly, serving one term. In 1874 he returned to placer mining on Washington Bar on Meadow Creek.

CHAPTER 8

1. Ward to Mumford, June 10, 1867, WP.

2. Ward to Mumford, August 18, 1867, WP.

3. *Montana Post*, November 9, 1867. This anonymous writer admitted to being in the employ of the Midas Company.

4. Record books A, C, E, and K, County Clerk and Recorder's Office, Madison County Courthouse.

5. Isaacs to McAndrew & Wann, September 29, 1867, *Isaacs v. McAndrew & Wann*, MCC.

6. *Montana Post*, December 28, 1867.

7. Ibid. Later, when Isaacs's costly expenditures for "Mountain Home" were challenged, he argued that in bringing his wife to Montana he had determined to provide for her a home and a standard of living in no way inferior to what she would have known in New York City. Deposition of Isaacs, *Isaacs v. McAndrew & Wann*, MCC.

8. Ward to Mumford, December 2, 1867, WP.

9. Mumford to Ward, August 14, 1867, WP.

10. Elizabeth S.S. Eaton to General Amos Eaton, August 29, 1867, in Blake McKelvey (ed.), Rochester Historical Society Publication Fund Series, vol. 21, *Post Civil War Economy and Politics* (Rochester, NY, 1943), 133–134; Office of the Midas Mining Company to the Stockholders, August 12, 1867, WP.

11. Ward to Mumford, August 1, 1867, WP.

12. Selden to Ward, August 10, 1867, WP.

13. Selden to Ward, August 6, 1867, WP.

14. Selden to Ward, September 6, 1867, WP.

15. Ward to Selden, September 1, 1867, WP.

16. Selden to Ward, October 17, 1867, WP.

17. Ward to Mumford, October 10, 1867, WP.

18. Ibid.

19. Mumford to Ward, October 24, 1867, WP.

20. Selden to Ward, November 6, 1867, WP.

21. Ibid.

22. Selden to Ward, November 12, 1867, WP. Selden had just read J. Ross Browne's 1866 government report on mining and an article published in a recent issue of *Mining Engineer*.

23. Ward to Mumford, September 6, 1867, WP.

24. Ward to Mumford, October 10, 1867, WP.

25. Ward to Mumford, November 19, 1867, WP.

26. *Montana Post*, September 21, 1867.

27. Ward to Mumford, October 10, 1867, WP. The Wheeling company did not build on Hot Spring Creek; instead, it erected its mill in Ramshorn Gulch on the western slope of the mountains. It failed within the year and was auctioned off at a sheriff's sale for indebtedness in November 1868. Q/201, R/452, MCC.

28. Ward to Mumford, November 19, 1867, WP. For a remarkably thorough description of the Midas mill and its operation, see the *Montana Post*, November 16, 1867.

29. Ward to Mumford, December 2, 1867, WP.

30. Ibid.

31. Ward was also critical of Pratt's habit of grinding his retort in a coffee mill and then utilizing it for commercial purposes as pure gold dust, not only debasing the true value of gold but in effect perpetrating a fraud. Ibid.

32. Weeks to Wisenall, December 28, 1867, Wisenall Papers, MSUSC.

33. Ward to Mumford, December 2, 1867, WP.

34. Weeks to Wisenall, December 28, 1867, Wisenall Papers, MSUSC.

35. Ward to Mumford, December 2, 1867, WP.

36. Ibid.

37. Ibid.

38. Ibid.

39. Selden to Ward, December 6, 1867, WP.

40. Selden to Ward, December 8, 1867, WP.

41. Selden to Ward, December 17, 1867, WP.

42. Selden to Ward, December 25, 1867, WP.

43. This issue of the *Tri-Weekly* no longer exists, but Ward's letter was republished in the weekly edition of the *Montana Post* on December 21, 1867.

44. Ibid.

45. Ibid.

46. Ibid.

47. Ward to Mumford, January 8, 1868, WP; *Montana Post,* December 28, 1867.

48. Ward to Mumford, January 8, 1868, WP; *Isaacs v. McAndrew & Wann, MCC.*

49. Notice of January 7, 1868, as printed in *Montana Post,* January 28, 1868.

50. Ibid., January 11, 1868.

51. Ward to Mumford, January 13, 1868, WP.

52. Bishop Daniel Tuttle to Hattie Tuttle, January 22, 1868, Bishop Daniel Sylvester Tuttle Papers, 1867–1911, SC 871, MHSA. Gamble roomed with Tuttle in Virginia City during this crisis.

53. *Montana Post,* January 28, 1868.

54. Ward to Mumford, February 10, 1868, WP.

55. R/175, MCC.

56. Ward to Mumford, January 13, 1868, WP.

57. Ibid.

CHAPTER 9

1. Ward to Mumford, January 25, 1868, WP.

2. Ward to Mumford, February 10, 1868, WP.

3. Hodge to Ward, August 5, 1866, WP. Hodge was unable to dispose of these lodes.

4. Eaton Report to Gov. Green Clay Smith on the "present and prospective condition of the Territory," *Montana Post,* November 16, 1867. See also Eaton's report, "The Professor's Rambles," *Montana Post,* October 26, 1867.

5. Selden to Ward, March 15, 1868, WP.

6. Ward to Mumford, February 10, 1868, WP.

7. This is the J. T. Conner who was in partnership with Tufts and Hagaman in New York and was simultaneously representing the Upper Missouri Mining and Prospecting Company's interest in the old Ragland, Cope, and Napton mill in the Norwegian District.

8. Q/226, MCC.

9. *George Atkin v. J. T. Conner,* File no. 1004, Civil Cases, MCC; *Montana Post,* December 28, 1867. There is no record of settlement either way.

10. *Chandler J. Dow v. the Gold* [sic] *Ore Mining Company,* File no. 743, Civil Cases, MCC.

11. *Montana Democrat,* July 18, August 1, 1868.

12. In 1888, Cope sold his placers for $35,000 and moved to Helena. He later settled in Los Angeles, California, where he died in 1910.

13. Clark to Rockfellow, undated, but October 1867, WP.

14. Clark to Ward, November 15, 1867, WP.

15. Clark to William Y. Lovell, May 15, 1868, Estate of Gad E. Upson, Probates, MCC. See also *Copelin v. Clark & Upson*, File no. 739, Civil Cases, MCC.

16. Clark died in Stony Creek, Connecticut, in 1909.

17. P. Henry Woodward, "Insurance in Connecticut," in William T. Davis (ed.), *The New England States: Their Constitutional, Judicial, Educational, Commercial, Professional and Industrial History* (Boston, 1897), 2:552–555.

18. Woodward, "The Manufacturing Interests of Hartford," ibid., 2:822.

19. *Montana Post*, January 11, 1868; *Montana Democrat*, January 11, 1868.

20. *Copelin v. Clark & Upson*, MCC.

21. Pratt to Ward, April 4, 1868, WP.

22. R/111, MCC.

23. Q/158, MCC.

24. Rolle, *Road to Virginia City*, 103.

25. *Montana Post*, February 2, 1867; *Montana Democrat*, April 18, 1868.

26. *Montana Democrat*, March 21, 1868; Q/269, MCC.

27. Estate of John S. Rockfellow, Probates, MCC.

28. *Montana Democrat*, February 22, 1868; Unauthored letter to the *Democrat*, March 12, 1868, printed March 21, 1868.

29. *Montana Democrat*, March 21, 1868; Ward to Mumford, March 22, 1868, WP.

30. Q/325–329, MCC; W. D. Wann to Ward, May 16, 1868, WP. How Maria Josephine Isaacs fared in this reorganization is not clear.

31. *Montana Post*, September 4, 1868.

32. *Montana Democrat*, October 24, 1868.

33. Ibid., March 21, 1868.

34. Ward to Mumford, March 22, 1868, WP.

35. *Montana Democrat*, April 4, 1868.

36. Tuttle to Hattie Tuttle, April 12, 1868, SC 871, MHSA. James Gamble had advised Tuttle of the same.

37. Selden to Ward, March 10, 1868, WP.

38. McKelvey, *Rochester: The Flower City*, 116–117; Ward, *Henry A. Ward*, 151; *Rochester Union and Advertiser*, April 9, 1868; *Rochester Daily Democrat*, April 10, 1868. On April 9, when Ward and Brothers closed its doors, civil disorder was narrowly averted when frustrated creditors besieged the bank and threatened to inflict personal violence on its officers.

39. Ward to Jackson, May 7, 1868, WP. Rochester's banks were fully recovered by 1872, and the city's surplus investment capital continued to be ventured in distant mines, railroads, and other speculations. McKelvey, *Rochester*, 117.

40. Selden to Ward, May 6, 1868, WP.

41. Ward to Jackson, May 7, 1868, WP.

42. Clark to Ward, August 6, 1868, WP.

43. Selden to Ward, May 14, 1868, WP.

44. Selden to Ward, May 13, 1868, WP.

45. Ward to Jackson, July 6, 1868, WP.

46. Selden to Ward, August 9, 1868, WP.

47. Ward to Jackson, September 18, 1868, WP. Samuel Selden never ceased to hope that the Midas would be revived. Finally, on death's threshold in 1876, he transferred title of the mill and Midasburg to Peter V. Jackson, along with a generous stipend to Jackson for having served as the company's superintendent from 1868 onward.

48. "To the Stockholders of the Midas Mining Company," October 14, 1868, WP.

49. Ibid.

50. The firm Ward founded in Rochester, Ward's Natural Science Establishment, provides educational institutions with specimens to this day. In 1906, at age seventy-two, Ward died of injuries suffered when struck by an automobile in Buffalo, New York.

51. *Montana Post,* May 16, July 31, September 11, 1868.

52. Ibid., July 31, 1868.

53. R456, 458, T/90, MCC; Madison County Liens and Mortgage Record Books, Book 2, "Liens," 21, 25, MCC; *Nathaniel Bailey v. Carroll T. Hobart,* File no. 900, Civil Cases, MCC.

54. *Montana Post,* July 31, 1868.

55. Ibid., September 11, 1868.

56. In September Maltby crushed twenty-three-dollar ore at a cost of only twelve dollars. See Jackson to Ward, August 15, 1868, WP; *Montana Democrat,* October 3, 16, 1868; Maltby to Ward, August 23, 1870, WP.

57. Selden to Jackson, November 11, 1868, referencing Jackson to Selden, September 29, 1868, WP.

58. *Montana Democrat,* November 7, 1868.

59. Maltby to Ward, August 23, 1870, WP.

60. Jackson bill of sale, December 2, 1868, WP.

61. Maltby to Ward, August 23, 1870, WP.

62. Mary J. Maltby to Ward, November 20, 1871, WP.

63. Ward to Jackson, May 1, 1869, WP.

64. T/278, MCC. The Madison County Treasurer Record Book for January 13, 1868–April 14, 1891, which details offerings of property for which taxes were delinquent, provides additional evidence of how rapidly Sterling was abandoned. See sales of April 27, 1868, 6–12, and March 1, 1869, 17–22, MCC.

65. Col. A. G. Brackett, "A Trip Through the Rocky Mountains," *Contributions to the Historical Society of Montana,* 10 vols. (Boston, 1966), vol. 8, 343.

66. *Montana Post,* March 21, 1868.

67. Ibid., July 31, 1868.

68. Ibid., July 17, 1868.

69. *Montana Democrat,* August 15, 1868.

70. Jackson to Ward, August 15, 1868, WP.

71. Corbett, "Field Notes."

72. *Montana Post,* January 18, 1868; William Y. Lovell, "Our Business Interests," *Montana Post,* February 15, 1868.

73. *Montana Democrat,* October 3, 1868.

74. *Montana Post,* July 31, 1868.

75. Montana Inspector of Mines, *Second Annual Report Ending November 30, 1890* (Helena, 1890–1912), 55–56.

76. *Montana Democrat,* August 15, 1868.

77. Ibid., October 3, 1868.

78. *Montana Post,* November 6, 1868.

79. For a Coloradan parallel, see Gardiner, *Mining Among the Clouds,* 39.

80. J. Ross Browne, "Mineral Resources of the States and Territories West of the

Rocky Mountains," March 5, 1868, H. Ex. Doc. 202, 40th Cong., 2nd Sess.

81. Bassett and Magee, *Statistical Almanac for 1869*, 29.

82. "Report of Professor A. K. Eaton," *Montana Post*, November 16, 1867.

83. For a Colorado-California comparison, see Greever, *The Bonanza West*, 167–168.

84. For an early comprehension of the cost problem, see *Montana Post*, August 12, 1865.

85. Clark to Ward, July 20, 1867, WP.

EPILOGUE

1. Samuel T. Hauser to Robert Harris, May 18, 1887, Records of the Northern Pacific Railroad Company, Engineer's Office, 86-1, Minnesota Historical Society, St. Paul, Minnesota.

2. *Fourteenth Annual Report of the Inspector of Mines of the State of Montana* (Helena, December 1, 1902), 3–6.

Bibliography

MANUSCRIPT SOURCES

BANCROFT LIBRARY, BERKELEY, CALIFORNIA
  Mining Company Prospectuses
CONNECTICUT, HARTFORD
  Office of the Secretary of State
    Incorporations
  State Historical Society
    Census Records
JACKSON FAMILY PAPERS, MADISON COUNTY, MONTANA
  New York and Montana Mining and Discovery Company, Journal
  Peter V. Jackson Papers
MADISON COUNTY, MONTANA, CLERK AND RECORDER'S OFFICE, VIRGINIA CITY
  County Treasurers Records
  Grantor and Grantee Records
  Journals of the County Commission
  Liens and Mortgage Record Books
  Quartz Lode and Land Preemption Record Books
MADISON COUNTY, MONTANA, CLERK OF THE COURT, VIRGINIA CITY
  Civil Cases
  Probates
MINNESOTA HISTORICAL SOCIETY, ST. PAUL
  Records of the Northern Pacific Railroad Company
MISSOURI HISTORICAL SOCIETY, ST. LOUIS
  Census Records
MISSOURI STATE HISTORICAL SOCIETY, COLUMBIA, WESTERN HISTORICAL MANUSCRIPT COLLECTION
  Daniel Jones and Three Sons . . . "Travels Across the Plains" (1865)
  Dr. Wade Howard Journal
MONTANA HISTORICAL SOCIETY, HELENA
  MC 33. Hedges Family Papers
  MC 262. Henry Elling Papers
  SC 78. Ellen Fletcher Papers
  SC 147. Diary and Reminiscences of David J. Bailey
  SC 262. Nowland and Weary Bank Records, 1865–1869
  SC 267. Adobetown Justice of the Peace Records
  SC 296. John S. Rockfellow Papers
  SC 302. Neil Howie Diaries
  SC 438. Henry N. Blake Oration
  SC 517. Isaac Irvine Moore Letter
  SC 553. Lyman Ezra Munson Papers, 1865–1899
  SC 585. Northwestern Mining and Exploring Company Prospectus

SC 613. Richard Owen Diaries, 1864–1865
SC 629. William Y. Pemberton Papers
SC 644. Diary of James H. Morley
SC 816. Robert Hedge Letter
SC 822. F. George Heldt Reminiscences
SC 871. Daniel Sylvester Tuttle Papers
SC 874. A. M. Hough Reminiscence
SC 962. Joseph Culton Walker Reminiscence
SC 986. Henry Hauser Diary, 1865–1869
SC 1275. Charles W. Baker Diary, April 21, 1864–September 1867
SC 2074. Benjamin Dailey Diary, 1866
Microfilm 460. Abram H. Vorhees Diary
Record Series 160. Records of the Montana Territory, Secretary, 1864, Poll Lists
    for Election of 1864
Vertical Files
Montana Census, 1870
MONTANA STATE UNIVERSITY, BOZEMAN, RENNE LIBRARY, SPECIAL COLLECTIONS
    Collection 42. M. A. Switzer, "Reminiscences of a Trip Over the Bozeman Trail
        in 1865"
    Collection 43. Letters of Franklin Luther Kirkaldie
    Collection 326. Benjamin Dailey Diary
    Collection 708. Merrill G. Burlingame Papers
        William W. Alderson Diary, 1864–1879
    Collection 1504. J. E. Haynes Papers
        "Excerpts From the Personal Diary of the Late William Emory Atchison in 1864"
        Mrs. William J. Beall Scrapbook
    Collection 2462. John B. Wisenall Papers
    Manuscript File 450. A. C. Peale Diaries, 1871
NEW YORK HISTORICAL SOCIETY, NEW YORK CITY
    "Montana Misc. Records"
PHILLIPS EXETER ACADEMY, ANDOVER, MASSACHUSETTS
    "Reminiscences of Henry Nichols Blake"
RICHMOND COUNTY (STATEN ISLAND, NEW YORK) CLERK AND RECORDER'S OFFICE
    Census Records
    Letters of Administration
    Liber Books
    Probates
    Surrogates Office Records
ROCHESTER (NEW YORK) HISTORICAL SOCIETY
    Rochester Historical Society Publication Fund Series
SENECA FALLS (NEW YORK) HISTORICAL SOCIETY
    Historian's Files, Seneca Falls Gold Mining Company
SILVER BOW COUNTY, MONTANA, CLERK AND RECORDER'S OFFICE
    Grantor and Grantee Records
UNITED STATES, BUREAU OF LAND MANAGEMENT, BILLINGS, MONTANA
    Montana Territorial Surveys, Field Notes
UNIVERSITY OF MONTANA, MISSOULA, MANSFIELD LIBRARY, SPECIAL COLLECTIONS
    James Fergus Papers
    Collection 72. State of Montana, Business License Receipts

University of Rochester, Department of Rare Books and Special Collections, University of Rochester Library
  Henry A. Ward Papers
University of Utah, Salt Lake City, Marriott Library
  Hampton Godbe Papers
Washington, D.C., Library of Congress, Rare Books Collection
  Hezekiah L. Hosmer address, "Montana"
Washington, D.C., National Archives
  Record Group 15. Records of the Veterans Administration
  Record Group 28. Records of the Post Office Department
  Record Group 29. Bureau of the Census
  Record Group 48. Records of the Office of the Secretary of the Interior, Indian Division
  Record Group 49. Records of the Bureau of Land Management
  Record Group 94. Records of the Office of the Adjutant General
Yale University, New Haven, Connecticut, Beinecke Library
  Hezekiah L. Hosmer Papers
  William Robertson Coe Collection

PRINTED SOURCES

Albion, Robert Greenhalgh. *The Rise of the Port of New York, 1815–1860.* New York: Charles Scribner's Sons, 1939.

Atwater, Francis (comp.). *History of Southington, Conn.* New Haven: Atwater, 1924.

Barry, Patrick. *Over the Atlantic and Great Western Railway.* London: S. Low, Son and Marston, 1866.

Barsness, Larry. *Gold Camp: Alder Gulch and Virginia City, Montana.* New York: Hasting House, 1962.

Bassett, S. P., and Joseph Magee (comps.). *Statistical Almanac for 1869 and Year Book of Facts Showing the Material Resources of Montana.* Helena: Montana Publishing, 1869.

Beckert, Sven. *The Monied Metropolis: New York City and the Consolidation of the American Bourgeoisie, 1850–1896.* New York: Cambridge University Press, 2001.

Brackett, Col. A. G. "A Trip Through the Rocky Mountains." *Contributions to the Historical Society of Montana,* 10 vols. Vol. 8. Boston: S. S. Canner, 1966.

Browne, J. Ross. *Mineral Resources of the United States.* Washington, DC: U.S. Government Printing Office, 1868.

Bruffey, George A. *Eighty-One Years in the West.* Butte: Butte Miner, 1925.

Burlingame, Merrill G. *The Montana Frontier.* Bozeman: Montana State University Foundation, 1980 [1942].

Burpee, Charles W. *History of Hartford County, Connecticut, 1633–1928.* 3 vols. Chicago: S. J. Clarke, 1928.

Burrows, Edwin G., and Mike Wallace. *Gotham: A History of New York City to 1898.* New York: Oxford University Press, 1999.

Campbell, J. L. *Idaho: Six Months in the New Gold Diggings: The Emigrant's Guide Overland.* New York: author, 1864.

Chadwick, Robert A. "Investigations of the Geology and Ore Deposits of the Red Bluff–Norris Area, Madison County, Montana." Unpublished manuscript, 1984. Bozeman, Montana. Copies loaned to author.

Clark Bros. Bolt Company. *100th Anniversary: Clark Bros. Bolt Company, 1854–1954.* Milldale, CT: Clark Bros. Bolt Company, 1954.

Clark, Victor S. *History of Manufactures in the United States*. New York: Peter Smith, 1949.

Crampton, C. Gregory, and Steven K. Madsen. *In Search of the Spanish Trail: Santa Fe to Los Angeles, 1829–1848*. Layton, UT: Gibbs-Smith, 1994.

Cushman, Dan. *Montana: The Gold Frontier*. Great Falls: Stay Away, Joe, 1973.

Dick, Everett. *The Lure of the Land: A Social History of the Public Lands from the Articles of Confederation to the New Deal*. Lincoln: University of Nebraska Press, 1970.

Dimsdale, Thomas J. *The Vigilantes of Montana*. Norman: University of Oklahoma Press, 1976 [1866].

Doty, Lockwood R. (ed.). *History of the Genesee Country*. Chicago: S. J. Clarke, 1925.

Doyle, Susan Badger. *Journeys to the Land of Gold: Emigrant Diaries from the Bozeman Trail, 1863–1866*. 2 vols. Helena: Montana Historical Society Press, 2000.

Eaton, Asahel K. *A Text-Book on Agricultural Chemistry for the Use of Academies, Schools, and Agriculturalists*. Utica, NY: D. Bennett, 1847.

Fatout, Paul. *Meadow Lake Gold Town*. Lincoln: University of Nebraska Press, 1974.

Fellman, Michael. *Inside War: The Guerrilla Conflict in Missouri During the Civil War*. New York: Oxford University Press, 1989.

Fisher, Vardis, and Opal Laurel Holmes. *Gold Rushes and Mining Camps of the Early American West*. Caldwell, ID: Caxton, 1990.

Fite, Emerson David. *Social and Industrial Conditions in the North During the Civil War*. New York: Peter Smith, 1930.

Fowler, William Worthington. *Ten Years in Wall Street*. Hartford: Worthington, Dustin, 1879.

Gardiner, Harvey N. *Mining Among the Clouds: The Mosquito Range and the Origins of Colorado's Silver Boom*. Denver: Colorado Historical Society, 2002.

Gayetty, P. C. *The Miner's Guide: A Practical Treatise on Prospecting for the Precious Metal*. Oakland: W. B. Soule, 1897.

Geer's Hartford City Directory, 1865–1866. Hartford: Elihu Geer, 1866.

Goodrich, Thomas. *Black Flag: Guerrilla Warfare on the Western Border, 1861–1865*. Bloomington: University of Indiana Press, 1995.

Greever, William S. *The Bonanza West: The Story of the Western Mining Rushes, 1848–1900*. Norman: University of Oklahoma Press, 1963.

Guice, John D.W. *The Rocky Mountain Bench: The Territorial Supreme Courts of Colorado, Montana, and Wyoming, 1861–1890*. New Haven: Yale University Press, 1972.

Hayden, Ferdinand V. *Preliminary Report of the United States Geologic Survey of Montana and Portions of Adjacent Territories, Being a Fifth Annual Report of Progress*. Washington, DC: Government Printing Office, 1872.

Hine, Robert V., and John Mack Faragher. *The American West: A New Interpretative History*. New Haven: Yale University Press, 2000.

Hollister, Ovando J. *The Mines of Colorado*. New York: Promontory Press, 1974 [1867].

Homsher, Lola M. (ed.). *South Pass, 1868: James Chisholm's Journal of the Wyoming Gold Rush*. Lincoln: University of Nebraska Press, 1960.

Hosmer, Hezekiah K. "Montana." New York: New York Printing, 1866.

Hunter, Louis C. "Waterpower in the Century of the Steam Engine," in Brooke Hindle (ed.), *America's Wooden Age: Aspects of Its Early Technology*. Tarrytown, NY: Sleepy Hollow, 1985.

Jackson, W. Turrentine. *Treasure Hill: Portrait of a Silver Mining Camp*. Tucson: University of Arizona Press, 1963.

Jameson, Elizabeth. *All That Glitters: Class, Conflict, and Community in Cripple Creek*. Urbana: University of Illinois Press, 1998.

Johnson, Dorothy M. *The Bloody Bozeman: The Perilous Trail to Montana's Gold.* Missoula: Mountain Press, 1983.

Johnson, Susan Lee. *Roaring Camp: The Social World of the California Gold Rush.* New York: W. W. Norton, 2000.

Kelley, Robert K. *Gold vs. Grain: The Hydraulic Mining Controversy in California's Sacramento Valley.* Glendale: A. H. Clark, 1959.

Kennedy, Michael (ed.). "Infernal Collector." *Montana: The Magazine of Western History* 4 (Spring 1954), 13–23.

King, Joseph E. *A Mine to Make a Mine: Financing the Colorado Mining Industry, 1859–1902.* College Station: Texas A&M University Press, 1977.

Lass, William E. *A History of Steamboating on the Upper Missouri.* Lincoln: University of Nebraska Press, 1962.

———. *From the Missouri to the Great Salt Lake: An Account of Overland Freighting.* Lincoln: Nebraska State Historical Society, 1972.

Leng, Charles W., and William T. Davis. *Staten Island and Its People: A History, 1609–1929.* 2 vols. New York: Lewis Historical Publishing, 1930.

Lewis Publishiing Co. *The Bay of San Francisco: A History.* Chicago: Lewis Publishing Co., 1892.

Lord, Eliot. *Comstock Mining and Miners.* Berkeley: University of California Press, 1959 [1883].

Louis, Henry. *The Dressing of Minerals.* New York: Longmans, Green, 1909.

Madsen, Betty M., and Brigham D. Madsen. *North to Montana: Jehus, Bullwhackers, and Mule Skinners on the Montana Trail.* Salt Lake City: University of Utah Press, 1980.

Malone, Michael P., Richard B. Roeder, and William L. Lang. *Montana: A History of Two Centuries.* Seattle: University of Washington Press, 1991.

Marks, Paula Mitchell. *Precious Gold: The American Gold Rush Era, 1848–1900.* New York: William Morrow, 1994.

Mattes, Merrill J. *The Great Platte River Road: The Covered Wagon Mainline via Fort Kearny to Fort Laramie.* Lincoln: Nebraska State Historical Society, 1969.

May, Robert E. *The Southern Dream of a Caribbean Empire.* Baton Rouge: Louisiana State University Press, 1973.

McClure, Alexander K. *Three Thousand Miles Through the Rocky Mountains.* Philadelphia: J. B. Lippincott, 1869.

McKelvey, Blake. *Rochester: The Water-Power City, 1812–1854.* Cambridge: Harvard University Press, 1945.

———. *Rochester: The Flower City, 1855–1890.* Cambridge: Harvard University Press, 1949.

Montana Inspector of Mines. *Second Annual Report Ending November 30, 1890.* Helena: Journal; Independent, 1890–1912.

———. *Fourteenth Annual Report of the Inspector of Mines of the State of Montana, December 1, 1902.* Helena: Journal; Independent, 1890–1912.

Mullens, Patrick Aloysius, S.J. *Creighton: Biographical Sketches of Edward Creighton, John A. Creighton, Mary Lucretia Creighton, Sarah Emily Creighton.* Omaha: Creighton University Press, 1901.

Muscatine, Doris. *Old San Francisco: The Biography of a City from Early Days to the Earthquake.* New York: G. P. Putnam's Sons, 1975.

Napton, William Barclay. *Past and Present of Saline County, Missouri.* Indianapolis: B. F. Browne, 1910.

———. *Over the Sante Fe Trail.* Santa Fe: Stagecoach, 1964 [1905].

National Historical Company. *History of Howard and Cooper Counties, Missouri*. St. Louis: National Historical Company, 1883.

Nealley, Edward B. "A Year in Montana." *Atlantic Monthly* 17 (August 1866), 236–250.

Nelson, Raymond P. "Edward Creighton and the Pacific Telegraph." *Mid-America* 24 (1942), 61–74.

Niven, William John, Jr. "The Time of the Whirlwind: A Study of the Political, Social, and Economic History of Connecticut from 1861 to 1875." Unpublished Ph.D. diss., Columbia University, 1954.

Olsen, James C. (ed.). "From Nebraska City to Montana, 1866: The Diary of Thomas Alfred Creigh." *Nebraska History* 29 (September 1848), 208–237.

Oviatt, Alton B. "Steamboat Traffic on the Upper Missouri River, 1859–1869." *Pacific Northwest Quarterly* 40 (April 1949), 93–105.

Pace, Dick. *Golden Gulch: The Story of Montana's Fabulous Alder Gulch*. Virginia City, MT: Virginia City Trading Company, 1962.

Paul, Rodman W. *California Gold: The Beginning of Mining in the Far West*. Lincoln: University of Nebraska Press, 1947.

———. *Mining Frontiers of the Far West, 1848–1880* (rev., expanded ed. by Elliott West). Albuquerque: University of New Mexico Press, 2001.

Peavy, Linda, and Ursula Smith. *The Gold Rush Widows of Little Falls*. St. Paul: Minnesota Historical Society Press, 1990.

Polk's San Francisco City Directory, 1865–1866. San Francisco: R. L. Polk & Co., 1866.

Prospectus of the Atlantic and Great Western Railway of Pennsylvania and Ohio. N.c., 1858.

Purple, Edwin Ruthven. *Perilous Passage: A Narrative of the Montana Goldrush, 1862–1863*. Ed. Kenneth N. Owens. Helena: Montana Historical Society, 1995.

Rohe, Randall E. "The Geography and Material Culture of the Western Mining Town." *Material Culture* 16 (Fall 1984), 99–120.

———. "Hydraulicking in the American West: The Development and Diffusion of a Mining Technique." *Montana: The Magazine of Western History* 35 (Spring 1985), 18–35.

Rohrbough, Malcolm J. *Aspen: The History of a Silver Mining Town, 1879–1893*. New York: Oxford University Press, 1986.

———. *Days of Gold: The California Gold Rush and the American Nation*. Berkeley: University of California Press, 1997.

Rolle, Andrew (ed.). *The Road to Virginia City: The Diary of James Knox Polk Miller*. Norman: University of Oklahoma Press, 1960.

Ryan, Benjamin W. "The Bozeman Trail to Virginia City." *Annals of Wyoming* 19, 2 (July 1947), 77–104.

Safford, Hugh D. "Outline of the Geology and Ore Deposits at the Hot Spring Mining District, Madison County, MT." Unpublished manuscript, 1993. Bozeman, Montana. Loaned by the author.

Safford, Jeffrey J. "Baited by a 'Color' of Gold to a Mountain of Granite: Connecticut Capital at Work in the Montana Goldfields, 1865–1868." *Montana: The Magazine of Western History* 47 (Summer 1997), 2–13; (Autumn 1997), 34–45.

———. "'What's in a Name?': Christening Early Madison County, Montana Quartz Lodes." *Montana: The Magazine of Western History* 50 (Autumn 2000), 66–69.

Sanders, James U. (ed.). *Society of Montana Pioneers: Constitution, Members, and Officers, with Portraits and Maps*, vol. 1. Helena: Society of Montana Pioneers, 1899. [Only this volume was published.]

Shinn, Charles Howard. *Mining Camps: A Study in American Frontier Government*. New York: Alfred A. Knopf, 1948.

Silversmith, J. (comp.). *The Miners' Companion and Guide: A Compendium of Most Valuable Information for the Prospector, Miner, Geologist, Mineralogist and Assayer Together with a Comprehensive Glossary of Technical Phrases Used in the Work.* San Francisco: J. Silversmith, 1861.

Smith, Duane A. *Rocky Mountain Mining Camps: The Urban Frontier.* Bloomington: University of Indiana Press, 1967.

———. *Rocky Mountain West: Colorado, Wyoming, and Montana, 1859–1915.* Albuquerque: University of New Mexico Press, 1992.

Spann, Edward K. *The New Metropolis: New York City, 1840–1857.* New York: Columbia University Press, 1981.

Spence, Clark C. *British Investments and the American Mining Frontier, 1860–1901.* Ithaca: Cornell University Press, 1958.

———. *Mining Engineers and the American West: The Lace-Boot Brigade, 1849–1933.* New Haven: Yale University Press, 1970.

———. *Territorial Politics and Government in Montana, 1864–1889.* Chicago: University of Chicago Press, 1975.

———. *Montana: A Bicentennial History.* New York and Nashville: W. W. Norton and the American Association for State and Local History, 1978.

Spude, Robert L. "To Test by Fire: The Assayer in the American Mining West, 1848–1920." Unpublished Ph.D. diss., University of Illinois, 1989.

Stanley, E. J., Rev. *Life of Rev. L. B. Stateler, or Sixty-Five Years on the Frontier.* Nashville: Publishing House of the Methodist-Episcopal Church, 1907.

Taylor, George Rogers. *The Transportation Revolution, 1815–1860.* New York: Rinehart, 1951.

Thompson, Robert L. *Wiring a Continent: The History of the Telegraph Industry in the United States, 1832–1866.* Princeton: Princeton University Press, 1947.

Timlow, Heman R., Rev. *Ecclesiastical and Other Sketches of Southington, Conn.* Hartford: Press of the Case, Lockwood and Brainard Co., 1875.

Trimble, William Joseph. *The Mining Advance into the Inland Empire.* Madison: University of Wisconsin History Series, Bulletin 638, 1914.

Trow, V. S. *Trow's New York City Directory for Year Ending May 1, 1865.* New York: J. S. Trow, 1865, 1866, 1867.

Tufts, James. *A Tract Descriptive of the Montana Territory, with a Sketch of Its Mineral and Agricultural Resources.* New York: R. Craighead, 1865.

Tyler, S. Lyman (ed.). *The Montana Gold Rush Diary of Kate Dunlap.* Salt Lake City: University of Utah Press, 1969.

Ward, Roswell. *Henry A. Ward: Museum Builder to America.* Rochester: Rochester Historical Society, 1948.

Wells, Merle W. *Gold Camps and Silver Cities: Nineteenth Century Mining in Central and Southern Idaho.* Moscow: Idaho Bureau of Mines and Geology, Bulletin 22, 1983.

West, Elliott. *Contested Plains: Indians, Goldseekers, and the Rush to Colorado.* Lawrence: University of Kansas Press, 1998.

White, Helen McCann (ed.). *Ho! for the Gold Fields: Northern Overland Wagon Trains of the 1860s.* St. Paul: Minnesota Historical Society, 1966.

White, Richard. *"It's Your Misfortune and None of My Own": A New History of the American West.* Norman: University of Oklahoma Press, 1991.

Wilbur, William R. *History of the Bolt and Nut Industry of America.* Cleveland: Ward and Shaw, 1905.

Wolle, Muriel Sibell. *Montana Pay Dirt: A Guide to the Mining Camps of the Treasure State.* Denver: Sage, 1963.

Woodward, P. Henry. "Insurance in Connecticut," in William T. Davis (ed.), *The New England States: Their Constitutional, Judicial, Educational, Commercial, Professional and Industrial History.* Boston: D. H. Hurd, 1897.

———. "The Manufacturing Interests of Hartford," in William T. Davis (ed.), *The New England States: Their Constitutional, Judicial, Educational, Commercial, Professional and Industrial History.* Boston: D. H. Hurd, 1897.

Young, Otis E., Jr. "The Craft of the Prospector." *Montana: The Magazine of Western History* 20 (Winter 1970), 28–39.

———. *Western Mining: An Informal Account of Precious-Metals Prospecting, Placering, Lode Mining, and Milling on the American Frontier from Spanish Times to 1893.* Norman: University of Oklahoma Press, 1970.

Zanjani, Sally. *A Mine of Her Own: Women Prospectors in the American West, 1850–1950.* Lincoln: University of Nebraska Press, 1997.

NEWSPAPERS

Atchison [NE] *Daily Champion*
Brooklyn Daily Union
Butte Weekly Miner
Cleveland Herald
Connecticut Courant [Hartford]
Deseret News [Salt Lake City]
Hartford Daily Courant
Montana Democrat [Virginia City]
Montana Post [Virginia City and Helena]
Montana Post Tri-Weekly [Virginia City]
New Northwest [MT]
New York Evening Post
New York Herald
New York Tribune
Richmond County [Staten Island, NY] *Gazette*
Rochester Daily Democrat
Rochester Evening Press
Rochester Union and Advertiser
Sacramento Bee
Sacramento Daily Union
Salt Lake Daily Tribune
Seneca County [Seneca Falls, NY] *Courier*
Seneca Falls [NY] *Reveille*
Southington [CT] *Mirror*
Virginia City [MT] *Times*

Index

179